Please return or renew by
latest date below

LOANS MAY BE RENEWED BY PHONE

PRAIRIE PEOPLE

Dr. Peter Lorenz Neufeld

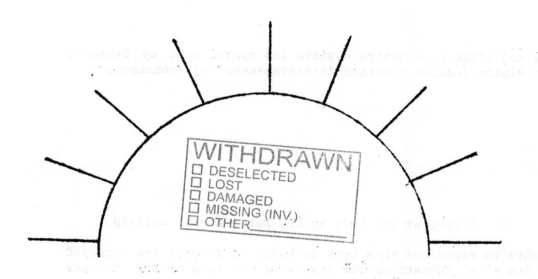

GLENDOSA RESEARCH CENTRE
Minnedosa, Manitoba, Canada

ACKNOWLEDGMENTS and PREFACE

I wish to express sincere personal appreciation to the many people whose interest, encouragement and help made this book possible. It would be virtually impossible to name every person who has through co-operation in an interview, supplying information and suggestions become involved in a book of this nature. Frequently the articles themselves make such acknowledgments whereas in others these are inherent in the material itself.

Many persons whose names are mentioned in these articles were not aware at the time of their original publication that these would eventually also be included in a book; though perhaps most suspected it due to the format of my previous book PRAIRIE VISTAS. I had hoped eventually to publish these articles as a sequel to that book but was not at all sure it would become a reality until quite recently. However, as none of the material involving individuals is slanderous in nature--in fact, usually quite complimentary--I've taken the liberty of re-publishing them in book form without specifically asking each person's permission. The articles have of course already been published once in newspapers and magazines and individuals involved were aware of and consented to that first publishing.

Although according to Article 12 of Chapter C-30 (commonly called the Copyright Act), specific permission is not required from newspapers and magazines involved for an author to re-publish his own articles in BOOK form, I do however wish publicly to acknowledge appreciation to them for friendly advice, co-operation, and for publishing them in the first instance. They are: The Brandon Sun, The Whitehorse Star, The Western Producer, North/Nord magazine, Parkland Bottle Collectors magazine, Manitoba Welsh Pony News, Minnedosa Collegiate Yearbook, Canadian Frontier, The Birtle Eye-Witness, The Winnipeg Tribune, The Minnedosa Tribune, New Bedford Whaling Museum, The Shepherds' Dir, Manitoba Pageant.

All articles are virtually as previously published. In some instances I've cut out a sentence here and there to avoid repetition from other articles, modified slightly a particular statement because of feed-back from readers, etc. I think it's fair to say that 98% of the writing is exactly as first published.

An intriguing sidelight regarding the fascinating Tanner saga of which I've written much in this book and my previous one that warrants further research, involves a recent comment made to me by an elderly Saulteaux gentleman whose ancestors were of the same tribe as the Tanners (Red Lake Chippewas) that emigrated to Canada from the USA in the 1860s. According to him, the Tanner family of Gambler reserve should really be called 'Henry' as their Saulteaux surname was 'Zanarie' which interprets thus.

This is most interesting for at least three reasons. First, 'Henry' is one of four surnames about which I've written (see Article 27) involving white children captured by Indians. 'Tanner' undoubtedly is by far the most prominent of these. Second, it may mean that Chief Picheito Tanner's wife was a Henry and possibly her tribe once traced surnames through maternal rather than paternal lines as did some tribes. Third, there is a slight chance that I was incorrect in my conclusion that John Tanner of Gambler was a son of Picheito. He definitely was John Falcon Tanner's grandson, was not Rev. James Tanner's son, was a cousin of Minnedosa's founder. Picheito spent his last years in that district and none of Falcon's other sons, or their descendants, lived in Manitoba. But if maternal rather than paternal lines were used to denote surnames, there exists the possibility that Falcon and Morning Sky's daughter may instead have been the parent of John Tanner of Gambler, and her husband a Henry.

Other historical research in which I became deeply involved in these two books I hope especially someone will continue because aspects of it are still incomplete includes: Who murdered Rev. James Tanner and why? What was the true identity of 'Jimmy Tanner'? More details on the quarter century Minnedosa's John Tanner lived in Prince Albert region. The fate of Hubert Darrell of Birtle. More details on why Mennonites are still excused from jury duty. Details of John Bunn's fate after Beautiful Sky with children fled to Canada. Why did two American Sioux chiefs living in the same general area and during the same time have the same name--Red Cloud? More details on the kidnapping of Rev. John Sargent's daughter. Search for the lost box of personal papers belonging to poet Robert Service which may perhaps include interesting information on Hubert Darrell. Search for log books etc. which may have been rescued when the Frances

Allyn burned and sank as they may include data on Hubert Darrell; as well as that of Charlie Darrell's effects. A check on the effects of John Tanner of Gambler. The identity of George Campbell Jr., and the ultimate fate of the George Campbell Sr.'s daughter.

I am indebted to my daughter Verna for the cover layout, to my wife Elsie for constructive criticism involving the various articles.

Since I began writing professionally in July of 1967 I've written three types of books--a psychohistorical novel, an applied science reference book with underlying psychological theme, some 200 historical articles re-published in two books. Though writing has to date been anything but FINANCIALLY successful for me, the books have been well received and widely read resulting in considerable recognition--such as that by eight internationally-published 'Who's Who?' books--for which I'm sincerely grateful. At the same time, I don't wish to fall into a rut. During the next half decade I hope to do some entirely different type of writing--short stories. I hope to get them published in North American or European magazines, perhaps eventually re-publish them as my fifth book.

I firmly believe that the fascinating history of our Canadian Prairies and its people has been severely minimized by historians generally. It is my hope and prayer that this book--my final attempt at historical-type research and writing--may prove a small contribution towards giving it greater emphasis.

Peter Lorenz Neufeld
Minnedosa, Manitoba
August, 1975

TABLE OF CONTENTS

Seventy-five years ago thousands of gold-seekers trekked north to seek fortunes and overnight Yukon Territory became a separate part of this nation. Commemorating these phenomenal events which then reached deep into the lives of many Canadians, Klondike '73 celebrations are currently under way in places like Dawson and Whitehorse.

Of numerous Manitobans who followed 'The Trail of '98', at least three West-Manites played major roles in northern development. One was none other than James Duncan MacGregor, who in 1929 became our lieutenant-governor.

A son of David MacGregor and Annie Smith, born Aug. 29, 1860 in Amherstburg, Ont. and educated at Windsor, James left in 1877 to seek fame and fortune. Before and after his sojourn in the Yukon (1897-1905) he owned and operated world-famous Glencarnock Farms in the Brandon and Portage la Prairie districts. A leading breeder of Angus cattle on this continent, he won the world championship two years running at Chicago in 1912 and 1913, contributed greatly to the success of Brandon (now Royal) Winter Fair. At one time he also owned 200,000 acres near Medicine Hat, Alta. In 1882 he married, had four children.

During MacGregor's years in the Arctic he was chosen as one of the pioneer administrators of Yukon appointed during the Klondike gold rush and during the height of that struggle for riches, 1897-99, served as Yukon's mine inspector. He died in Winnipeg March 15, 1935.

Although Canada became a nation in 1867 much of her vast northwest still belonged to Hudson Bay Company for a while. Though mail service became a federal responsibility then, that historical company provided postal deliveries to Arctic outposts in many areas of Keewatin, Mackenzie, Yukon well into this century. A phenomenal undertaking in a harsh, frequently inaccessible land where extraordinary events and situations more often were rule than exception, mail carrying too didn't follow the orderly predictable development of our settled south. Unusual developments called for unusual solutions.

That Hubert Darrell and Hudson Bay Company should meet was inevitable. An Arctic phenomenon who left his older brother's farm near Birtle to join the Klondike gold rush, this short, stocky, energetic young man of tremendous stamina within one short decade explored and mapped, prospected, hunted-trapped-fished, guided North West Mounted Police patrols and government officials in virtually every region of Keewatin, Mackenzie, Yukon and eastern Alaska. Explorers like Roald Amundsen, Vilhjalmur Stefansson, David Hanbury (whose 16 month Arctic exploration expedition he guided) can't praise him enough. Northerners concur few men if any--white or native--knew Canada's northland as well 70 years ago as did Darrell. Had he not mysteriously disappeared in 1910 he would have accompanied Amundsen on his South Pole expedition and undoubtedly written about his work. Stefansson planned one article in 1912, an editor of a prominent international magazine another in 1964. Somehow neither materialized. Hubert's brief association with Hudson Bay Company as mail carrier is one important aspect of this remarkable West-Manite's Arctic achievements.

Darrell and several Hudson Bay Co. men became close friends. In letters to parents in England (originals owned by Scott Polar Research Inst. and microfilm by Glenbow-Alberta Inst.) he frequently mentions them. One was "company manager Mr. Gaudet" with whom he first became acquainted at Fort Resolution on Great Slave Lake in 1900. Another in that vicinity was "Mr. Brabant at Hudson's Bay Co. post who always treats me well. He had an organ there and I played three nights." Later he writes his mother, "If I had a house I should want a piano for I like music better than anything." He and Joseph Jacquot, prospector and trading post manager of Fort Arctic Red River, were close friends until his tragic disappearance. They hunted, trapped, explored, mapped, prospected, bought furs together. On June 20, 1906 he writes his father from Fort McPherson "All Hudson's Bay officers treat me with great kindness." Another fur trader with whom he became good friends was Dan Cadzow of Rampart House. On March 20, 1910 he informs his father from Dawson that recently he had "made a trip to Red River on the Mackenzie to see my old friend Campbell of Hudson's Bay Company and J. Nagle of Hyslop and Nagle". Also a friend was John Firth, long time Hudson Bay Co. manager at Fort McPherson. Stephen North of Birtle, son of Hubert's closest friend there, told me, "he was an extremely quiet and retiring man, not given to making friends quickly, and possessed an almost Thoreauvian honesty".

When funds ran low Darrell sometimes did odd jobs at Hudson Bay Co. posts -- operated these in absence of managers away buying furs, loaded furs onto boats, accompanied traders on fur-buying excursions. An unfortunate liaison in 1905 with an American explorer of sorts, A.H. Harrison--author of the 1908 book IN SEARCH OF A POLAR CONTINENT and most incompitent Arctic expedition leader, ended in late fall with Darrell quitting the party resulting in much bitterness, a fist fight and lawsuit. Destitute, Darrell contracted to carry mail for Hudson Bay Company for six months between Fort McPherson and various Arctic outposts.

Roald Amundsen first met Darrell as mail carrier February, 1906, "face black with smoke accompanied not even by a dog, and dragging his toboggan behind him" loaded with mail from Fort McPherson destined for trading posts in northwestern Yukon across Richardson Mountain range "hundreds of miles from the nearest human being, with not a soul to aid him in case of illness or accident, cheerfully trudging through the Arctic winter across an unblazed wilderness". Needless to say the two quickly became close friends. Dr. Margaret Dudley of Winnipeg, younger sister of Hubert's fiancee Agnes Dudley of Birtle, recalls that period in his life as "I believe Hubert carried mail between two Arctic posts, about 500 miles apart, travelling alone over uninhabited territory".

Famous explorer Stefansson, whom Darrell first met in November, 1906, at Shingle Point on the Arctic coast just west of the Mackenzie mouth when the former brought him a packet of letters and the latter was guiding a Mountie patrol from Herschel Island to Fort McPherson, pays tribute to Hubert's accomplishments. "To travel alone and without dogs," he states, "is an unheard of thing even among Eskimos". Especially noteworthy he finds Darrell's mail delivery trip to and from an American whaling fleet wintering in the Bailey-Herschel islands region of Beaufort Sea.

To get mail to these ships frozen in shifting Arctic ice and word out in time to summon a relief ship to that beleaguered fleet was undoubtedly extremely risky and required an extraordinary mailman. In Hubert Darrell Hudson Bay Co. fortunately then had just such a man. Some ships had been icebound as long as three years. The lives of 500 whalers depended on the long-delayed mail getting through.

Later, writing his father from Fort Yukon, he describes briefly this incredible undertaking. "They are on rock bottom and have to be supplied by ships which have more supplies. I agreed to carry the mail over and as the snow was so deep, no trail, so cold, I had to haul my toboggan, I had a very hard time of it as far as work went. The distance I came was 480 miles and it took 30 days of actual travel. My last day into Fort Yukon I did nearly 50 miles—a vast difference to four to five miles per day in the upper part of Porcupine and Peel rivers. I passed right over one range of Rocky Mountains which are so low in these parts but for all that absolutely bare of vegetation near the summit".

John A. Cook, American whaler and author of the 1937 book THAR SHE BLOWS, in charge of the ship Bowhead and wintering some distance from the main fleet containing vessels like Belvedere, Beluga, Herman, Narwhal, describes Darrell's arrival April 22, 1906. "I saw something that looked like a man dragging a sled. As sled-outfits included both a number of dogs and two or more men commonly, my curiosity was instantly aroused. Forthwith I fetched binoculars and discovered a man without companions or dogs was approaching my ship, dragging a small sled (about eight feet long) of the Itkilik toboggan type. That sled contained nothing apparently except sleeping equipment and rifle and ammunition.

"The stranger came directly to the Bowhead—haltingly as if practically exhausted, halted on the ice below me and, in a weak voice, asked permission to come aboard and get something to eat and rest. He showed us letters of authorization given him by Firth at the trip's commencement and one signed by the postmaster at Fort Yukon."

Stefansson describes the finish of Darrell's amazing mail trip. "Although he travelled alone he had no adventures and no mishaps—adventures and mishaps seldom happen to a competent man—and when he arrived on the Yukon the telegraph dispatches recorded the simple fact that mail had arrived from imprisoned whalers in the Beaufort Sea, and not a word of who had brought it or how it had been brought". Writing to Agnes Dudley in 1912 (letters owned by Stefansson Collection, Dartmouth College library) he states, "Darrell had to his credit more real achievement than many who are famous for their work in the north". Saving the lives of 500 whalers while temporary mail carrier for Hudson Bay Company was one such achievement; an achievement for which public recognition—though posthumously—is very long overdue. As Stephen North remarked to me recently, "Nothing would've pleased my father more than to think Hubert was finally receiving, however belatedly, the recognition he so rightly deserves".

Hazardous ventures never daunted the intrepid Darrell but instead spurred him on to yet greater ones. Immediately upon reaching Fort Yukon with word from the starving whalers he's already eagerly outlining plans to his mother of a proposed exploration and prospecting excursion through the same wilderness he'd just traversed. "There are no settlements and no Hudson's Bay Company posts and no living residents more than a few wandering Eskimos," he confides. "I don't expect to see any wheat crops either," he quips. Three months later he writes his father from Fort McPherson that, "my idea is to get a job here for one year and then engage as dog driver on the US mail service in the Yukon 1907-08 and perhaps 1909". In July, from Fort Good Hope, he reiterates these intentions to his father, "I want to go to Alaska and drive mail a couple of seasons".

But fate intervenes. That fall, while packing his gear to leave for Alaska, the NWMP persuade Darrell to guide a patrol they hope to establish between Fort McPherson and Herschel Island through the uncharted No-Man's Land he had successfully challenged the winter before as mail carrier. Hubert consents, and during the next four years guides several long patrols through unexplored Yukon territory. Only once does he mention mail carrying again to his family. On Oct. 30, 1907, he writes his father from Dawson, "I missed a good job carrying mail for $100 per month by not being on the spot at the right time".

The American whalers whose lives he saved are often on Hubert Darrell's mind. To his sister Kathleen in England he writes from Dawson, Sept. 18, 1908, "You know of McLure's Cache where the Investigator wintered many years ago. I'm very anxious to go there and am going to make inquiries from the Herschel Island whalers whether they will give me a landing on Bank's Land. If I can get landed with a good companion and plenty of provisions I could do something". The last white men to see him alive before he vanished into thin air in late 1910 was the crew of the Rosie H at Cape Bathurst on Baillie Islands where he stopped briefly for supplies.

2. DARRELL, ARCTIC GUIDE Freelance article, North/Nord magazine, Summer, 1973

What the invaluable Metis guide Jerry Potts was to the North-West Mounted Police in frontier southwestern Canada during the 1870s, Hubert Darrell became in frontier Arctic Canada during the first decade of this century. Had he not mysteriously disappeared on an exploration-prospecting trip, his career with the Force would undoubtedly have extended beyond four short years.

The 1890s suddenly brought white civilization to Mackenzie Bay, a region which the Klondike gold rush had virtually ignored. New England whaling ships had for years been hunting Greenland whales, usually wintering in the Bering Strait area. As the whales moved northeastward the ships followed. By the mid-1890s whalers began wintering in Herschel Island harbour, often as many as 500 to 700 men.

Despite most whaling captains ruling with iron hand, rough crews bored by long idle hours of Arctic winters soon created many problems for Herschel Island's Cogmollick and Nunamiut Eskimos. As Henry A. Larsen, skipper of the RCMP St. Roch which first navigated the North-West Passage from west to east, writes years later, "Many moved in with Eskimo women, and a period of wenching and home-brewing followed that is still remembered in the North. In return for their hospitality the natives received only the diseases of whites." Writing to his mother in England from Great Slave Lake on April 9, 1903 (letters owned by Scott Polar Research Inst., microfilm by Glenbow-Alberta Inst.) Hubert Darrell mentions the many problems created by "the whiskey traffic on Herschel Island and Peel River by American whalers." Although a priest was sent north from Fort McPherson, Larsen indicates that "law and order did not follow until 1903-04 when two policemen from the then NWMP arrived and started to clean up conditions". They were Sgt. Francis Fitzgerald and Cst. Sutherland. In addition to protecting Eskimos from unscrupulous whalers they collected customs duties and 'occupied' this island for Canada.

When Larsen first wintered on blizzard-ridden Herschel Island in 1926-27 just prior to enlistment in the RCMP, many natives recalled vividly those lawless days a quarter century past. One of his closest friends and co-workers was Jorgen Klengenberg who wintered there during that terrible season in 1905-06, when some 500 whalers almost starved. It was Hubert Darrell who had carried to an outside world the beleagured whalers' cry for help.

Darrell became a legend in the Arctic during the early 1900s. A farmer from Manitoba, he joined the 1898 Klondike gold rush and fell in love with the North. Explorers Hanbury, Amundsen, Stefansson lauded his achievements. Eskimos and Indians respected him as they did few other white men of his decade. Luta Munday, in her 1930 book A MOUNTY'S WIFE remarked, "It should also be remembered, with almost the single exceptions of Hubert Darrell and Hornby, two Englishmen who travelled far and wide in the Arctic at different times and quite alone, all white people in the far North are dependent upon native people for guidance to their desired destinations and for game by which to live."

That the recently knighted Royal North-West Mounted Police should make use of Darrell's unique talents to live off frozen tundra and travel at will over vast unexplored Arctic regions comes as no surprise. The Force's 'B' Division headquartered in Dawson on the Yukon River, with Fort McPherson as major sub-post. Small outposts were scattered in the Mackenzie River region in places like Arctic Red River, Peel River, and the newly-created Herschel Island post. David Laird, with whom Darrell became acquainted in spring of 1906, was then Indian commissioner of the Northwest Territories. Commissioner of the Yukon district was James Morrow Walsh, the Mountie who accepted Sitting Bull's surrender a quarter century before. Commanding the Mackenzie River sub-district was Inspector W.J. Betys. The problem was not that of furnishing outposts with supplies, for this was readily accomplished in summer months via ship to Herschel Island and steamboats down the Mackenzie. In that pre-wireless era the real problem was developing a satisfactory overland winter communication and mail service system between Dawson, Fort McPherson and outlying detachments like Herschel, hundreds of miles away.

In November, 1906, Darrell guided his first RNWMP patrol from Fort McPherson to Herschel Island, some 300 miles of treeless, trackless Arctic wilderness unfamiliar to white men. Writing his father on January 21, 1907, following his return from that barren rock he explains, "I was just 36 hours away from starting for Alaska when the police came and asked me to go on patrol to Herschel Island. Only Corporal Haylow and I went with one dog team. We went half way and reached the coast in quick time, and then the storms came. We were storm-bound by a blinding gale and blizzard three nights in an unsheltered spot. We luckily secured the tent by piling driftwood and supporting it by many poles inside before the wind got too strong and then the whole was bound by lashing it to logs." About crossing the Mackenzie Bay ice he confides, "I carried on and tried the ice all the way for eight miles. Cpl. Haylow does not know to this day how near he came to getting a ducking or worse. The dogs and sled did go through at the crack but I jumped across. There was great excitement among the Huskies (Eskimo) when we arrived. Sgt. Fitzgerald and Walker (who had replaced Sutherland) of course put us up. Cpl. Haylow is a most excellent man and if any of the other police had gone in place of Haylow there would, I really believe, have been a funeral with no service or mourners."

Vilhjalmur Stefansson first met Darrell at Shingle Point on the Arctic coast just after this patrol started back for Fort McPherson. "That was always his way," he writes. "He was about as new to that country as the policemen were, but still he was a competent guide, for he never lost his head." Stefansson had brought Darrell some mail from England and the two men became close friends. Writing his friend's fiancee, Agnes Dudley of Birtle, on September 30, 1912 (letter owned by Dartmouth College) Stefansson tells her the world should "know about such men, men who quietly and unostentatiously do remarkable things."

Next winter saw Darrell sworn in as special constable to guide a patrol from Dawson to McPherson. The previous winter he had roomed for a while with Cst. W.J.D. Dempster, who was in charge of this patrol, and the two had become friends. His salary was $4 per day of patrol duty.

Upon their return Dempster, in typical formal, low-key police language, filed his report on this five-man patrol March 24, 1908. Part of it reads, "Left Dawson on December 26, 1907. We carried 24 pounds of mail for Fort McPherson and Herschel Island. Fitzgerald with team accompanied us up the 12 miles to Tombstone creek, a distance of 53 miles from Dawson. The transport consisted of four toboggans. The two oak toboggans were too thin, one of them split badly. They were also too long, making them very inconvenient for making short turns on the trail. Our snowshoes were very poor. We arrived at McPherson on January 25, 1908, having been 31 days on the trail. We remained at McPherson 24 days to feed our dogs and procure snowshoes. On our return trip we left McPherson with 26 pounds mail. One dog 'Ned' played out; 'Ben' died on the trail, one private dog ran away, another one played out one day from McPherson. Regarding the members of the patrol who were with me I cannot speak too highly; all performed their work cheerfully and willingly."

Darrell writes his father later from Dawson. "I was trail-breaker all the way there and back, which is to say guide as three of them had never been on a trip of any account before and Dempster was always with the dog teams as it required his entire attention to get the green fellows along at all. We did not lose trail for 10 miles in a 525 mile (one way) journey." Two years later, in an attempt to set a new record for the trip, Francis Fitzgerald (now Inspector) and constables Carter, Kinney and Taylor, all perished from extreme cold, blizzards and starvation. Dempster was sent to investigate the tragedy and bring back the bodies. His closest friend in Dawson, Darrell tells his father, is Cst. Bob Forrest--the man who had established this record the previous winter.

During the winter of 1909-10 Darrell guided the same patrol, again a five-man detachment with Dempster in charge. The trip took 33 days, waiting for mail 23 days, return 23 days. Toboggans performed better but snowshoes as badly as before. They learned that pemmican made of dried meat scraps and tallow provided the best dog food, their teams consuming 280 pounds on the return trip. Besides meeting a party of prospectors outfitted by Harry Waugh, American explorers Stefansson and Anderson, Canadian scientist Ernest Leffingwell, Angus McDonald of the Yukon Gold Company, they reported on the whalers at Herschel Island which included fining S.S. Karluk's second mate $100 and costs for giving whiskey to an Eskimo woman.

Darrell's last patrol with the Mounted Police occurred in June 1910 when a detachment from Dawson travelled to Fort McPherson to meet the Hon. Frank Oliver, Minister of the Interior. A former journalist of the Toronto Globe and Mail and of the Winnipeg Free Press and founder of Alberta's first newspaper, the Edmonton Bulletin, Oliver was also Superintendent General of Indian Affairs in the Laurier cabinet and a vital force in encouraging immigration to western Canada. His wife was Harriet Dunlop of Prairie Grove, Manitoba. It was Oliver who later said, "Ordinarily speaking, no more wildly impossible undertaking was ever staged than the establishment of Canadian authority and Canadian law throughout Western Canada by a handful of mounted police."

Writing his mother two days before the trip Darrell said, "I was roused from bed by the police who were very excited and asked me to take a patrol over to Peel River to meet Frank Oliver, the Minister of the Interior, who is coming to Dawson by way of the Mackenzie River and Fort McPherson. It appears there is no one here who knows the way right through." To his father he writes from Arctic Red River on July 4, 1910, of the many mosquitoes on that trip. "On July 1st the R.C. Mission 'St. Marie' arrived here, and to our surprise had Mr. Oliver on board who was in a hurry and had not waited for the Hudson's Bay boat. He of course asked to see me when he heard I had come over with the party from Dawson to meet him and was at this place. I told him a good deal about the portage and the Porcupine River. When he would reach Fort Yukon on the mouth of the Porcupine he would catch a steamboat for Dawson."

Sgt. A.E. Acland was in charge of Darrell's last patrol. Reporting on it Acland refers to the gasoline police launch 'Frontiersman' utilized for part of the trip down the Yukon and up the Bell to La Pierre House. "On the 21st at 8 P.M.", reads his report, "I left La Pierre House with Waters and Darrell and five days' grub, leaving Simons and Small at La Pierre House to await our return, and started over the portage to Peel River, packing about 25 pounds each. We found the walking very bad indeed, being mostly swamp country."

RCMP historian S.W. Horrall wrote me that "The Arctic explorer, Hubert Darrell, was employed by the Force as a Special Constable on a number of occasions on patrols in which he participated. As Mr. Darrell was employed temporarily for patrol work we do not have a service file on him." Acland's report indicates, "H. Darrell was paid off on the 27th." So ended Darrell's Arctic career as guide for the RNWMP. The words of Canadian poet Robert Service, whom Darrell knew in Dawson, may well have been meant for this remarkable Arctic wanderer, "This is the law of the Yukon, and ever she makes it plain. Send not your foolish and feeble; send me your strong and your sane." Hubert Darrell exemplified this ancient Law of the North.

3. HISTORICAL HIGHLIGHTS OF RIVERS   Valley Vistas column, Brandon Sun, July 28/73

Clare Swain, a former Boissevainite and now secretary-treasurer of R.M. of Daly, tells me Rivers will be celebrating its Diamond Jubilee August 3-6. Clare, I feel, may want to prolong celebrations a further two weeks for he's contemplating matrimony Aug. 18--and as fellows like me who've been hitched two decades well know, all further celebrations cease as of that date!! (I doubt if his intended, Betty Wiley, will appreciate that prediction).

Rivers, like Brandon, sprang up over night when a major railway passed through the site. And like Brandon it's situated in a valley on a pleasant meandering river. A huge dam built recently created popular Wahtopanah Lake.

The mile-long trestle bridge spanning the valley in 1908, constructed by Grand Trunk Railway, was then one of the longest of its kind in Western Canada. Named after railway president Charles Rivers-Wilson, this railway centre was incorporated in 1913 after less than three years as a booming village which had witnessed events like a rail strike culminating in traditional western shoot-out at the Cecil House hotel resulting in one dead and two injured. For some residents, like Percy Bayliss, Rivers wasn't booming enough for he started walking north in quest of gold, got as far as Rice Lake before discovering "warm weather was scarcer than gold, doubled back, walking 24 hours without anything to eat" after which through kindness of a Transcona cafe owner "slowly began recuperating from frostbite and gold-fever." Six years later Providence remembered the penitent Riversite when a severe summer storm ripped off the Anglican church tower and roof leaving Percy inside shaken but uninjured.

Both world wars brought many enlistments from Rivers and troop trains through it, decorations like the Victoria Cross to Lce. Cpl. Michael Leary for conspicuous bravery in the first conflict, and Distinguished Flying Cross to F/O Walter Daniel who released the six-ton bomb which destroyed Hitler's mightiest battleship Tirpitz boosting greatly Allied morale at expense of Axis plus a posthumous VC to CSM John R. Osborne for heroism at Hong Kong in the second. During the last war the nearby air base was one of its kind under Commonwealth Air Training Plan and those terrible years saw the name 'Rivers' become wider known internationally than any other Canadian Prairie centre.

Located on a major railway and for years near a major RCAF base, Rivers frequently became the scene of visiting royalty and political dignitarians. The year 1951 saw 50,000 people over-run this town to catch a glimpse of Princess Elizabeth (queen several months later) and Duke Philip while 1923 saw HRH the Prince of Wales walk the last mile into town accompanied by a solitary escort. The Depression years brought visitors of another kind-- hordes of 'riding the rails' hoboes descended on the town panhandling while the freight trains refuelled.

Rivers has produced several famous personalities; Earl Dawson of hockey fame, nuclear scientist Dr. Harry Messel, metropolitan opera star Iva Withers to cite three. Occasionally a weekly newspaper 'scoops' the big dailies, like when Rivers Gazette carried a major news story of a record established by a Sabre-Jet from Edmonton to Rivers in 1952 several days before the dailies got wind of the story.

Magazine articles by RCAF personnel did much to focus attention on West-Man. One I'm particularly familiar with was by F/O P.M. Simpson which appeared in the May 1955 issue of The Roundel. A most interesting and informative article its objective was to introduce newly-posted personnel at Canadian Joint Air Training Centre (which then had a population of 22,000) to the base, to the town of Rivers, and to recreation and other facilities of southwestern Manitoba.

From the beginning Rivers seems to have had cordial relations with Indians of the vicinity. Back in 1910 Sioux Chief Charlie Okupaw was organizing Indian pow-wows in town. In 1943, when the 86-year-old chief whom Rivers had learned to know and like well died, historian G.F. Barker notes his passing with the comment he now "could roam the happy hunting grounds in peace." Perhaps it's fitting Canada's unique co-operative experiment with her native citizens should take place at Oo-Za-We-Kwun near this particular town.

Writing to commemorate Rivers' Golden Jubilee 10 years ago Barker suggests that "reuniting sons and daughters may roam again the banks of the Little Saskatchewan with its memoried swimming holes and picnic spots--and visit their modern counterpart in Wahtopanah Lake; or wander their yesteryears' school classroom; or worship amid new surroundings on the same sites they knew long ago. They will find along the streets, among more recently built dwellings, that many early homes still stand--perhaps their own birthplace, included." The same will apply, perhaps even more strongly, next weekend in Rivers.

4. BABIES   Valley Vistas column, Brandon Sun, August 4, 1973

Ever judged a Beautiful Baby Contest? Don't feel too depressed if you haven't. I had not either until two weeks ago--and feel I'd sooner judge at a dozen school science fairs or shoot a charging lion. As family counsellor I'm hoping I didn't break up as many homes in half an hour as I pride myself I helped salvage in six years. Oh well, Mother warned me there would be days like that.

It's really strange how very little personality a baby of several months exhibits when you, a total stranger, stop and stare at it (her? him?) for a moment. Especially when we are so used to thinking of people in terms of personalities. Most very young babies reveal about as much personality as pumpkins in a garden, and considerably less than after those become jack-o-lanterns. Don't tell anyone but I prefer babies between ages 3 to 5 years--and 25 to 50.

Some categories like 'most hair', 'best finger or thumb sucker', 'chubbiest', 'most curls', 'baldest', are impersonal enough and easy to judge objectively. When you get to 'happiest', 'prettiest eyes', and 'cutest dimples (anywhere)' things start getting more sticky. The real doozer is the trophy-winning 'most beautiful baby' category, being entirely subjective and a much more personal thing for both judges and mothers. Believe you me it becomes hard at this point to differentiate between the mother--whose physical beauty and personality are virtually inseperable and reasonably obvious--who is holding the baby, and the little tyke who doesn't yet show much of either attribute.

Of the three categories: 0-6 months, 7-12 months, 13-18 months, I was involved in the middle one. Fortunately the two judges with me--Nancy Taylor, a former most capable student of mine and now a successful insurance agent--and Valerie St. John--formerly a doctor here to whom I'm still indebted for giving a biology class a guided tour of the local hospital which undoubtedly rates as one of the best of some 75 tours of one sort or other in which I was involved as teacher--had their feet solidly on the ground and their heads out of the clouds.

The three most beautiful baby trophies went to Michael Syslak, Barbara Gillishammer, and Craig Boyd. Being a male chauvinist I was overjoyed to discover that boys are more beautiful than girls, but also being a realist I was forced to conclude that because two out of three judges in each division were women, females probably instinctively find males more attractive. (These hypotheses may require further research before being fully acceptable to the scientific community as theories).

Kidding aside, I feel the Lambda Chapter of Beta Sigma Phi's venture proved remarkably popular and the contest committee itself--composed of Marilyn Hoffman, Maxine Proven and Fawn Scott--every bit as attractive themselves as you could find in any beauty contest. Unfortunately the club neglected to provide a category for that particular age.

President of the club Dianne Nylen, a former school teacher who still hangs in there substituting, indicates the organization consisting of two chapters is "well over 20 years old". Like most clubs its purpose combines social interaction and community service but Dianne feels Minnedosa stresses the latter more than do most city counterparts. Projects the group's involved with include providing annual scholarships for sudents entering nursing and related fields, Christmas hampers, financial assistance to organizations like Children's Aid and Touchwood Park.

Minnedosa's recent beautiful baby contest wasn't the only focus on babies during local Fun Fest celebrations. The Railroaders Association, composed of numerous CPR employees living here and first organized four years ago for centennial purposes but never disbanded because of its popular projects, introduced an added attraction to Railroaders' Day by awarding a $50 Canada Savings Bond to the "first baby arrival on Railroaders' Day Time 0001 to 2359". Winning the award hands down (bottoms up?) was Jennifer Lynn Freeman, daughter of Ernest and Lorraine Freeman of Minnedosa, who arrived at the local hospital at precisely 0705 hours (7:05 a.m. to most of us) with some assistance from Dr. Ray Bright. Headed by Ken Harris the railroaders have, in addition to this popular annual day of celebrations, given valuable assistance to the skating rink, baseball club, Tanner's Crossing Park.

The emphasis on babies here brings to mind this town's first two babies. Minnedosa's first boy--appropriately named Minnedosa and later shortened to Mindo--was a son of Dr. and Mrs. Kenning while the first girl was Minnedosa (Dosa) Armitage (later Mrs. Rook of Calgary), daughter of J.S. and Elizabeth (Schwalm) Armitage. Little Dosa, as the Feb. 16, 1882 edition of Minnedosa Star (copy owned by Evelyn Erickson) attests, quickly made news by setting the Armitage home on fire and then calmly watching her mother battle the blaze and finally manage to put it out.

In sharp contrast to focus on babies was a most attractive display of hobby craft by senior citizens at Minnedosa Fair last week. People like Dave Cannon, the Wm. Hoods, Howard and Ralph Shorrock, Frank Usick had created an exceptionally popular display of items like horse-drawn vehicles, lamps, miniature furniture, diamond willow cane, spoon rack, souvenir commemorating 'Minnedosa Inn 1887-1972' whittled from one of its beams, a 'bottle cap' figure of a man. Maybe it's time we did focus more strongly on babies and senior citizens and somewhat less on youth at whose shrine we've worshipped for the past quarter century.

5. JERRY STOUDT'S DUCK RESEARCH   Valley Vistas column, Brandon Sun, August 11, 1973

Although I'd known of Jerry Stoudt for several years and even written an article about a project in which he was deeply involved, I'd never met him personally until last week. Tall, stately, greying, pleasant, this wildlife biologist sat in his room at the new Minnedosa Inn and described some problems and highlights of a 42-year career, the last 22 summers of which were spent on the Canadian prairies.

Jerome H. Stoudt was born and grew up at Hastings on the Mississippi River near St. Paul, Minnesota; son of dentist Frank Stoudt and Mary Hanna whose father Jerome was an early pioneer there. After high school he attended University of Minnesota where he was one of the first two masters graduates in wildlife management. He's employed by the US government's Fish and Wildlife Service, operates out of Jamestown, N.D., but makes his permanent home with wife Marian in Aberdeen, S.D., has a son and daughter, three grandsons.

Through the past two decades Jerry's been involved in three major Canadian duck research projects near Red Deer, Alta., Redvers, Sask. and Minnedosa's pothole region. His specialty's canvasbacks, which nest on water in reed cover. He's the author of several US government wildlife publications, one he gave me being based on the Redvers project. His 12-year canvasback research here, in raw form a volume an inch thick, will be published shortly.

Canvasback nesting success this year's possibly the worst on Canadian prairie record. Although the 70 square mile project area between Minnedosa and Forrest contains what Jerry's convinced is the best canvasback breeding habitat in North America, nesting success this summer was less than three per cent. Canvasback nesting success since 1960 has never been especially high (45% average here) and the blow this fine game bird is currently suffering is phenomenal. If you have visions of hunting that particular species this fall, forget it! Redheads and coots have suffered a somewhat less severe setback.

Jerry explained why canvasbacks couldn't raise young this summer. Although these birds prefer large lakes and sloughs much of the year, they nest on very small secluded potholes. Probably because redheads transmit parasites to them and elude their closely related cousins by nesting on hidden, easy-to-defend ponds. Last year's water level was the highest in at least 12 years. A dry fall plus little snow in winter caused a drastic drop in pond levels away from natural shore cover like cat tails. Instead of nests being on 18" - 24" deep water and hidden by vegetation as in past years, they now were on water 6" deep and exposed. Predators like racoons, skunks, and to lesser degree red foxes, wiped out virtually all nests.

Jerry's four decades of wildlife research have convinced him a large part of our current increasing small predator problem's due to past government policies on both sides of the border of destroying coyotes. True, coyotes also destroyed some nests—but comparatively few for rarely was there more than one pair per five square miles, and they kept small predators in check. With coyotes gone, skunks, racoons and foxes multiplied rapidly. In short, where 25 years ago two coyotes roamed, today upward of fifty smaller predators hunt.

Jerry isn't too worried about foxes because recent sharp rise in price of their fur will keep them under control. He cited one instance of a Minnedosa mink rancher, Albert Kruger, having trapped 58 foxes last winter. Skunks and racoons are another matter entirely.

I questioned Jerry on his views concerning bounties on predators and he indicated this method can be effective if employed over a short time period and a very high bounty paid, making it extremely costly to municipalities. Most bounty systems reduce predator populations by only about 30% and this has virtually no effect on game bird populations. To be effective a system must wipe out at least 80% of predators and defiitely destroy adult females. When bounties are small extending over many years, hunters deliberately avoid killing the goose that lays golden eggs.

Current high long-haired fur prices have no effect on skunk and racoon populations. Skunks hibernate in winter, and racoons much of it. Farmers could help most in controlling these two predators by destroying old abandoned farm buildings and burning and levelling the countless bulldozed brush piles near recently-cleared fields. And if farmers would just stop burning grass and reeds around sloughs every fall a major waterfowl increase would result. Not only does this burning destroy next spring's nesting cover, it also destroys small rodents like mice on which predators commonly feed and these then turn to duck and upland game bird eggs instead. Even if we could bring coyotes back, says Jerry, this alone would not turn back the clock for skunks and racoons are too firmly entrenched in walls of buildings and brush piles. Racoons and skunks could be sharply controlled with strychnine-injected eggs near their homes; a method outlawed in the US and frowned on in Canada.

Perhaps the canvasback wouldn't have been hit so hard if it didn't possess such a strong homing instinct. Most lay eggs on the same ponds each year. Not so coots and redheads. When these encountered nesting problems here this year, they simply headed further north. Canvasbacks stayed.

13

Jerry Stoudt has just retired and by the time this article's published will have returned to the USA. In an era when the cry 'Yankee, go home!' rings out in many countries and sometimes here, this particular American and his colleagues have contributed much to the welfare of Canadians. To him, and others like him, a most sincere 'Welcome, Yankee; come again!'

In the same column on October 27, 1973:
Recently Jerry Stoudt wrote clarifying the statement concerning redheads transmitting parasites to canvasbacks stating, "redheads are parasitic and lay their eggs in canvasback nests. About 57% of 2,500 canvasback nests found from 1961 to 1972 in Minnedosa-Shoal Lake area contained redhead eggs." In connection with fall burning he wished I'd included "spring burning, because burning in spring is even worse because it destroys many nests of ducks as well as nests of other birds, mammals and insects."

6. DARRELL'S MYSTERIOUS DISAPPEARANCE   Free lance article, The Whitehorse Star,
Aug. 15/73

After 12 years of Arctic exploits unmatched by any man of his era Hubert Darrell suddenly vanished in the Anderson River region. The past 63 years have shed little light on the fate of one of Canada's most remarkable Klondikers. Anniversaries being celebrated in the Arctic this year--75th birthday of Yukon as territory, Klondike Gold Rush of 1898, White Pass and Yukon Route, 100th birthday of RCMP formed as NWMP--would hardly be complete without reference to the intriguing mystery that shrouds the disappearance of a northerner who played major roles in these Arctic events being commemorated.

How a man of Hubert Darrell's amazing abilities could vanish without trace in the land he knew like the back of his own hand has puzzled Canadians for six decades. The mystery of his disappearance is every bit as intriguing as was the much-publicized mystery surrounding the death of famous artist-outdoorsman Tom Thomson in Northern Ontario just seven years later.

There are certain striking similarities between the two men and the two mysteries. Both men were physically robust, excellent canoeists, reserved with strangers, dark of complexion, in their 30s. William T. Little's comment on Thomson that "The north country gradually got him, body and soul" applies as strongly to Darrell.

Both were secretly engaged to be married; both deeply patriotic, highly independent, courageous, honest men--well liked and highly respected by their peers. Both made at least one bitter enemy. However, whereas evidence presented by Little strongly suggests Thomson was murdered by his foe, no evidence exists that Darrell's greatest rival did more than fight with him, sue him, attempt to discredit him throughout the Arctic and prevent his obtaining employment, publicly denounce him in at least one book.

Writing for the Dawson News July 6, 1911, from Fort Arctic Red River (reprinted in London Daily News August 1, 1911), Darrell's trader-prospector friend Joseph Jacquot tells of a lengthy exploration-prospecting trip his wife and he made with Darrell the previous summer. Some of this time was spent correcting his enemy, A.H. Harrison's inaccurate maps of the Anderson region. On September 21 they parted with the understanding they would meet on December 5 after freeze-up, return to Arctic Red River together and continue on to Dawson.

Jacquot waited until December 15, but no sign of Darrell. He writes that his friend "was pretty well outfitted" when they separated. "Of grub he had enough to last him a month without having to resort to any game. He had a good shotgun and good 30-30 carbine", plenty of ammunition.

Arctic explorer Vilhjalmur Stefansson, who knew Darrell well, wrote a lengthy letter to his friend's school teacher fiancee Agnes Dudley of Birtle, Manitoba, on September 30, 1912 (letter owned by Dartmouth College) describing Darrell's whereabouts since leaving Jacquot and speculating on his disappearance.

"In the fall of 1910," writes Stefansson in part, "Mr. Darrell visited the Eskimo village at the Baillie Islands (Cape Bathurst); I think the time was early November, though I am not sure of the date. There was wintering there at the time the whaling schooner 'Rosie H', Capt. Fritz Wolki, mate Harry Slate.

"At this time I was in Coronation Gulf perhaps 400 miles east of Cape Bathurst. Cpt. Wolki, I believe, was absent and Mr. Darrell was entertained by Mr. Slate. Mr. Darrell did not stay long, for he wished, he said, to return at once to Fort Macpherson (about 400 miles SW), intending to cross over to Dawson in December or January.

"When Mr. Darrell left the Baillie Islands he travelled alone--which was a perfectly safe thing for so competent a man as he was, except for the possibility of accidents or illness. He was going toward a permanent camp he had, which I suppose to have been 30 to 40 miles SW of the Baillie Islands.

"He had Eskimo neighbors near--but not at--his camp. These people say that he arrived at his camp safely from the Baillie Islands. About this time he wrote a letter to Mr. Slate, containing a Post Script for me. In it he re-iterates his intentions to proceed to Fort Macpherson. This letter he gave to one of his Eskimo neighbors and it was by him carried to Mr. Slate and by Mr. Slate later forwarded to me.

"I received the letter before we began to suspect that anything might have gone wrong with Mr. Darrell, and so I took no particular care of the letter--I think, however, that it is preserved somewhere in my baggage which should arrive in San Francisco in November. If I find the letter I shall send it to you. I fear it may prove to be the last certain trace we have of him.

"The Eskimo, so far as I know (and I think I have spoken with all of them) did not see Mr. Darrell leave his camp. He must however have left it in late November or early December, no doubt heading for MacPherson as he had intended. This was not a more difficult trip than he had already made more than once; in other words, there was nothing to be feared from blizzards or cold, nor was there danger of his missing his way and suffering starvation for that reason--some other men might have been in danger from these things, but not Darrell.

"I think I shall be doing you the greatest kindness in my power by ending all suspense, so far as my opinion in the matter goes: I admired Darrell too much to concede that any incompetence can have been the cause of his loss, which I fear is now only too certain: some serious accident or a sudden illness must have come upon him.

"As for the writing found on a tree by some Eskimo: several days' journey up the Anderson River there was seen a blazed tree with some writing on the blaze. It is not, of course, impossible that Mr. Darrell may have gone up the Anderson River towards Good Hope, though why he should do so I cannot see--for one thing, that would presuppose a sudden change of plans entirely uncharacteristic of him. I think it therefore most probable that this was the writing of some Good Hope Indian--for these Indians hunt in the district where the writing was seen, and many of them can write. I told the Eskimo, however, if they went to this locality again, to cut the tree down and to bring the piece with the writing on it to the 'Rosie H' at the Baillie Islands to be read. These instructions I gave the Eskimo in March 1912, and the first week of the following May I reported the facts to the Mounted Police (Inspector Betys) at Herschel Island.

"For a year and more after Mr. Darrell left the Baillie Islands we considered him safe--had no reason to think that he had failed to reach Dawson; personally I thought the chances of his safety good till I saw the Police in May last--I thot, in other words, that he had got safely south and that we had merely thru some accident failed to hear from him. I speak not only for myself and Dr. Anderson but also for Captain Wolki and Mr. Slate of the 'Rosie H' when I say that had we realized the situation while yet there was any hope we should have made a search, not only for mere reasons of humanity but because of the admiration we all felt for his ability and character."

Because of Hubert Darrell's phenomenal ability of walking and canoeing alone through the Arctic while living off the country, no one seems to have really missed him or initiated a search until many months after his disappearance.

Luta Munday, in her book A MOUNTIE'S WIFE, attributes his death to "an attack by a polar bear". She may of course be right in her speculation. That polar bears inhabited the region is pointed out by Jacquot when he writes, "We saw a polar bear track, a very fresh and large one. It resembled more than anything else the bottom of a barrell".

RNWMP records show polar bears frequently were killed by Indians and Eskimo of that area. But why then was no trace ever found; like clothing, rifle, shotgun, bedroll? The RNWMP, for whom Darrell worked as guide on several occasions, themselves don't appear to have looked for him. RCMP historian S.W. Horrall wrote me recently "There does not seem to have been any search conducted for him or, if there was, we do not have a record on it."

In fact, the Mounties had serious other problems just then. Inspector Fitzgerald with constables Carter, Kinney and Taylor had just perished on the mail trip from Fort Macpherson to Dawson while attempting to break the speed record for the run held by Cst. Bob Forrest--Darrell's best friend on the Force. The route was one along which Darrell had guided policemen several times. Jacquot, in his article, indicates that had his companion not vanished the four Mounties would likely not have died, for the two men were planning to follow the same route and would have caught up with the policemen before tragedy overtook them.

Had Darrell not disappeared he would have accompanied Roald Amundsen to the South Pole the following year. "He would certainly have been a member of that expedition," writes Amundsen, "had not fate intervened....one of the finest men of the northern breed it has ever been my good fortune to meet."

Stephen B.W. North of Birtle, son of William Ivor Wolseley North who was Hubert's best friend in this province, told me recently, "Nothing official was ever learned of his disappearance although Charlie (Hubert's older brother with whom he farmed until the gold rush) did his very best, contacting whomsoever he could from the north. Actually, Stefansson and Amundsen, by expressing admiration for his courage and independence, foreshadow his probable end. Various rumours filtered out of the Arctic for years -- Eskimos had discovered his remains, he'd been killed by polar bears etc. but absolutely nothing authentic."

Dr. Margaret G. Dudley of Winnipeg, younger sister of Hubert's fiancee, told me, "Agnes wrote many letters--to Stefansson, Robert Service etc. and hoped against hope Hubert would turn up. His untimely death was a great shock to her." Eleven years later Agnes married Charlie; a marriage that had serious problems and produced no descendants. Both are dead now.

During the year Darrell disappeared a strange double killing took place in the same Keewatin area Hanbury and Darrell had explored nine years previous. Two American explorers-prospectors-hunters, Radford and Street, were killed by two Eskimo in what was later ruled self-defence because the two had threatened the Eskimo when they refused to guide them further. Coincidently, it had been Harry Radford--an avid trophy hunter--who during most of the past year had pestered Darrell to guide him on an extended hunting trip in the barrens. Despite a most attractive financial offer and personal recommendation from a bishop, Darrell had flatly refused because of Radford's infamous reputation with Eskimo, Indians and Whites in Mackenzie and Yukon--much to Radford's anger. If Darrell had two enemies, Radford could be considered the second one.

It's been speculated Darrell may have committed suicide or simply left the Arctic and vanished on purpose. That he had numerous bitter disappointments can't be discounted. Several stand out.

The loss of the schooner Francis Allyn, under Captain Santos, by burning at sea near Cape Fullerton July 15, 1902 with most of Darrell and Hanbury's specimens of their 16-month exploration-scientific expedition depressed him somewhat as letters to his parents reveal. Being unable to capitalize on a major copper discovery, and later one of gold ore the potential of which he underestimated while a passing acquaintance to whom he described it became rich. Not being selected for Captain Joseph Bernier's expedition for the Canadian government. The death of close friend and co-explorer Major David T. Hanbury in San Francisco the same year Darrell vanished. The extreme lengths to which A.H. Harrison went to discredit Darrell simply because the latter quit his expedition.

Following publication of Harrison's 1908 book IN SEARCH OF A POLAR CONTINENT in which he harshly criticizes him, Darrell's younger brother Claud in England planned to take Harrison and his publisher to court and force them both to apologize publicly. "I don't know how to answer him," Hubert writes his father June 19/09 from Dawson where he lived much of the time from 1907-1910. A year after he left the Harrison expedition in fall of 1905, Darrell confides to his mother in a letter from Fort Good Hope that "Things turned out as Harrison predicted. He said that no one would give me a job if they really knew me and so far he is right."

However, considered in light of the indomitable type of man he was, his approaching marriage to Agnes Dudley, the proposed trip to the South Pole with Amundsen he eagerly contemplated, it's highly unlikely Darrell committed suicide. Nor is it likely he left the Arctic of his own accord for all available evidence suggests otherwise.

The farm which Hubert and Charlie once operated in Warleigh district near Birtle was, indicates Stephen North, "on the same section where I was born. As a matter of interest, the old Hudson's Bay trail crossed it, and until quite recently the ruts were clearly visible. Charlie died on the home place in the late fifties, still in the same house-- a veritable wreck by then--and it has since burned down. Bulldozers cleared all the trees off the house quarter, and at present it is simply another farm, a source of deep regret to me personally, for I had a deep affection for the old farm."

Whatever happened to Hubert Darrell that fateful fall day of 1910 will probably remain an unsolved Arctic mystery. Perhaps Canada's famous poet Robert Service, who lived in Dawson during the same years as Darrell and knew him well, provides us with the answer when he writes "I have clinched and closed with the naked North, I have learned to defy and defend, Shoulder to shoulder we have fought it out--yet the Wild must win in the end." Possibly Hubert Darrell did simply underestimate the naked North--and the Wild did win in the end.

7. DARRELL, ARCTIC EXPLORER   Free lance article, Western Producer, August 16/73

Few men knew the Canadian Arctic as intimately at the turn of the century as did Hubert Darrell. One of seven children of Lily Elizabeth and Charles Darrell of Worthing, Kent, England, he emigrated to western Canada alone in 1892 to join his older brother Charlie who had preceded him two years previous to farm at Warleigh near Birtle. "He went up north to improve their joint fortunes and help pay for the farm", explains Stephen North of Birtle, "but undoubtedly the love of wilderness and adventure played an important role." Darrell himself, Vilhjalmur Stefansson, Roald Amundsen corroborate this. Although lure of gold and adventure drew Hubert into the Arctic in '98, unlike countless prospectors who failed to strike it rich returning bitter and disillusioned, he fell in love with the vast northland and remained.

Writing his parents (letters owned by Scott Polar Research Inst. and microfilm by Glenbow-Alberta Inst.) from a shack on Great Slave River Jan. 20, 1900, he remarks, "Mr. Hanbury of survey brought me your last letter." During his first two years in the Arctic Darrell had prospected and explored the Great Slave region alone. He'd come to know well Joseph Burr Tyrrell--geologist, mining engineer, historian, surveyor--and James Bell, nephew of Robert Bell who explored vast areas of Canada's Arctic. Almost he accompanied James on an expedition to Bear Lake and Coppermine River but plans fell through. He and James corresponded regularly in succeeding years. His chance Oct. 1, 1899 meeting with famous explorer David T. Hanbury played a major role in Hubert's destiny.

In July, 1901, Hanbury engaged Darrell to guide his second fact-finding expedition into the Arctic which lasted 16 months spanning much of the north and uncovering valuable data. Characteristically, Hubert makes light of this immense undertaking in letters to parents who worried readily. Hanbury, however, wrote a long, detailed book with numerous photographs called SPORT AND TRAVEL IN THE NORTHLAND OF CANADA published 1904 by Macmillan of New York and London.

Stefansson pays tribute to the expedition saying, "Although Franklin's parties, Richardson's, Dease and Simpson's, and many others have been over ground adjacent or overlapping that covered by Hanbury, I have always found that in all practical matters related to means and method of travel, distances etc., and especially in my intercourse with the Eskimo, I have derived greater help from Hanbury's book than all the others put together." Darrell's own sketch maps and record of experiences remained unpublished till now.

The Hanbury-Darrell expedition began at Fort Resolution on Great Slave Lake and ended at Fort Norman on junction of Mackenzie and Great Bear rivers. Roughly it followed a giant curve running east northeast to Chesterfield Inlet on Hudson Bay through lakes like Artillery, Campbell, Abbott, Beverly, Schultz, Baker and along the river later named Hanbury, continuing down the Arkilinik (Thelon) River.

Stopping briefly at Marble Island in Hudson Bay the small party wintered in the Daly Bay region making exploratory excursions and hunting forays northwestward into the Tehek Lake, Quoich and Back rivers area. In early spring they continued north to Garry Lake, down Perry River to the Arctic coast, Melbourne Island, westward past Kent Peninsula, through Coronation Gulf to mouth of the Coppermine, up the Rae arcing southward to Dismal Lake, Kendall and Dease rivers, into Great Bear Lake exploring it, and finally down Great Bear River.

Besides guiding-exporing, Darrell's duties included hunting and fishing for food, paddling and steering canoes, building shelters, helping gather scientific data like rock samples, fossils, butterflies, examples of Eskimo culture, sketching maps. Accompanying the two white explorers was Sandy Turner--a Metis interpreter--and several Indians and Eskimo who remained for varying lengths of time.

To his parents Darrell generally speaks highly of Hanbury making comments like: "He has a clever head and his experience has taught him that small parties are best in this country for if you're going a long distance you can't carry grub and must live on the country, it's easier to hunt for two than three. The bigger the party the greater the risk of starvation. He was very kind to me. He is very well known in Canada from end to end and has a marvelous constitution."

There appear to have existed only three mild differences of opinion between the two explorers; one of these following their parting in fall 1902. Stephen North indicates, "While acting as guide to Hanbury's expedition Hubert left the party and climbed a ridge of hills and noted a river on the far side. Returning he mentioned this fact to the explorer and Hanbury subsequently named the discovery after himself. Other members of the party were unanimous that it should have been the Darrell River."

The second instance involves Hanbury's scepticism about Darrell's being surrounded by a pack of Arctic wolves during a solitary side trip. Darrell, Hanbury and North refer to this incident. Dealing with the third, Darrell writes his father from Great Slave Lake March 26, 1903 that he disagrees with Hanbury's account as it appeared in the Edmonton Journal, that he himself can't publish anything without Hanbury's permission, but does not elaborate. Unfortunately most of Darrell and Hanbury's expedition mementos were lost when the Francis Allyn burned and sank shortly after their trip.

Writing his parents from Edmonton July 7, 1905 following a lengthy visit to Birtle he states, "I went to Brandon and met Harrison at Calgary just as I was boarding the train for Edmonton." Unlike his fortunate encounter with Hanbury, Darrell's meeting this fellow had far-reaching negative results starting a feud which never died.

A.H. Harrison was an American surveyor-explorer of sorts planning to traverse the Mackenzie to Herschel Island, winter there, and as Darrell writes, "next year go over the ice as far as the Lord will let us to explore the hitherto unknown region of Bank land." Harrison claims he hired Darrell in Winnipeg, Darrell that he was hired "to run the boat" as "navigator".

Darrell had reservations about this expedition before it even began, writing, "I feel rather uneasy as to prospects and chances of success as the man is not Hanbury and has not the instant resources of my former boss." A month later he writes his father, "I understand currents pretty well but Harrison is as green as you can make them although he should not be, having been engaged in this kind of thing for the past 15 years. I have to tell him everything. He will pull the oar the wrong way and cut wood on a stone with an axe just as cheerfully as you please. I am very sorry I've gone with him. He will never do anything by himself."

In his book Harrison berates Darrell's poor navigation in "running the scow onto a sand-bar." At Arctic Red River Darrell returns the salary advanced him and quits the expedition. A fist fight ensues. Harrison takes Darrell to court charging him with breach of contract. The case comes before RNWMP Inspector Howard who rules Harrison's accepting the cheque terminated the agreement.

Writing his father from Fort Yukon, Alaska March 5, 1906 and his mother Oct. 20, 1907 from Dawson, Darrell indicates that Harrison "was utterly incompetent to be in charge of a party and misrepresented everything to me. We had four months journey to Peel's River, which should have been done in two, with the result it ended in hardship. He nearly drove me crazy talking about his theories and every day it was a different proposition. He said he will publish the reasons for not being able to carry out his plans and throws the blame on me. He wants to see Mr. Hanbury and find out what sort of fellow I was with him. Harrison treated me most dastardly. Those who know him in the north don't pay much attention to his stories. His so-called survey of the Red River-McPherson portage created great amusement and was very much wrong at the time although he may have found out his mistake afterward and rectified it. Count de Sanville spent three years, about 1893-96, all over the district Harrison was in and far beyond but died before making public his survey which can be had from some French academy. Harrison's way of showing a river uniform in width is absurd. He shows no bays or winds or points; no one can locate himself."

Darrell next met explorer John A. Cook, author of THAR SHE BLOWS and PURSUING THE WHALE, on the whaler Bowhead in April, 1906. His association with Harrison had left him destitute and he contracted to deliver mail to a whaling fleet frozen in at Baillie Islands. He visited Cook a few days and left. On March 23, 1910 he writes his mother from Dawson, "I see that Cook has been denounced as a fraud. I was positive from the first accounts that he was, although when he started north three years ago I thought it was a good man going."

Darrell's association with Roald Amundsen gave direction to the remainder of his short life. Amundsen first met him February, 1906. "We came up to a solitary man, his face black with smoke, accompanied not even by a dog, and dragging his toboggan behind him", writes Amundsen in MY LIFE AS AN EXPLORER. "Here was a man, hundreds of miles from the nearest human being, cheerfully trudging through the Arctic winter across an unblazed wilderness, and thinking nothing at all of his exploit. I was lost in admiration of this hearty and cheerful Scotsman. We became warm friends and subsequently he wrote me many letters, in the last of which he asked to include him in my impending expedition to the South Pole. I was delighted at the opportunity to get him". Stefansson quotes him exclaiming, "With a crew of men like that, I could go to the moon."

Darrell's opinion of Amundsen is equally high and to his parents writes warmly of him ending with, "I should very much like to go on the next expedition with Amundsen for bar accidents like crushing the ship and losing everything Amundsen is going to reach the Pole, of that I've not the slightest doubt." This goal helped lessen deep disappointment he felt over being excluded from Captain Joseph Bernier's 1910 expedition for the Canadian government to emphasize claims to waters and islands of Arctic Canada.

In spring 1906 Darrell had been asked to join the Leffingwell-Mikkelsen expedition aboard the 'Duchess of Bedford'. He refused, confiding to parents the main reasons being exceptionally low salary and the fact the ship wasn't equipped with motor power. He predicted failure. Stefansson, slated as ethnologist for the same expedition, also recognized the latter drawback in negotiating Arctic ice and decided instead to join the vessel at Herschell Island should she make it that far. She doesn't. Darrell, exploring on foot in the vicinity, is the first to bring news of the expedition's problems to the outside world. At about the same time he'd rejected an offer from Canadian Forestry Commissioner Stewart to accompany him to Fort Yukon, continuing instead to explore alone. Stefansson pays high tribute to Darrell's lone exploration trip across the Endicott Mountains as a vastly greater achievement than one performed by Amundsen and acclaimed by the world.

Hubert Darrell has sharp criticism for one of Ernest Thompson Seton's noted achievements and nothing but scorn for Robert Edwin Peary's claim to be the first to reach the North Pole April 6, 1909. Of Seton's trip to the barrens with Darrell's friend Edward A. Preble he writes his mother from Dawson Dec. 17, 1907, "Only last week I see according to a Winnipeg paper that 'Thompson Seton travelled with Preble into the barren lands from Slave Lake and is the first white man to have undertaken the great journey since Franklin'. Where do I come in I wonder? Seton and Preble were never there; they might have gone towards there but I do not believe they were on the barrens for it is far from Resolution—at least 400 miles and many portages—and they did not have time to do it. Anyone who knows Hanbury knows that anyone taking the trip that he did would have taken at least a year longer, even supposing they had accomplished it at all."

Concerning Peary, Darrell writes his mother from Dawson March 23, 1910, "If they should denounce Peary it would complete things to my satisfaction as I want to know by what means he knocked off 120 geographical miles in a straight line in four days without Bartlett's pioneer work when he could not do that distance with Bartlett's aid and less loads and more men".

8. FATHERS   Valley Vistas column, Brandon Sun, August 18, 1973

Attended my father's 70th birthday in Boissevain recently. Being of a Neufeld lineage from which the males invariably die young we tend to over-react when one of ours does happen to reach that magic Biblical age of three score years and ten.

Like many immigrants from central Europe, Dad's had his share of problems (besides raising me, that is) during those seven decades. From age 11 to 18 his country (Russia) was at war or in revolt, with much hatred directed against members of his ethnic group. During that period his mother died leaving husband and three sons without a woman in the home. I'm not convinced the picture Ben Cartwright and his boys portray is all that rosy in real life. His older brother and several friends and relatives fought on the losing side of a revolution. Moving to new homeland without knowing a word of English, deep in debt before even beginning to farm, when things just start to improve a depression hits you, must be problems difficult to face without becoming bitter.

The influence of the father in the home today is often ignored by social scientists. Because wives have been more accessible to researchers most studies on parental influences in the home have focussed on mothers. What little data there is indicates the father has an extremely significant role to play in a family's stability. Dad also has a major effect on the psychological growth of sons and daughters, this influence becoming increasingly consequential as his children reach puberty and adolescence.

If modern fathers were with their children continually and took care of them from babyhood, they would undoubtedly exert a vastly greater effect on their families. Where fathers have through choice or necessity assumed more responsibility--fed and burped them, etc. --such children invariably turned to their fathers for comfort and counsel when ill or hurt in later years. This strongly suggests a father's role in the family as we understand it today is more likely forced upon him by economics than by psychological drives.

A father's own unique personality and feeling towards rearing his children strongly colors the role he plays in his family. If he's gentle and moderate always allowing Mom to hold the reins, his masculine effect on his children may be quite negligible. If he's an autocrat whose decisions are never questioned his effect on his children will be readily seen. A normal, democratic father who stays at home quite often exercises at least three vital influences on his children.

First, Dad brings the outside world into his home. This helps his children develop personalities better equipped to cope with today's modern world.

Second, Dad's essential for sex typing his sons. Boys need to identify with a man they admire to help them develop masculine personalities and learn appropriate male behavior. Thus sons become masculine in their interests, wants, motives and evolve male attributes. Further, Dad helps them broaden interests, develop leadership traits, self-discipline and self-direction vital in striking out on their own later.

Third, Dad's equally essential for sex typing daughters. Girls require frequent association with their fathers to learn how males behave and how girls should act toward men. This helps them clarify femininity with respect to masculinity. Without good male standards during childhood, daughters often have trouble establishing normal relationships with men later. Not only does Dad provide his daughter with manly shelter traditionally attributed to fatherhood but also he's a momentous factor through which she makes the transformation from normal childhood to healthy adjustment to the opposite sex as mature, adult woman.

While in Boissevain district we dropped in to see Joe Wilson who operates a horse ranch near Whitewater Lake. Joe owns a pony we raised which now has a beautiful filly eligible for registration as an Ara-Wel. Joe's ranch offers an exceptionally fine view of the huge marshy lake, which he says is higher than it's been for many years; in sharp contrast to Minnedosa area where lakes and ponds are at their lowest level.

Stopped for a picnic at Camp Koinonia on Max Lake in the Turtle Mountains. This camp is operated by the Mennonite Church and is one of the most interesting I've seen. Strong wilderness setting is emphasized with cabins well separated by bush and connected only by trails, much canoeing etc. Two cabins added this summer are intriguing being octagon in design with window in each wall and bunk bed alongside resulting in a most sensible arrangement. Director is Rev. Ed Cornelson, who grew up on a farm next to ours. Max, of course, also has a public beach worth visiting.

Chatted with minister brother Jake (actually I'm the only black sheep in the family) who's just back from another Mennonite camp--on the Assiniboine in Springstein area -- which played host to a number of Saulteaux kids from Little Grand Rapids-Bloodvein area where he spent three years recently as minister. This camp's just developed a somewhat unique and highly popular innovation, a 'Tarzan obstacle course'. From start to finish you remain 'in the jungle' off the ground, swinging on ropes from tree to tree, climbing up ropes, walking on logs suspended from trees, walking hand-over-hand along ropes.

When we arrived home we were overjoyed to find our own Ara-Wel mare had just produced a beautiful filly--the first second generation one in Canada, daughter of the same stallion that sired Joe Wilson's foal. Our mare's the same one I described July 28/72 as having both stallions to whom I tried to breed her. She must read this column faithfully for a month later she completely succumed to the charms of the younger (naturally!) one.

9. HUBERT DARRELL AND AGNES DUDLEY   Valley Vistas column, Brandon Sun, Aug. 25/73

Driving around in Warleigh district recently I decided to visit the old Darrell farm. Set on a natural ridge near the famous Carlton Trail, the buildings have unfortunately been demolished. Only ruins of a basement, some partly-burnt logs, pieces of farm machinery, broken glass remain. An excellent crop of chest-high wheat surrounded the ridge, golden rod blanketed the site, a flock of fine sharp-tailed grouse greeted me.

Letters to his parents in England during 12 years Hubert spent in the Arctic frequently refer to brother Charlie and their farm at Warleigh. From Fort Resolution on Dec. 13, 1902 he informs his mother of his brother's misfortune when several colts died. Four months later he indicates to his father that his fbrother's good wheat crop should help recoup some losses. During spring 1905 he returned to Warleigh to seed the crop while Charlie visited England. On July 7 from Edmonton while returning north he tells his mother "I certainly hope things go well with him for he's a good farmer and has the best farm around." June 1, 1906 he writes his father from Fort McPherson that Charlie had a bumper crop, "large farm with all machinery necessary. I enjoyed putting the crop in immensely and think the reason was I was my own boss and could go out in the field just when I saw fit." Frequently he tells his parents Charlie ought to get married. "It would be the making of him."

Charlie Darrell's supposed to be buried in Shoal Lake cemetery. If he is, he lies in an unmarked grave for Elsie and I checked every headstone carefully.

Hubert's fiancee was Agnes Dudley of Warleigh. A school teacher, she was the oldest daughter of Joseph Charles Dudley, born at Wedbley in Herefordshire, England, Oct. 18, 1851, died May 11, 1932, and Ada Birch, born at Birmingham in England, Nov. 29, 1855, died July 18, 1924; both buried in a family plot in Birtle cemetery. Agnes Clarissa was born at Birmingham May 2, 1877, died April 3, 1959 and is buried in the same plot.

On Feb. 3, 1921, in Winnipeg—almost 11 years after Hubert vanished in northern Yukon—Agnes married his older brother Charles Harrise Darrell. Although the marriage was a failure from the start, neither she nor Charlie ever remarried. Each went his own separate way: she continued teaching, he farming.

One of several schools in which Agnes Dudley Darrell taught during her career was a one-room country school called Oxford (1901-60; first building of logs, 1883-1900) in Wattsview district southwest of Birtle. Following consolidation with Birtle in 1960, it was converted into a farm house.

Chatted for a while with one of Agnes Darrell's former students, Edward McDonald. Ed's a son of William J. McDonald who farmed in Wattsview (once called Invercoe) all his life, grandson of William McDonald who in 1882 with wife Elizabeth Forbes (Astor estate employee) and seven children came from Iverness district where he'd been a gamekeeper and his father chief forester on the Edward Ellice estate. Quarantined two weeks for measles in Brandon the family continued up the Assiniboine by flat bottom boat (last boat of its kind to make the trip) to Birtle (Wattsview) Landing. Two miles east of Fort Ellice, where William Sr.'s brother Archibald then was HB CO.'s last chief factor, they farmed raising some of Canada's finest purebred Highland cattle. Several of this McDonald clan have played major roles in Manitoba, Canadian, American, international history.

Agnes taught Ed during both Grades 7 and 8. Ed liked her very much, found her strict but pleasant. In those days (1922-24) Grade 8s wrote provincial high school entrance exams. These he passed easily, an achievement for which he thanks Agnes. A severe bout of rheumatic fever during Grade 10 ended his formal education. Ed showed me where Birtle Landing used to be, where Hudson Bay Co. had a wharf and warehouse. Nothing remains of them or the old Red River cart trail past the landing which joined the Carlton five miles north.

Chatted briefly with J. Peeler, a farmer one-waying his summerfallow next to the Birtle Landing site. By coincidence, he grew up near Charlie and Hubert's farm, remembers Charlie well but Hubert had left for the Arctic long before his time. Of interest is the fact CNR marks this historic spot with the sign WATTSVIEW at their railway crossing despite the fact this siding's long gone. This is one site an historical society should definitely mark with a cairn. While in Warleigh district, Elsie and I visited briefly with Mrs. Stephen North who knew both Charlie and Agnes well. She recalls particularly the fast, rather wild horses Charlie drove.

Wattsview derives its name from the Will Watt family who farmed and once operated a post office and held church services and community meetings in their home. A.A. Wood, originally from Neepawa, today farming the Watt place, was in process of building a new barn and busy teaching a young calf to lead. He showed us the ruins of the original farm house which had been a combination of barn, granary and house. All-in-all, that short trip into Hubert and Charlie Darrell country, and that of Agnes Dudley who played a major role in the lives of both brothers, proved quite fascinating. And the Assiniboine Valley in the Birtle-Binscarth region plus the Birdtail Valley certainly rate high among West-Man's more spectacular scenic spots.

In the same column on October 6, 1973:
"I have been very interested in your write-up about Mr. Darrell," writes Florence Swainson of Upton Apts., Brandon. "Agnes Dudley taught at the Seeburn school for four

years, 1918-22. She boarded at Otto Seebach. The school was three miles south and one mile west of Angusville, has since been moved away. Some of her pupils are still around and remember her." Florence is a sister of J.L. Swainson, author of the book OUR ANCESTORS ARRIVE IN MANITOBA.

Miss Swainson's not the only one who's become interested in Hubert Darrell. Even a Toronto CBC producer phoned me with intentions of doing a program on this remarkable northerner from Birtle. Because I didn't want to impose too much Darrell on faithful readers of this column I'd written several other articles for various magazines on different aspects of Hubert's Arctic career and each one sparked considerable interest. Hope this West-Manite finally gets the recognition he rightly deserves--even if 65 years late.

Dr. Margaret Dudley of Winnipeg wrote me recently and enclosed a homestead map. This 1875 map lists the Darrell place (16-16-25) as first being homesteaded by J.H. Mason, Alexander and John Young, W. Hattey. The Darrells arrived later. She indicates, "I made inquiries at the vital statistics branch and Charlie Darrell died in Birtle hospital April 10, 1952 and was buried in Shoal Lake cemetery in a plot belonging to J.B. Findlay, who was an intimate friend of Charlie's. It is sad that his grave is unmarked."

In the same column October 27, 1973:

A recent letter from Thomas M. Young of Holland, Man., states in part, "I have read with very much interest your articles on Hubert and Charlie Darrell of Birtle. I was born in February, 1905, on SE¼ 16-16-25. My father was John Young who died in March, 1923. Alex Young was my uncle, never married and lived I think until 1937 or '38. I lived on that farm from 1905 to 1926 and then again from 1933 to 1951. Charlie Darrell died at his home on NW¼ 16-16-25, not in Birtle Hospital. He was discovered by a neighbor. I also knew the Miss Dudleys quite well, and their brother Ernest. My uncle Alex Young, I am given to believe, helped set the type for the first Brandon Sun that was issued. This was when they came West from Ontario."

10. TANNER OF TANNER'S CROSSING   Valley Vistas column, Brandon Sun, Sept. 1/73

That the one-armed Metis postmaster who founded Tanner's Crossing owning much of the land on which Minnedosa's located interests me must be obvious. When I learned recently John Tanner had been an American Civil War veteran I immediately inquired of appropriate US sources. Considerable red tape and $3 elicited the following:

John Tanner was born Aug. 17, 1839 or '40 at Torch Lake (Lac du Flambeau), Wisc. A farmer, he lived in Sterns County in Minnesota, postal address being St. Joseph. In August, 1862, he enlisted at St. Cloud as private in the Union Army's Ninth Regiment of Minnesota Voluntary Infantry from which he was honorably discharged in August, 1865, at Fort Snelling near St. Paul. Records list John at heights varying from 5'4" to 5'7", weighing 130 pounds, eye color grey or blue, complexion both dark and light, hair dark or sandy or brownish-black.

When John first applied for an American disability pension Oct. 5, 1904, he describes his disability as "right arm amputated above elbow" stating he's lived in Minnedosa 1869-80 and Prince Albert 1880-1904, mailing address being "Kirkpatrick, Canada." He indicates his wife is Katherine Trucher whom he married in Portage la Prairie Anglican Church in mid-June, 1869. He states he's a farmer and has no children.

It seems John is initially refused a pension. On Feb. 27, 1915, he reapplies -- from Kinosota on Lake Manitoba northeast of McCreary. Filed before commissioner of oaths J.G. Lockhart the application's "accepted as a claim under the act of May 11, 1912." He indicates since discharged he's lived in Minnesota until 1869, Manitoba until 1895, Saskatchewan until 1910, he sustained a rupture "while scouting at Fort Abercrombie, 1863."

On March 31, 1915, John files additional data and appears to have been living at Kinosota since May 28, 1907, at least. He states his wife died at Prince Albert on Jan. 17, 1907, spelling her name Catherine Troutchee. He indicates he has "no children by marriage. I have an adpoted son." Regarding his deceased wife, John says "her former husband's name was James Sinclair. I do not know the date of this marriage. James Sinclair died at Shoal Lake, Man. He never served in military; he was a Hudson's Bay Co. chief trader. I do not know the date of his death." Minister marrying Catherine and John was Rev. George.

On June 12, 1924, John appears before police magistrate J.W. Shuttleworth of Kinosota to file a new Declaration of Pension "to have regular personal aid and attendance of another person" due to "rupture, loss of one arm, and old age." Witnesses were Mrs. J.W. Garrioch and Susan Moar. He lists his occupation as carpenter. The increased pension claim is approved, this time under "Sec. 2, act of May 1, 1920."

Minnesota infantry muster rolls show John Tanner was 25 at time of discharge, retained his knapsack, haversack and canteen for which he still owed $6 but Uncle Sam owed him $15.79 clothing account and another $75. He's designated as scout, his company (G) at one point (September to October, 1864) having been in action at Pleasant Hills, Nev.

US Army medical records reveal John Tanner was treated for ruptured scroti Sept. 27 to Oct. 15, 1862, and related complications of orchitis Nov. 25-29, 1862 and Oct. 4-7, 1863, blenorrhagia Dec. 2 and 3, 1864, catarrh and hydrocele May 5-10, 1865 and "no additional record of disability found." An Oct. 14, 1932 pension "drop report" states John was last paid $100 per month to Sept. 3, 1932, having "this day been dropped from the roll because of death, Sept. 6/32", a Miss Halloran having notified them. His Kinosota address is still given.

Driving through Gambler reserve area southwest of Binscarth recently I decided to check the story that a John Tanner lived out his final years in that district about the same time. Eventually Elsie and I located the still-used old Indian-Metis cemetery overlooking Assiniboine Valley in a huge PFRA pasture near the former Metis settlement Madeline.

Of some 75 to 100 graves most are marked with simple wooden crosses, or with shield-like sandstone headstones--some with cross designs. A few have steel crosses; only about seven have names. A damaged figurine of Christ stands propped up. A white, rectangular marble tombstone of fairly recent origin near a foot-deep depression contains a cross design and inscription: John Tanner, 1842-1937. Adjacent is the largest and most ornate marker resembling a shield merging into cross with crucifixion design. Inscription reads: May, Wife of John Tanner, died Nov. 25, 1922, age 60 years. It's obviously been there long. Other designated graves belong to John E. Fleury, Pte. John Vermette, Alfred L. Demontigny, Mrs. Ambroise Fisher, Mrs. Julie L. Ducharme. The great grandson of this John Tanner, who inherited his personal effects, told me his ancestor too had fought in the US Army which owed him money upon discharge. (About six months after writing this article I learned the two John Tanners were cousins, the latter being a son of Chief Picheito Tanner of Portage la Prairie who was a half brother to Rev. James Tanner, the father of Minnedosa's founder).

In the same column October 6, 1973:

The Diocese of Rupert's Land, Anglican Church, was able to add information on John Tanner, founder of Tanner's Crossing. At 29, John, settler and son of James Tanner and mother's name not stated, of St. Mary's la Prairie near Portage got married. His bride was Catherine Sinclair, widow, daughter of Joseph Trottier and mother's name not stated, of St. Mary's la Prairie. The wedding took place July 14, 1869; witnesses were James Tanner and John Jas. Setter with Rev. Henry George officiating.

Mrs. Vermette, a granddaughter of John Tanner of Madeline, told me her ancestor was definitely not the founder of Tanner's Crossing. She remembers her grandfather well, also that he had both arms. She thought some family relationship did exist between the two John Tanners though--cousins or step brothers.

Craig Stewart too found the Tanner article interesting, indicated his father and uncle both farmed at Silver Ridge near Kinosota. Craig's father and uncle knew the one-armed Metis well. It was common knowledge there John once lived in Minnedosa, and was receiving an American disability pension because $100 per month was much money in those days and quickly made local news. Craig's father is dead but his uncle lives in a senior citizens home in Pine Falls and may have something to add about John's later years some time. John's loss of arm, by the way, seems not to have interfered with participation in sports for MINNEDOSA MEMORIES indicates he was one of this town's star football players in 1879.

In the same column October 27, 1973:

Came across some information on the Mr. Charles who tried to persuade John 'Falcon' Tanner (grandfather of Minnedosa's founder) to go to England and tell of his 30 years of living with Indians. Undoubtedly he was George Charles, a HBC trader at Nelson House and vicinity, close friend and former classmate in London's Grey Coat School of famous explorer-surveyor David Thompson. Full name of the officer commanding Selkirk's soldiers whom Falcon guided from Ontario to Red River was Capt. P.D. Orsonnes.

-11. CRANBERRY PORTAGE PROJECT   Valley Vistas column, Brandon Sun, Sept. 8/73

Of countless STEP, OFY and similar projects initiated and operated by hundreds of capable young people across the province this summer, one that interested me especially was conducted midway between The Pas and Flin Flon at Cranberry Portage. Perhaps because our oldest was involved in it and the 'Cranberry Project' had been a central topic of conversation in our home for the past half year. Perhaps because of the deep involvement of my favorite university--Brandon. But I like to think it's more because the whole concept's good.

In a nutshell, the project consists of uprooting several hundred of Manitoba's most strongly urban-bound 10-14 year olds and placing them in a diametrically opposite wilderness-type setting for two weeks under direction of university students with camping experience and training as teachers, receiving a fair but not high salary plus some university credits for their efforts.

The schools from which the youngsters were drawn were John M. King, Margaret Scott, Montcalm, Pinkham, River Elm, Victoria Albert, William White; all from downtown Winnipeg where most students live in apartments and seldom if ever get to leave the city. Project director was phys. ed. professor David Johns of U. of M. with his wife doing the nursing and Rob Vipond assisting, Benjy Levin of Youth Secretariat as field advisor and Rick Cooper accountant. Of some 25 camp counsellors, 17 came from BU. Besides Lory, they included Hendrica Trudeau, Kathy Quinn, Clara Underwood, Debby Simes, Don Johnston, Sharon Milburn, Janet Gara, Shirley Vandoorne, Compton Khan, Beverly Mayuk, Penny Abar, Valerie Wallis, Joy Dell, Brenda Kersell, Marie Gross, Art Esuke.

Last summer I wrote an article about Gord Vidal who was provincial co-ordinator of STEP and indicated we would likely hear more of him in years ahead. Gord's been deeply involved also in launching this program, which seems may become a permanent one and expand beyond summer vacation months. Brandon University faculty of education professors and Frontier school division played no small roles either.

To begin with, the staff underwent an intensive four week training - orientation - planning period in Winnipeg during June, met with and helped select prospective campers and consulted with their teachers and parents. A week of canoeing, camping and last minute planning at Cranberry Portage further prepared the staff for the three highly - active two-week camps.

The youngsters' program was divided into six phases. Arts and crafts included developing skills like candle making, beading, writing letters on birch bark, and making kites. Sports included horseback riding, ball of all types, track and field. Eight field trips evolved to places like mines at Flin Flon and Snow Lake, wildlife reserves and parks and museums. Camping trips involved Wukusco Falls near Snow Lake, Baker's Narrows; canoe trips on three Cranberry lakes, Goose Lake and River, Lake Athapapaskow. Special events saw canoe regattas, wiener roasts, films. sock hops, music workshop by a group of Brandon high school students under government grant, trappers' day, The Pas Indian Days as well as Baker's Narrows Days with competitions like goose-moose-wolf calling, flour packing and endurance events. About 30 Cranberry kids were included in the program. The cost to individual families for the two-week excursion (including a 600-mile there plus return train ride) was a nominal $5.

Cranberry Portage was especially suited for this project for at least two reasons. It's located in the heart of one of Manitoba's finest vacation areas being surrounded by lakes and rivers teeming with fish; trees, wildlife. Thanks to poor planning on someone's part in the defence department in the early 1950s, an RCAF station constructed and used briefly in connection with the DEW Line and then abandoned has subsequently been taken over by Frontier SD and provides ideal facilities. Undoubtedly a most worthwhile project; one that hopefully will become a permanent feature and expand in years ahead. Any project where youngsters stowaway on the train for a repeat performance must have something going for it.

12. CENTRALIZATION OF MANITOBA SOCIAL SERVICES Valley Vistas Col., Brandon Sun,
Sept. 15/73

I'm a firm believer in the concept of decentralization of industries, armed forces bases, federal and provincial government services. Both Canadian and Manitoba governments profess, publicly at least, to subscribe to this philosophy and to certain degree have made it policy in the past decade.

During the 12 years we've lived in Minnedosa we've seen an excellent example of one provincial government department take decentralization seriously. The municipal assessment branch had a single employee, Barry McPherson, when we arrived. Minnedosans saw the local branch grow under Barry's guidance, and later under Garry Grant overflow its ground floor offices in the court house spilling into basement and just over a year ago take up a complete floor of the new civic centre. I've known several of these employees through the years and a friendlier, more courteous and capable crew would be hard to find.

Other provincial departments in this rural district that have continued to expand or at least hold their own and thus support the decentralization concept are highways, agriculture, health, attorney general. Federal ones are postal, health of animals, veterans land administration.

A provincial department that seems to be operating in direct opposition to declared government policy is social services. Unless one classifies expanding Brandon facilities while phasing out those in other West-Man areas decentralization. Personally, I consider that type of 'decentralization' (Brandon emphasized in addition to Winnipeg and to heck with the rest of the province) a complete farce.

The closing of Minnedosa Juvenile Detention Centre on June 30 was about the final step in West-Man of withdrawing the last remnant of meaningful service in rural areas by social services and concentrating it instead in an urban centre. And the manner in which it was done leaves much to be desired; especially coming from a department that prides itself in dealing with people as human beings.

Without a word of warning, detention centre officers (guards) received separation certificates by mail from accounting services co-ordinator P. Crook of the Winnipeg office. This despite the fact guards were paid on a monthly, though hourly, basis. Legal, perhaps. But any private employer who pulls this kind of stunt is severely criticized by people and black listed by unions. Only after protest was made to the Brandon office were letters sent out explaining Brandon would in future "serve as the sole detention facility for juveniles within the western judicial district." Great! Next time your 13-year-old son or daughter is arrested--regardless whether you live in Birtle, Killarney, Deloraine, Neepawa, Minnedosa or wherever--at least you can look for him or her in Brandon.

So poorly co-ordinated was the 'phasing out' of the detention centre here that several weeks later when a juvenile in this area was arrested he was inadvertently booked in Minnedosa. Someone in social services had somehow neglected to notify the RCMP the centre had been closed. When a former guard explained the situation to a policeman the constable was unable to reach the single over-worked probation officer on duty in Brandon. As Flip Wilson would say, "Amen, for Rene Toupin's co-ordination!"

I have no axe to grind with individual social workers and probation officers. I know many personally and most are highly dedicated, good people. But the system is wrong--and is becoming more so instead of less. At least when the attorney general looked after juvenile detention centres until recently, an effort was made to keep them operative where most needed.

First, there should be more juvenile detention centres created in western judicial district and not the number reduced. Kids should not be dragged a hundred or more miles, and booked long distances from their homes. Even if it is only for several days until juvenile or family court convenes. You can bet your hat such court will also most likely sit in Brandon for it's highly unlikely children will be transported back to courthouses nearest their homes. This makes attendance of parents at their children's trials less probable and more difficult than ever. Further, Mounties should not be expected to waste valuable time playing taxi driver to transport children long distances to Brandon.

Second, instead of congregating social workers and probation officers in cities, why not scatter them around? A worker in Brandon can hardly be classed 'readily accessible' to youngsters or adults faced with immediate problems, contemplating suicide, etc. in Boissevain, Erickson, Russell, Shoal Lake, Binscarth. Ever tried to get hold of a probation officer quickly? I have on several occasions, knew where to call and whom. Still took over an hour sometimes. A 15-year-old trying to decide whether or not to run away from home, steal a car in Hamiota, Melita, Reston isn't going to try hard. Even if by chance he does happen to know one personally way off in Brandon; which isn't likely. Maybe if there was one living in Hamiota, Melita, Reston he might try. You don't see Mounties operate out of Brandon--they LIVE where they're needed.

Third, a social worker or probation officer's weekends should be Tuesdays and Wednesdays or Wednesdays and Thursdays. Any person dealing regularly with problems of juveniles and adults can tell you 90% of problems which erupt into action do so between late Friday afternoons and early Sunday mornings (early Tuesday mornings on long weekends). That's when all real action occurs and not during regular work and school hours. Yet social services keeps only a small staff on duty those crucial hours. Do you see Mounties and Brandon city police close shop 5 p.m. Fridays? Hardly!

So Mr. Toupin, if our highly trained and dedicated social workers and probation officers are to be worth a tinker's hoot and not degenerate completely into impotent corpses, let's scatter them throughout the province LIVING right in at least the larger towns near where people they're supposed to help live--not come driving in from the city in Buicks a day or two 'after the fact'. Let's decentralize detention centres instead of building one huge one in the 'big city'. Let's make certain juvenile and family court will probably be held increasingly more often in smaller centres in future instead of continually less frequently. Finally, let's make most of our social workers and probation officers work weekends. Some of the rest of us do, you know. As our minister quipped the other day, "So do I." Amen, again!

13. ROBERT BELL OF RATHWELL   Valley Vistas column, Brandon Sun, Sept.22 & 29/73

In connection with Klondike gold rush celebrations currently under way, Griswold UCW in their 1967 centennial publication BRIDGING THE YEARS mention J.D. McGregor repeatedly. It seems J.D. purchased the farm Deer Park located about seven miles south of Griswold and first homesteaded by John Smith Hitchcock in 1882 who when later asked by a son why he chose that particular piece of land had replied, "It was the only land sticking up out of the water." Robert Brown lived on this farm many years managing McGregor's world-famous herd of Angus cattle.

Another southwestern Manitoba Arctic pioneer was Robert Bell who selected a farm about 50 miles southeast of Brandon in Rathwell district for his balmy south retirement haven following countless northern excursions. Among other accomplishments, Bell is credited with naming over 3,000 Arctic geographical features while employed from 1856 to 1906 by Geological Survey of Canada, of which he was chief geologist the last 16 years and director six.

Born in Toronto June 3, 1841, son of Rev. Andrew Bell and Elizabeth Notman and a grandson of Rev. Wm. Bell, Robert was educated at McGill where he won a gold medal acquiring doctorates in both medicine and applied science. In official circles this man is known as Robert Bell, ISO, FRS, MD, CM, DSc, LLD, FGS, FGSA. The farm on which he retired, Rathwell elementary school principal Ron Bell (no relative) told me recently, was "a show place in the wilds and included a golf course and tennis court. A page wire fence with iron gates surrounded the farm. A grain elevator with railway tracks was planned but abandoned when Robert died" June 19, 1917. The local district and school were named after him.

During his half century of geological survey and exploration work Robert Bell covered vast areas of northern Quebec and Ontario, Hudson Bay region, northern Manitoba and Alberta and Northwest Territories. Frequently he was the first to map Arctic lakes and streams; one river--a branch of the Nottaway--officially named after him. As early as 1884 he was on the staff of the steamer Neptune exploring Hudson Bay, returning the following year on the Alert. In 1897, the year gold was discovered on the Klondike, he was in charge of a party working on southern Baffin Island.

Dr. Bell's writings include some 200 reports and pamphlets dealing with his explorations involving geology, geography, forestry, biology, folk-lore. R.A.J. Phillips claims "the bold and painstaking work of Bell around Great Bear Lake had its sequel 29 years later when Gilbert La Bine read the report of cobalt-bloom and copper green at Echo Bay. La Bine followed it up and found the enormously rich deposits of pitchblende on which he built the Eldorado mine ... first ounce of radium in 1936, when radium was worth about $2½ million an ounce." Robert's geological exploration work also paved the way for subsequent mining developments at Cobalt and Sudbury in Ontario.

Historian W.L. Morton credits Bell's "surveys of the Nelson and Hayes rivers" in 1880 with providing necessary "scientific evidence in support of the feasibility of a railway to the bay" and the federal government expedition of 1884-86 under command of Capt. A.R. Gordon, Bell supervising the scientific aspect, with laying the foundation for its ultimate completion. It's my sincere belief construction of that railway to Churchill and development of this port will in years to come produce far-reaching effects on both northern and Prairie development.

Recently the Brandon Sun carried a news item that the Swedish freighter Greta Thulan left Chuchill with 1,537,200 bushels of barley, "the largest shipment of grain ever taken out of the port on a single ship." Events like this support what Hudson Bay Route Association's trying to accomplish. This organization, which celebrated its 50th anniversary in Yorkton in June, estimates it's saved Manitoba, Saskatchewan and Alberta $50 million--an average of a million per year. Instead of allowing US controlled St. Lawrence Seaway to be pushed down our throats as the best thing that's ever happened to Canada, every Prairie citizen, journalist, MLA and MP should be advocating the development of Churchill's port and shipping facilities. Robert Bell pointed the way almost 90 years ago. The $10 million joint federal-provincial 220,000 square foot complex just begun there is certainly a step in the right direction.

Although Bell's father was a minister, he too pioneered in Canadian geology playing a major role as advisor when the united provinces of Upper and Lower Canada established a geological survey. As youth Robert often accompanied his father on fossil collecting trips in Ottawa Valley and at 15 eagerly joined James Richardson's party in Gaspe Peninsula. At 21 he became professor of chemistry and natural science at Queens University in Kingston where he taught five years.

The Royal Society of Canada pays tribute to this Arctic pioneer stating, "In his religious views he was very broad-minded, and though a Presbyterian by birth and persuasion he took a keen interest in the missionary activities among the northern Indians of other denominations, and the Church of England missions on Hudson Bay are indebted to him for material assistance in carrying on their work."

Robert Bell strongly influenced the work of his nephew James Mackintosh Bell (1877-1934) who followed his uncle's footsteps closely and left his own unique mark on the rocks of the Arctic, especially Mackenzie Valley. Author of at least three books, James went overseas in the First World War with the CEF and in 1917-19 played a significant role on staff of the British military mission to Russia together with such other noted Prairie Canadians like Col. John Stoughton Dennis Jr.

James Bell and Hubert Darrell were close friends. Darrell, writing his mother in England from a shack on Great Slave River on Jan. 20, 1900 states in part, "I know young Bell, son of the great Dr. Bell, very well indeed and correspond with him. He half promised to take me on his survey to Bear Lake and Coppermine River this summer but was unable to carry it out."

Darrell was however wrong when he called his friend a 'son' of Robert Bell for James was a nephew. Robert married Agnes Smith in 1873 and they had one son and three daughters. Donald, the only son, died young. Rathwell old timers remember only two daughters --Alice and Olga;, perhaps the third also died young, or was already married and settled somewhere before the Bells moved to Rathwell.

After Dr. Bell died on his Rathwell farm in 1917, his wife and daughters continued to live in that district until 1924 at which time they moved back to their former home in Ottawa where they were active in government circles. Mrs. Alice (Bell) Outram had a daughter named Alice and thus Robert's granddaughter. Although most Canadians unfortunately know little of Robert Bell's remarkable accomplishments, many remember his granddaughter Alice Outram better because of her marriage to a central Canadian political figure who became involved in two political scandals that shook this nation.

At 22, Alice Outram, an exceptionally attractive RCAF public relations officer stationed in Toronto, married 46-year-old former House of Commons speaker Louis Rene Beaudoin following his Reno divorce from his wife Margaret. A central figure in the heated closure controversy Beaudoin, after his divorce from Alice later, moved to the US where he was involved in illegal sales of Canadian government information.

Rene Beaudoin, a federal government official wrote me recently, "died in the United States and his personal papers were dispersed there. The Outram family home in Ottawa was destroyed by fire some time ago and I understand that many of the books were given by Mrs. Outram to the National Archives. The geological survey is in the process of having an extensive history written." It goes without saying that the work of Robert Bell of Rathwell will comprise a significant part of that history.

14. GRIFFITH, BOULTON, McKAY   Valley Vistas column, Brandon Sun, Oct. 6 & 20/73

Back in June, in connection with early West-Man art, I mentioned the 1884 oil painting 'Scene in the Valley at Minnedosa' by J. Russell Griffith owned by Don Ritchie of Winnipeg and expressed the desire to know more about this artist. Well, Evelyn Erickson's Feb. 16, 1882, issue of Minnedosa Star sheds some light.

This edition carries the following notice: "T.R. Griffith, Artist (Late of Toronto), Student of Bridgman & Forster, Wishes to inform the inhabitants of Minnedosa and surrounding country that he has located in Minnedosa for a short time, and is prepared to execute Portrait and Landscape Paintings, Oil and Crayon Pictures, etc., etc., in the highest style of art. Portraits of deceased friends enlarged from a photograph to life size. Paintings from sittings can be arranged for." Artists' signatures being similar to doctors' prescriptions, it seems the book 150 YEARS OF ART IN MANITOBA erred slightly on Griffith's first initial (or the Star made a slight typing error) for obviously this is the man who painted the valley scene.

On several occasions I've written about West-Man's Major Boulton who fought in both Riel rebellions. Most historians simply call him Major Boulton, as does his own book. Because one historian called him John I also began calling him that. This may have been his nickname but his real name was Charles Arkoll. He was born Sept. 17, 1841, in Cobourg, Upper Canada and died May 18, 1899, at Shellmouth, Man. A son of Lt.-Col. D'Arcy Edward Boulton and Emily Heath, he was appointed to the Canadian senate in 1889, married a Miss Latter and, according to Canadiana Encyclopedia, had one daughter. J.L. Swainson, however, states they had two sons, Everat and Lawrence, who spent their lives in Russell.

The Angus McKay who tied with Dr. Lynch as first MP of Marquette constituency back in 1871 was undoubtedly the same one described as a "prominent Metis" by historian W.L. Morton. He, together with other noted Metis like M. Nolin, Joseph Hamelin and John F. Grant, was among those arrested by Louis Riel and imprisoned in Fort Garry.

15. PAT BURNS OF CLANWILLIAM   Valley Vistas, Brandon Sun, October 13 & 20/73

It's not that I didn't know Pat Burns, founder of one of the largest neat-packing firms in the world, came from Minnedosa district. I'd known that for a decade from a local history book which states in part, "he and his partner Dave Drysdale took up adjoining homesteads and in order to qualify for their deeds they built a shanty, half on each homestead, where they slept at opposite ends, or each on his own land." But millionaires turn me off generally—unless they've led fascinating lives, or performed a significant public service.

Leafing through Grant MacEwan's book FIFTY MIGHTY MEN recently I came across the interesting article 'Cattle King Burns'. Pat must have been quite a guy, I thought. Maybe I should write about him. Less than an hour later I received a phone call from Allan James—local lawyer and one of Minnedosa's most popular and nicest men. "I was in Horseman's Hall of Fame in Calgary the other day," he volunteered. "Did you know Pat Burns came from Minnedosa district and is featured in the Hall of Fame there?" "Yes, to your first question, no to the second," I replied. Coincidence? Fate? Next day he gave me a pamphlet on Calgary Brewing and Malting Company's Horseman's Hall of Fame.

Of Irish descent, industrial tycoon-cattle king-senator Pat Burns was born the son of Michael O'Byrne (later changed to Byrne and then Burns) and Bridget Gibson on July 6, 1856, in Oshawa and died in Calgary Feb. 24, 1937. MacEwan states young Pat attended Kirkfield school with two other Canadians who later also became famous—railway builders William Mackenzie and Donald Mann—where he participated in "at least one famous shirt-tail wrestling match for school supremacy." Local historian Pax Crawley, in his booklet LAKELET SCHOOL AND ITS PIONEERS, set in the school district where Burns later lived, disagrees stating, "As far as we know he took no part in school affairs, which is understandable when we know that he could neither read nor write at that time." Another most reliable person concurs with Crawley, and indicated to me that even in later years Pat signed with an X. It would seem that if Pat did attend school at all it didn't appreciably shape his destiny; perhaps he was too busy fighting.

In 1878 Pat and brother John left their parents and nine siblings, heading west to Winnipeg. Reports of fertile soil around Tanner's Crossing (Minnedosa) interested them, says MacEwan, and the brothers walked "six days and sleeping out at night" to select and file on quarter sections. I don't know where John homesteaded but Crawley shows a homestead map with Pat on NW 18-16-17 and buying the NE quarter, with the quarter that Dave Drysdale supposedly filed on as "Sale T.A. Moynes." The only Drysdale this map includes is a J. Drysdale homesteading 2½ miles west.

MacEwan indicates that because the Burns brothers owned no equipment they walked back the 160 miles to Winnipeg, worked on a construction crew building the CPR east of Winnipeg at $25 per month with Pat purchasing a team of oxen, wagon and plow to return to live on his homestead the following year.

The Burns (and Drysdale?) shanty was located on what's now the northern outskirts of the hamlet Clanwilliam; about 100 yards northeast of Immanuel Lutheran Church and just east of a large grey brick farm house owned since 1938 by Nellie Zynger of Minnedosa, in which her daughter now lives. Nellie informed me that just this summer a cave-in occurred in the yard, suggesting a basement or ice house or well was once there.

Crawley includes an anecdote illustrating Pat's genius for money-making as told by his early neighbors. It seems Pat purchased old oxen each fall, fattened them during winter and toward spring borrowed sleighs and harness from neighbors, built racks of dry poplar poles on the sleighs, loaded them with hay and "with his own ox team leading and the others following" drove to Brandon. There he sold the hay, sold all the oxen except his own team for beef, sold the poplar poles for firewood. He then loaded the borrowed sleighs and harness on his own sleigh and returned the 40 odd miles to Clanwilliam.

Grant states Pat also "hauled freight from Winnipeg" and did "custom breaking with his oxen--anything to make a dollar." His first cow was bought on credit, sold for a profit and this method expanded so that by 1886 he was furnishing beef for Mackenzie and Mann's railway building crews in Maine, and later for "construction camps along the railroad being built from Regina to Saskatoon and Prince Albert." For the decade 1880-90 MINNEDOSA MEMORIES carries the listing "Pat Burns, Farmer and Cattle buyer." By 1890 Calgary had become his main headquarters while furnishing beef to railway crews on the Calgary to Edmonton line.

The Klondike Gold Rush of late 1890s brought riches to Pat Burns in different form. Buying up all cattle he could lay hands on he shipped them north from Vancouver by boat, drove them inland "over forbidding passes and dangerous wilderness," slaughtered them on the bank of the Lewes river and floated the carcasses downstream to Dawson City to qualify "for the reward of a dollar a pound for beef" to gold-rich but hungry prospectors. Thus Pat quietly accomplished what several others had tried desperately but had failed--the most famous failure probably being that of British Columbian Norman Lee on whose diary the popular book KLONDIKE CATTLE DRIVE is based. In succeeding years Pat shipped "thousands of tons of Prairie beef northward to fill the Alaskan-Yukon needs."

By 1912 Burns had become not only a major Canadian cattle buyer but owned six of Alberta's largest ranches qualifying as that province's 'Big Four' cattlemen who that year "backed the first ambitious Calgary Stampede and saw it achieve success". Horseman's Hall of Fame features these four in a large painting with the stocky, moustached Irishman wearing his ever present fedora while relaxing in an armchair.

Chatted recently with old timer Ed Taylor, a former Minnedosa mayor. Although he didn't know Pat personally, his older brother who was a banker in Calgary knew him very well. It seems Burns was a great gambler, especially loved poker. He and rancher friends had a little private room in the old Palliser Hotel tucked midway between two floors accessible only by elevator to someone who knew precisely when to press a particular button. Here Pat and his cronies gambled regularly. Herb Taylor sat in on one game, but the $1,000 poker chips were too rich for his blood and he declined future invitations.

Pat Burns was a highly sensitive, very human, humble type of person. It's generally conceded he achieved the impossible--became a millionaire without losing a friend. He cared deeply for his employees. For example, when the wife of one plant worker fell ill Pat arranged to have her sent to a famous US hospital at his own expense. He contributed generously to those charities in which he believed. When a tiny mascot pig walking beside a float in a Calgary Stampede parade tired, Pat emerged from his limousine to give the dejected piglet a ride. People loved the guy--and that in itself is worth more than millions.

In 1910 Pat Burns married Eileen Ellis of Penticton, B.C., and they had one son. Even his love life had style. The story goes Pat was sitting in the Vernon Hotel discussing a big cattle deal with a local rancher when Thomas Ellis and his two daughters walked in. When Pat noticed the girls his conversation ceased abruptly. To his friend's query regarding their identity Burns answered, "Never saw them before"; then he added, "See the girl on this side? She's the future Mrs. Burns." She was!

When Pat Burns was called to the Canadian senate in 1931 Calgary threw a mammoth birthday party for the 75-year-old pioneer, complete with two-ton birthday cake cut into 15,000 pieces for Canadians from all walks of life. By then he held directorships in several important banking, engineering and insurance companies while his meat packing firm had branch offices in exotic places like London, Liverpool and Yokohama. In 1936 he relinquished his senate seat, died the following year.

In the same column on May 18, 1974:

Ran across an interesting anecdote recently about Pat Burns about whom I wrote last October. Josephine Phelan, in THE BOLD HEART dealing with Canadian Oblate missionary Father Pere Albert Lacombe, describes how the Lacombe Home for down-and-out senior citizens and orphans at Midnapore near Calgary came into being.

The eminent missionary had just retired to a ramshackle cabin on Pincher Creek and Pat, a close friend, offered to build him a new house. "If Pat Burns was so wealthy," reasoned the good Father who'd spent a lifetime serving others, "why shouldn't he do something really worthy of his noble nature? Why shouldn't he provide a big home where other poor old people could find shelter and orphan children be cared for?" The upshot was Father Lacombe persuaded Pat to donate 200 acres of land at Midnapore and travelling the country collected additional funds to complete his massive project. One $10,000 donation came from Manitoba's noted Lord Strathcona. By November of 1910 the Home was a reality.

And in the same column August 17, 1974:

A while back I wrote about Pat Burns. Local bookstore operator Mrs. P.M. (Londry) Day, whose grandmother of Rookhurst district south of Minnedosa knew him well, told me the latter used to stop at her grandparents' farm for water and refreshments enroute to Brandon on his annual pilgrimage to sell oxen, hay and wood. Later when he became senator and sent her a piece of his two-ton birthday cake her rather irreverent comment was, "Humph! Could have baked a much better one myself."

16. ANTIQUE BOTTLES   Valley Vistas column, Brandon Sun, Oct. 27/73

In March I wrote a news item about Parkland Bottle Collectors club of which George Crighton of Cardale's president. George had uncovered information about a brewery that operated in Minnedosa from 1890-93 by Charles L. Davis and Lalimond, hoped Sun readers might be able to give the club further information. Local history book MINNEDOSA MEMORIES adds only "A brewery, run by Sherrif and Davies, but burned in 1889, was east of Main Street and farther north on First Street."

Harvey Ebner, a young highways department employee well known in West-Man as an exceptionally good golfer and formidable hockey player, is an ardent local antique bottle collector. Hoping to unearth a rare bottle or two he became deeply interested in the old brewery and began making inquiries. A conversation with Sid Hancock, nephew of George Fairbairn whose father Sid Fairbairn once operated a brick factory in Minnedosa and supervised construction of historic buildings like the former Minnedosa Inn and present Tremont Hotel, paid off.

Mrs. Ellen Telford, 86-year-old daughter of pioneer businessman and early Minnedosa mayor Joe Burgess, remembered the building in which the brewery was located. As youngster she played in the wooden barn-like structure without foundation located either on the present site of their home or immediately across the street on the Ripley site. She feel's the 1889 fire's date's too early for she was only about two then, the 1893 (Manitoba Archives date) being more likely. Both properties today being nicely landscaped residential sites it's most unlikely club members will be digging up lawns looking for antique 'Made in Minnedosa' beer bottles that may have survived the fire.

Of the nation-wide Parkland Bottle Collectors club several other members come from West-Man. These include Mrs. James Olive of Oak Lake; Rene R. Gaudry, Lila Higginbotham and Lorne Reads of Virden; Ruth McCutcheon of Homewood; Muriel Westwood of Rivers; Jean Skilton, William and Joan Poole of Manson; Graydon Cummin of Strathclair; Brandon Library, Harold Kalynovich and Doug Smith of Brandon; Sam Foote of Oak River; Eldon Robinson of Bradwardine; Arthur Giley of Beulah; Helen Campbell of Shilo.

Harvey Ebner owns some 200 antique bottles and jars. Several he treasures especially are embossed 'Minnedosa Pharmacy, Pure Drugs, Minnedosa, Man.', with half a dozen just like these but not embossed. Others include Patterson's Camp Coffee, Burdock Blood Bitters, Chamberlaine Cough Remedy, Norway Pine Syrup, Eno's Fruit Salts, Fellows and Co. Chemists, Underwood's Ink, Empire Brewing (Brandon), Blackwood's (Winnipeg, soft drinks), numerous whiskey, wine, gin (cased) and other alcoholic beverage bottles, a two-gallon crock jug with hand-painted bird design from about 1850, whiskey (pocket) flask with metal cover, white 'milk glass' flask with curved neck, numerous medicine bottles—one with glass stopper—and pickle bottles; bottles of various colors, sizes, shapes.

Harvey also collects other antiques: Indian relics, light bulbs, license plates, ornate silver pewter pot. Especially he values a shiny long sabre once belonging to Gen. Hugh Dyer of the 12th Manitoba Dragoons, purchased recently from a descendant of the deceased general's.

Of special interest to antique bottle collectors are early village, town and city dumps—dating back to days when most combustible garbage was burned in cook stoves and bulldozers didn't crush and bury discarded bottles on dumps. Harvey Ebner's located both of Minnedosa's oldest ones. For sake of property owners involved and this young man's mushrooming antique collecting hobby I'll sign off before I divulge that cherished secret.

17. FOSTER PARENTS   Valley Vistas, Brandon Sun, November 3, 1973

'FOSTER POWER—Power of Love' is their motto, an adult's hand and a child's hand extended towards each other with a red heart between their symbol: Foster Parents Association for Western Manitoba. November is Foster Parent Month.

Less than eight months old the association developed out of a localized group of concerned foster parents who met several months previous in the home of Agnes Grant of Minnedosa. Mrs. Grant's well known to many West-Manites—especially teachers, students and school officials—as a dedicated Manitoba Metis Federation education project coordinator and Brandon University IMPACTE instructor.

Agnes, who's program chairman for the fledgling organization, readily admits she's not a typical foster parent, for both their foster children are permanent wards and thus she, husband Garry and own children Elaine, Robert and Nancy aren't vulnerable to sorrow generated when foster children suddenly leave foster homes in which they have lived as family members for months or even years. She points to the Len Borleys of Rapid City and Bob Saddlers of Rivers as typical members. I've known the Grants, who live less than two blocks from us, for some 10 years; feel I know them particularly well as our eldest daughters are very close friends.

A major aim of the association's to upgrade its members through discussing mutual problems and meeting with trained persons like psychologists, social workers and probation officers. The recent seminar held in Brandon Ag Centre with speakers like Rev. Cutham and Don Robertson's typical. President is Randy Atkinson of Brandon, treasurer Frank Thiessen of Cromer, secretary Mary Turton of Rapid City while Dawn Borley of the same district's membership chairman.

Driving in Rapid City area recently I paid a surprise visit on Mrs. Turton. A moment later Mrs. Borley, whom I'd hoped to surprise next, turned the tables on me by paying an unexpected call on Mary Turton. Both live on farms, in one of West-Man's more beautiful and pleasant rural districts. The hour passed swiftly and I left the Turton home with the conviction here's a group of people who have their hearts in the right place and heads on straight.

It was a seminar sponsored by the Child Welfare League of America held in Winnipeg in June, 1972, with message 'CHILDREN: chattels or choosers' that inspired parents here to organize. Divided into various locals the association's currently establishing a local in Neepawa. Dawn and Mary pointed out that although their association co-operates with various related government agencies and receives valuable expert assistance of resource personnel, in no way is it a government agency but a grass roots everyday-people group. To help publicize their objectives the group's had floats at fairs in Rapid City, Rivers, Cardale, Oak River this summer.

Mary Turton too feels she's not really a typical foster parent because their children also are permanent; although she's had some experience with short-term cases unofficially—friends of their own children living in their home for various lengths of time.

I first met Mrs. Borley back in 1964 when I was teaching at Minnedosa Collegiate where two of their children attended. We'd all been especially impressed with their oldest daughter Sandra who'd recently been featured as Sun 'Teen-Ager of the Week' (chosen by classmates and teachers). Thus my recent visit with this most pleasant vivacious woman was not unlike a reunion of old classmates. Sandra, whom readers may recall since then winning a 4-H talent-beauty contest (Shorthorn Lassie, or some such title), is happily married to a farmer in southeastern Saskatchewan with youngsters of her own.

Parents of six children themselves the Leonard Borleys have been foster parents to some 21 youngsters through the years. "Two weeks," feels Dawn, "is plenty to become emotionally involved with a child—enough to feel pain and sense of loss at separation. Well meaning persons say to me, 'I'm too warm-hearted to become a foster parent, could not stand giving up the child later', the implication perhaps being 'Dawn Borley is hard-hearted enough to do that sort of thing but not me.' That's a poor excuse really. It hurts alright; especially when you have someone for 2½ years as we had two little sisters. But someone's got to do it, or such children just don't get placed into a family at all."

Some problems foster parents face may involve severe medical conditions. Metis and Indian children frequently meet discrimination in white communities even though living in white families. Some are emotionally disturbed, physically handicapped; older ones sometimes are on probation, alcohol, drugs.

One foster child I'll never forget is a young man I taught, frequently visited with and with whom I hunted ducks on occasion. He joined the Intelligence Corps of US Marines, fought in Vietnam. During his last visit he talked of the brutal interrogation of prisoners on both sides with which he personally was familiar. Naive, like many of us, he'd fully expected this of the enemy—but never of his own side. The psychological shock he'd suffered was obvious when he'd learned of a method of interrogation employed by some of his own South Vietnamese and American colleagues.

Yes, November is Foster Parent Month. "If," as the Children's Aid Society of Western Manitoba recently appealed in this newspaper, "you're mature in judgment and possess a heart, willing to provide children with adequate care to prepare them for an eventful return home, help us to help them through you; also remember children do provide satisfaction and fair remuneration, call David Jones (social worker, Brandon office) for appointment."

18. ROSS JOHNSTON AND VLA   Valley Vistas column, Brandon Sun, November 10/73

"Recent news reports that Veterans Land Act offices across Canada will be closing soon," Ross Johnston of Minnedosa office indicated to me, "are misleading. That they may eventually become obsolete is possible. Last veterans accepted under the act were from the Korean War; and I've got only one of those in my district." That district covers some 15 municipalities plus all the hamlets, villages and towns involved.

VLA opened its offices just before the end of the Second World War to help veterans re-establish in and re-adjust to civilian society. This particular office first opened in Rapid City, soon moved to Minnedosa. Joe Menzies was first field man, followed in 1959 by Ross. At first offices were centralized in Winnipeg and Brandon but the department quickly realized closer personal contact between veterans and VLA field men was paramount. This human relations factor Ross has found most rewarding in his work. "It's like a giant family," he explains. "I know every veteran in my area personally. Many come to me about personal matters, family counselling and so on. If I can't help them myself I direct them to those who can. And I know also every one of them would help me if I need it."

VLA is obviously one of the most successful ventures ever undertaken by the Canadian government—both from social and financial viewpoint. It can point to less than one-half of one per cent failure rate as loaning institution—bankruptcy whereby either the veteran or people of Canada lost money. "It's this loaning aspect that's slowly being phased out," says Ross, "not the supervision role, which will continue for many years yet." This is readily understandable when most veterans have already utilized their loan privileges, many have died, retired. Current minor changes are due partly to the fact most young men who stayed in the Armed Forces after the war have reached retirement age.

The Ross Johnston family are a West-Man product. Ross was born and raised in Oak Lake district; his wife Audrey Curry comes from there also. Sister Lorraine Holland lives in Oak Lake, brother Norris is a fertilizer salesman in that district while brother Barry farms the 'home place' which their father John (Jack) and grandfather William had homesteaded and developed. Ross' mother Eileen Hall came to West-Man from Ireland, her father having died at the World's Fair in Chicago at 24 and mother shortly after from heartbreak and childbirth, Eileen having been brought up by relatives, receiving an excellent education and excelling in drama and singing. William Johnston, after whom the country school which Ross attended was named, had with three brothers emigrated to Oak Lake-Virden area as United Empire Loyalist. Ross looks back on high school at Oak Lake collegiate with much fondness, having been lucky enough to have had C.E. Heapy—a Golden Boy award winner—as principal and teacher.

Unlike many teen-agers Ross had a good relationship with his parents. "My father was the most honest man I've ever known." A 4-H club member, Ross attended Boys Parliament, sat on the provincial executive of Manitoba Young People's Association. At University of Manitoba he completed the diploma course in Agriculture on a scholarship. Then came the war!

Ross Johnston joined the RCAF, trained in Regina and Calgary, went overseas in 1941 where together with men from all over the Commonwealth and USA served in the RAF. While enroute there on the ship Cameronian, just out of Halifax the ship directly behind them in the convoy was sunk. On their third night in England their mess hall was bombed by the Germans. As part of 180 Squadron Ross flew a B25 bomber. For a while they used an old Roman road as runway, then operated from a base near Norfolk, from the Isle of Wight and various other fields.

"At first we had no fighter escorts and were shot up pretty badly," mused Ross. "After we received escorts it was flack from anti-aircraft guns mostly about which we had to worry. I had a press fellow along once and the window beside him shattered from the flack; he kept his head down the rest of the way. As pilot you didn't have time to be afraid during the action because you were too busy, but afterwards when you emerged from your plane your legs were rubber. The crew had plenty time to become afraid during the raid though. Most of it was daylight flying and at very low level." Especially he liked the RAF men, admired their tenacity and dogged determination and willingness to go after any target regardless how dangerous.

In 1944, after 30 operations, Ross was transferred to Boundary Bay near Vancouver as flight instructor, and before the war ended "married the girl from home." Until 1959 they farmed north of Oak Lake where Ross led 4-H clubs in his spare time; was secretary of Pool elevators and president of the Legion, chief ranger of the Foresters, director of St. David's United Church.

The Johnstons have six children: Gaye (Mrs. Richard McMillan) of Winnipeg, Sherrie who's in charge of commercial art in CKX and son Kim who works as writer-producer for the same station and writes songs as hobby, Cindy working in Eaton's in Winnipeg, April in grade 6 and Lisa in 2 at Tanner's Crossing school.

There are fewer VLA offices in Canada now than in 1959 and less staff, admits Ross. This is due to greater efficiency of personnel, retirement and death of field officers, reduced work load caused by death of veterans. Some centres that have closed and duties assumed by adjacent offices are Gilbert Plains, Neepawa, Swan River, Roblin, Virden, Melita. Portage is in process of closing and its work load will be divided between Killarney, Brandon, Minnedosa. Ross doesn't envisage other offices in southwestern Manitoba closing before 1977. Some non-veteran work VLA officers have done includes computations for National Revenue data banks, assisting Indian Affairs with off-reserve housing and feasibility studies regarding business ventures, appraisal studies and Crown assets disposal for National Defence.

"Of my own air crew with whom I flew many missions during the war," indicated Ross Johnston sadly, "not one survived. All were shot down and killed shortly after my transfer. I don't think one reached his 21st birthday." That these young men will be much in his thoughts again this Remembrance Day goes without saying. Let us too remember!

19. TEACHER TRAINING AND OPEN EDUCATION   Valley Vistas, Brandon Sun, Nov. 17/73

"Generally, it's been my observation universities often take more out of public schools than they put in. I intend to make an effort to serve as active resource for ANY teacher or student teacher who may have need of the services Brandon University can provide." That philosophy characterizes Jerry Christensen's attitude towards the role universities should play in education generally—a role Brandon University has taken increasingly more seriously in recent years, and considerably more than most Canadian universities.

For decades Canada's most gifted men and women emigrated south because grass seemed greener across the border. The last few years has seen a reversal in trend. The 31-year-old faculty of education assistant professor Gerald E. Christensen, masters graduate from University of North Dakota and bachelor graduate from East Stroudsburg State College in Pennsylvania, is typical.

Jerry's the man in charge of an experimental five month on-the-job training program for student teachers in Minnedosa. Although yet too early to assess, the project seems to have the blessing of teachers, administrators, students and student teachers.

Three professors especially involved in initiating this program, and several similar ones elsewhere, are Dr. Ralph Pippert, John Loughton, Jack Dienes. Dialogue with superintendents, principals and boards involved elicited favorable responses towards the concept—one that has in somewhat similar form been tried recently in Brandon schools.

Both superintendent Arnold Nicholls and assistant Max Schatz of Rolling River SD, with whom I chatted at length, were enthusiastic about the project. Under the old system, they feel, a student teacher invariably left the school just as he was beginning to know the teachers and pupils and starting to become effective. Both student teachers and schools hope to benefit. Max, as readers may recall, I wrote about June/72; Arnold, as many will know, is a West-Man product—Brandon University graduate who was principal at Bradwardine six years and Rivers seven before coming to Minnedosa.

I sat in Tanner's Crossing school's 'pit' and chatted with Jerry for an hour, felt here was an educator with very definite ideas about educating youngsters but who would never push these down unwilling throats of administrators, school boards, student teachers, children, teachers. And that, to those familiar with the many ups and downs of controversial education developments in Rolling River during 1968-72, is refreshing.

The following student teachers are involved in the Minnedosa project: Ken Edinborough, Allan Hall and Allan Rathbone of Winnipeg; Zelda Vance of Portage; Helen Hastings of Rivers; Jo-Anne Bernstrom of The Pas; Judy Cassils of Deloraine; Grace Vickers of Pierson; Marilyn Southward of Virden; Lory Neufeld and Gary Nicholls of Minnedosa.

Jerry and most of his students are proponents of an educational philosophy growing in North America called Open Education. The concept, as Jerry explains, is not synonymous with Open Area Classrooms and may or may not be involved in such schools.

Most people my age (good side of 40) will remember the American educational philosopher John Dewey whose 'learning by doing' methods educators tried to emulate during the 1930s and '40s. Many will recall the complete chaos that often resulted in 'progressive schools', chaos which resulted not because of the philosophy itself but poor interpretations thereof. 'Let kids do as they please' kind of thing, 'they're sure to learn SOMETHING in the process'. Yeah! Many too will know of the remarkable success of Italy's Maria Montessori in teaching young children with her 'learning while playing' method. Her revolutionary approach to teaching evoked considerably less criticism because proponents of her method were much less inclined to turning classrooms over to youngsters; teachers, though in the background, remained an integral part of it.

Later that day I watched Allan Rathbone show an hour long film comparing traditional and open teaching. The film, one which I sincerely hope CBC TV will acquire to show Canadian parents, was filmed by CBS over a period of six months with the open method portion based on a classroom currently taught at Prairie View elementary school about 175 miles southeast of Brandon at Devils Lake, N.D. I could almost hear Dewey muttering, "Now that's my philosophy, you fools; not what many of you tried to make it" and Montessori admonishing, "That's MY method. Watch how you treat it."

The danger, as the film stressed, is open education may simply become a fad and be pushed too fast and too hard. In hands of competent teachers who feel comfortable in such surroundings children will undoubtedly become more self-reliant and intellectually curious, while in hands of poor teachers or those uncomfortable in this setting it would quickly degenerate into bedlam.

At the end of the Minnedosa project I hope to conduct a follow-up by recording responses of children, teachers, student teachers, principals, possibly parents regarding the five month on-the-job training of teachers and reactions to open education to which they've been exposed. As superintendent Nicholls reminded me, "You and I both have sons as student teachers in this project and thus have a vested interest." That both of us are hoping the project succeeds goes without saying. All the more reason a less biased assessment be made.

20. CAPTAIN MUNN, ARCTIC SAILOR   Valley Vistas column, Brandon Sun, Nov. 24/73 &
Dec. 1/73

Klondike Gold Rush celebrations are drawing rapidly to a close. The more I dig around in Canadian Prairie history the more I'm convinced that most major Canadian historians have virtually ignored many truly remarkable Prairie people. Certainly those books most commonly used as texts or reference in our public schools are sadly lacking in Prairie history.

Bert McKay, Sun correspondent from Moosomin who writes fascinating historical articles, suggested another West-Man Arctic pioneer in a recent riding-to-hounds story. Correspondence with Bert touched off research that revealed an interesting tale. The man was Captain Henry Toke Munn.

Munn arrived in Canada from England in 1886 with a bang--being almost killed in Montreal by a lady shooting wildly at a man who had just raped her. Arriving in Brandon he stayed at the Langham hotel whose proprietor was an American called Shupe, took in the May 24 horse races with friends--the Pares, and with Jim and Archie Heard of Rapid City-Minnedosa district. He tells of wagon loads of snow geese being hauled into Brandon after tumbling out of the sky with broken wings following a violent hail storm.

Munn first settled at Milford (long since gone) on the Souris River. Former postmistress Effie Macdonald tells me that village was located in the Treesbank area. Founded by a Major Rogers it had a saw mill, hotel, stores, blacksmith shop. An avid hunter, Munn tells of elk and mule deer roaming the Tiger Hills near Pelican Lake, of a Methodist minister accidently blowing the top of his horse's head off with a shotgun while hunting.

One night Munn went to Brandon with his friend Charles Bagnall who homesteaded in the Morley (Rapid City-Minnedosa) district with a brother and was wanted in the US for "killing a man in a fair fight". Charles kicked open the Langham beer parlor door after it was closed; arrested next day he was surprised to learn it wasn't over the US killing and cheerfully went to Brandon jail and subsequently paid a $10 fine -- which he'd won from one of the guards gambling.

In 1889 Munn went into partnership with James Duncan McGregor, another Arctic pioneer about whom I've already written. At first they shipped mustangs to Manitoba from B.C., Oregon, Montana, Washington and North Dakota--breaking them and selling them to farmers. He describes McGregor as "a man of tremendous drive and energy, and with a remarkable imagination and vision as regards the development for the West. No man ever worked harder to impress its vast possibilities on other people and on the Dominion government itself." He describes unique Brandonites like 'Tip' Hellwell and Jim Kennedy. The partners next imported Percheron stallions to upgrade Manitoba horses, shipped large consignments of young cattle to Alberta ranches like Bar U and Quorn in exchange for range horses. But "four disastrous years of bad crops on the prairies" resulted in bankruptcy for the Munn-McGregor firm because farmers were unable to pay for their horses.

In 1894 Munn accompanied Walter Gordon-Cumming on a muskox hunting trip into the Arctic barrens. They proceeded on HBC steamer Wrigley down the Athabasca River to Grand Rapids, flat-bottomed scow to Ft. McMurray, S.S. Graham to Ft. Chipewayan on the Slave River where he met Dr. Mackay---the HBC chief factor known by Indians as 'One Eye' who hated and despised all free traders. Munn's subsequent advice to HBC commissioner Chipman to initiate modern competition methods and department stores like those of Eaton's wasn't followed--much to their disadvantage until "20 years too late". From Ft. Resolution the party tavelled by canoe to the eastern end of Great Slave Lake, "touring the multitude of islands known as the Simpson's group", onward to Ft. Reliance and on July 21 were stopped by ice on Artillery Lake. Although they viewed a two-week long caribou migration consisting of millions of animals of which they shot many and caught a 50-pound lake trout they saw no muskoxen. Returning to Great Slave Lake they waited until Oct. 29 and set out again, half their dogs starving during a blizzard but eventually killing a band of muskoxen on Nov. 13. Christmas was spent at Ft. Resolution where Gaudet was "the new trader". At Ft. Smith they hunted wood buffalo with Caspar Whitney, an American.

Returning to West-Man Munn spent most of 1896 with the Heard family, visited England and travelled to British Columbia the following year. In Vancouver he was hired by Whithaker Wright Co. to guide the Bank of British North America staff with capital to Dawson as gold had just been discovered on the Klondike.

Guiding the staff with $225,000 currency Munn otwitted the notorious Soapy Smith who terrorized Skagway, Alaska, during early gold rush days. He simply pretended to hire some of Soapy's own cut-throats to transport the money by pack horse, then really hired an honest man to do it several hours earlier--to the rage of Smith and his killers. Canada quickly served notice to these outlaws to remain on the US side of the border when Lake Bennett's NWMP Major Steele caught one member who ventured across, confiscated all he had and threw him out. Two weeks later Skagway vigilantes wiped out the entire gang.

After the bank was established Munn went prospecting with cashier Finlayson and Colin McGregor (J.D.'s brother) staking claims "up a creek 10 miles downstream from Dawson." However the only gold Munn obtained was an ounce he won in a canoe race in Dawson celebrating the queen's birthday. Almost he purchased the famous 'Gold Hill' claim that later yielded fortunes.

Loading a canoe with supplies Munn paddled alone down the Yukon some 1,600 miles to Bering Sea; was shot at, lost for a while, bought cord wood while waiting for his company's ship. Purchasing a second steamer they jammed it with prospectors and returned to Dawson, Munn as purser. Briefly he panned for gold, a single shovel of 'pay streak' yielding $147. Bank manager Doig and partner Jerry Lynch realized a profit of $500,000 on their claim, the bank company itself however losing money badly.

In fall of 1899 Munn returned to Brandon, lived briefly with the Heards of Rapid City-Minnedosa, visited England and left for South Africa to fight in the Boer War. June, 1903, saw him back in Brandon where Archie Heard was recuperating from a serious hunting accident, spent much time at Senator Kirchoffer's hunting lodge on Lake Manitoba, the two supplying Brandon "with ducks after one of these expeditions."

In 1904 Munn moved to Wilmer, B.C., where he and a cousin bought a 2,000-acre cattle ranch on which he lived three years. When silver was discovered in northern Ontario he rushed to Cobalt but missed by 30 minutes staking the fabulously rich Hollinger mine.

Autumn of 1911 saw Munn in Peace River country reporting on land for a British syndicate. By June, 1912, he was back East outfitting the SS Algerine with crew of 20 and Peary's former captain John Bartlett for an expedition to Baffin Island because he'd come across a secret treasure map describing a gold discovery made by a whaler 50 years before. The venture proved disastrous--no gold, and the ship sank in a gale. "Her hull," one historian writes, "was crushed like a paper box. Her crew barely had time to scramble out on the ice before the floes parted, releasing the ship. She sank within 20 minutes in 500 fathoms of water. The officers and men made their way across to Pond Inlet" where they found a cabin and cache left by Capt. Joseph Bernier two years previous. Rescued by the Newfoundland sealer SS Neptune, Munn was later charged with stealing fur and ivory (which one of its crew 'Lucky Scott' had done) but cleared by Capt. Bernier, with whom he subsequently became close friends.

In fall of 1913 Capt. Munn returned to England to organize a syndicate to establish trading posts on Baffin Island, outfitting the small whaling ketch Albert, which famous missionary Wilfred Grenfell had been using. Sailing in July, 1914, they established a post at Durban Harbor. In September he and one sailor left the Albert and founded a second post at Pond Inlet, stepped on a rusty nail and broke a bone in his hand. Bernier also had a post here and the two became friendly rivals. That winter Munn took numerous trading-exploring trips. On one of these he came upon a German called Franke who'd been on Cook's Arctic expedition and now with a brother-in-law was making a movie, discovered the latter frozen to death. July saw Munn again prospecting, finding much iron purite (fool's gold) concluding this must have been the sailor's 'discovery'. Caught on a floating ice floe he almost perished.

The Albert returned in August and Munn sailed to England and tried to enlist but considered too old. In 1916 he outfitted again, encountered gales and tremendous tides but managed to make Southampton Island in Hudson Bay, let his ship return. Here he stayed two years. The second winter he and some natives crossed the island to Roe's Welcome--"which I think I was the first white man to make." Today, Munn Hills in the southwest and Munn Bay on the south coast--five miles west of Coral Harbor containing an RCMP station, airfield, meteorological station and Eskimos--on the Kirchoffer River (undoubtedly named after his senator friend) commemorate this West-Manite's Arctic explorations.

In England, following Armistice, he purchased Bernier's trading post, returned to service it and his own in 1919 but ran into violent gales and much ice, losing his mate. For months Lloyd's of London listed them missing.

In 1920 Munn was back in the Arctic. This was the year the white man Janes was killed by natives, who were later tried at Pond Inlet in a widly publicized trial. Munn's version contradicts sharply those of most historians, his sympathies being entirely with the condemned natives—one being a close friend and he himself having had several unpleasant experiences with Janes. Munn takes Janes' furs to Newfoundland and buys them for $9,000 from the dead man's father, loses heavily on the transaction. Although he has no use for missionaries generally he has only praise for the Wesleyan Rev. James Evans. During this voyage he rescues the crew of the shipwrecked Easonian, is almost shipwrecked himself.

Hudson Bay Co. was now rapidly establishing trading posts on Baffin Island. Despite harsh criticism of that company's "economic enslavement of the Eskimo rather than genuine concern for their welfare" Munn and other independent traders—like the Moravians who did missionary work as well—agree to sell out. Munn makes representation to Ottawa to limit the slaughter of caribou in the North and appropriate legislation results, bids farewell for the last time to his native and white friends and leaves the Arctic.

Also in the December 29/73 edition of the same column:

"I was most interested in reading of the experiences of Captain Henry Toke Munn," writes Ellerton S. Hopper of Powell River, B.C. "I shall be looking forward to a report on a later visit he made to Brandon around the turn of the century. It was the occasion for a celebration, the details of which I am not in a position to state. However, he decided to throw a party to his friends. It was in late spring at a time when the skating rinks were about to close for the summer months, but the ice was still in pretty good shape for skating so he decided to lease the building from the owners, Murdock McKenzie and my brother William Hopper. It may have been through the latter connection I was one of the invited guests along with a couple of hundred others.

"It was the one and only affair of that kind so far as I am aware and it was surprising the number of friends Henry Toke Munn had. The two waiting rooms, I remember, were well supplied with liquid refreshments with counters set up for convenience in the dispensing of it." And it wasn't even New Year's Eve!

And in the March 16/74 issue:

Recent correspondence with Mrs. Jenny Gilbertson of Coral Harbour near Munn Bay, who produces documentary and educational films and programs, contributing to British magazines like Times, Guardian, Scotsman, Glasgow Herald and doubling as Justice of the Peace, adds a bit more data on this remarkable Arctic wanderer.

According to Memoirs of the Carnegie Museum, Vol. XII, which deals with a 1929-30 report on Southampton exploration by George Misch Sutton, Munn's home "was located near the head of South Bay, not far from Seal Point. During the summer of 1917 he made several journeys inland and along the coast, and in February, 1918, took some local natives from South Bay to Sir Thomas Roe's Welcome. He reached the coast of the Welcome about half way between Cape Kendall and Cape Frigid. According to the natives he was 'the first white man to cross the island'.

"Munn's map shows the location of Kirchhoffer River, which he named, and of Kathleen Falls (50 feet) which occur near the river's mouth. Several inland 'salmon ponds' are indicated, and the altitude of the mountains is suggested. According to this map Munn travelled, presumably by dog-sled or whale boat, about half-way down the coast from his headquarters at South Bay, to Cape Low: northward to the high country about thirty miles; northeastward almost to Fox Channel; eastward almost to Leyson Point; and also, in a circuitous route, to Native Point, thence quite a way inland, and finally back to his headquarters. Many of the Eskimos, with whom I came in contact, remembered Captain Munn very well. I walked about the site of his 'house' at Seal Point again and again and saw many of the beacons which he had erected from stones."

In the same volume, Mathiassen in 1931 writes that "Capt. Munn's map gives much information concerning the interior." T.H. Manning, in his book on Southampton Island, also credits Munn with being the first white man to cross this island. Thanks to Jenny Gilbertson, whom you may have seen on a recent CBC arctic film, for furnishing us with more information on a fascinating West-Manite.

"I often wondered how a person could last that long," Andy Sandstrom chuckled when we discussed his approaching 100th birthday recently. Grandfather of 16 children and great grandfather of 22, Mr. Sandstrom will be a century old Dec. 16. "Just missed being a Christmas present," he quipped.

Andy was born a son of Lars and Grinilla (Wall) Sandstrom in the village of Stromsund in northern Sweden the same year Canada put wheels in motion to create the Mounties. Eighteen years later he and his father played a major role in the destiny of one detachment—stationed south of Estevan on Souris River where Boundary Dam power plant now's located—by supplying its horses with hay for the winter. "They had much better food than we had," he recalls; and that there were buffalo bones piled high alongside fields.

Lars Sandstrom had been a lumberman in Sweden, cutting trees on mountains and then floating them downriver to the Baltic Sea. After his wife's death he took four of his five children and sailed to Canada on a cattle boat; a daughter, Anigaberg, remaining behind. Lars Jr. farmed at Estevan, Eli south of Minnedosa, Annie (Mrs. Neville) lived at Minnedosa but now's in Vancouver.

Andy was 14 when the Sandstroms arrived in Winnipeg where they lived in an immigration shed for several months, recalls the main street just then being paved with tarmac blocks and gravel. From there they moved to Brandon "which was my home off-and-on during my early wandering years" before he met and married Jenny Johnson—daughter of pioneer Minnedosa farmer Swan Johnson—and started farming southeast of Minnedosa 10 years later.

As young Brandon teen-ager Andy remembers vividly several logging operations with his father, himself usually as cook's helper because of his age. The Sandstroms were employed by Johnny Christie cutting lumber in Riding Mountains and floating the booms down Minnedosa River to Brandon. One spring he and his father walked to Birtle where they cut logs and floated them down the Assiniboine. To youngsters like Andy, Brandon of about 1887 meant huge mud puddles along Rosser Avenue; his friends and he bouncing on wooden sidewalks to make the water splash until the good ladies of that mushrooming metropolis chased them off. It meant watching in fascination at the CPR station Canadian soldiers return from Western Canada during the aftermath of the Northwest (Second Riel) Rebellion, many with sunburned toes protruding from boots.

One whole year involved living on a scow on Lake of the Woods where a giant boom of many thousands of logs from Rainy River had burst spilling all over the lake, Andy and his father being hired to gather and pile the logs. For two years they worked on a rail crew in Miami district where the hunting lodge in which they lived burned down with all their personal papers and family records from Sweden. When his father—who lived to be 95—took out a homestead in Estevan district, Andy continued to work on the railroad between that town and Brandon. Although offered the position of roadmaster he too decided to farm and moved to Minnedosa.

Andy and Jenny Sandstrom had six children: Mrs. Nellie Collard of Detroit, Harold (deceased), Milton of Minnedosa, Wilfred—well known popular auctioneer in this district many years but now deceased, Lila (Mrs. Albert Lamb) formerly of Clear Lake and now of Minnedosa.

Farming was tough in the 1890s and early 1900s but Andy, a most cheerful and optimistic man, seems to have taken it all in easy stride. "As long as we had a bit of pork and some potatoes we were happy," he remarked with a twinkle, "and strangers were always welcome in your home in those days regardless how poor you were." A large, tough man, in his prime tipping the scales at 217 pounds with little of it fat while today still holding steady at 170, his major concern is that he can no longer see well enough to read. Impaired hearing and a stroke that left his right side partially paralyzed don't seem to concern him greatly and he still gets around on his own remarkably well. His wife has been dead 30 years. In 1952, almost 80 then, he retired from farming and ever since has been living with Lila.

"I love Canada. It's the nicest country in the world," stated Mr. Sandstrom seriously. A former school trustee in Hazelwood S.D. (the school house still stands three miles east of Minnedosa), Andy was instrumental in building the former Covenant Church of which I've previously written. He enjoys an occasional shot of brandy, takes snuff. "I used to chew tobacco and once smoked a pipe but don't any more," he explains.

The excellent relationship that must have existed between Andy and his children is clearly evident in the Lamb home today. "Dad is never grumpy, never wakes up with a chip on his shoulder," volunteered Lila. "It's really a pleasure to have him live with us." And having elderly parents live out their lives in the home of a child, although common 30 or 40 years ago, is becoming a rare phenomenon.

22. THE WHITE SHEPHERD CONTROVERSY

Valley Vistas column, Dec. 8/73; Brandon Sun; Reprinted Sept./74 edition Shepherd's Din.

Dave Agnew's Canadian Press article 'These Dogs Earning Keep' in The Sun's Nov. 28 edition naturally caught my eye. It involved the remarkable work Sgt. Bryan Anthony of London, Ont., police force has been doing with German Shepherd police dogs.

Several thousand American breeders of dark Shepherds, as many from West Germany, one or two hundred in Canada would rejoice ne end should Sgt. Anthony and your beloved Valley Vistas columnist quietly fade into oblivion--the sergeant for proving dramatically white German Shepherds make at least as good police dogs as do their darker cousins, yours truly for writing the 1970 book THE INVINCIBLE WHITE SHEPHERD which refutes many old wives' tales about degeneracy of this variety in process of becoming separate breed. The 'White Shepherd Controversy' rages viciously in the United States, to more subdued degree in West Germany and with less furore in Eastern Canada. Except as involving my book (written after a decade's research), all's yet quiet on our western front.

The August edition of Dog Fancy--said to be the world's most widly read magazine about dogs--dealt impartially with this controversy in a major article by professional free lancer Gail Finkeldei of Sherman Oaks, Calif. Gail, who initiated correspondence with me in connection with her article, deals at length with Sgt. Anthony's work and displays a full page photo of the sergeant and his department's white German Shepherd police dog Prince.

Quoting Sgt. Anthony Gail's article states, "I was not aware Prince was white when I came to check the volunteers for the Canine Section. My immediate reaction, the result of 20 years of training and handling police dogs in Britain, was to walk away from a white German Shepherd. But I decided the dog at least deserved a chance. After a great deal of examining I put aside the prejudice of many years. This dog seemed to possess the qualities of intelligence, aggressiveness and strength that are required for police dog training. Prince was one of two dogs selected out of 60, the other being a standard Shepherd.

"The white Shepherd seemed to know exactly what was expected of him and performed beautifully. It was no surprise when he graduated at the head of the class. Prince's specialty is property search; with his nose to the ground he has helped solve many cases. Prince has made a believer out of me. I just hope he can open the eyes of others who think whites are inferior!"

In April of 1972 Elaine Twanow, White Shepherd Club of Canada's secretary, wrote me, "Shortly after the program was instituted, Sgt. Anthony had contacted the people of other clubs in town and volunteered to speak to them about the program. It seems he received a very poor reception from some members of the (dark) German Shepherd Club who caused a bit of trouble for the police department with the City Fathers. At this point Sgt. Anthony decided he had better keep out of the public eye." This he found impossible with numerous journalists vieing for his attention. Significantly, Dave Agnew studiously avoids ascribing colors to any of London's police dogs.

I've long lost count of how many times my book's been reviewed; unfortunately most of the time either highly favorably by white Shepherd fanciers or most derogatorily by dark German Shepherd breeders. Whenever I read reviews by the former I begin to feel perhaps I'm another Messiah, but the latter quickly convince me more probably Satan's foremost henchman.

I've been awarded a lovely plaque in recognition for research involving white Shepherds by the Canadian club with honorary life memberships in it plus the US club while the book's been utilized as text by at least one Canadian university class on one hand, received numerous hostile and sarcastic 'hate letters' on the other. A recent article in a dark Shepherd magazine from America, Midwestern Shepherd, informs me "the German Shepherd Dog Club of America's attorney is handling the matter of the erroneous statements in the book" while one of its three chief book reviewers Donald L. Bland sums up my valiant authorship with "I, for one, hope that Dr. Neufeld, in the future, will confine his literary efforts to the grocery list and leave more serious and entertaining writing to those who know how." But then, it's easier writing a book today than composing a week's grocery list at current prices.

So, if by next week I haven't been canonized by white Shepherd promoters, or drawn-and-quartered (at least kidnapped and spirited across the 49th parallel to answer charges of literary perjury) by dark Shepherd forces, I'll be back to regale you once again in my usual witty, refreshingly scintillating and fascinating style. Meanwhile Sgt. Anthony would be well advised to avoid all dark alleys on night patrol—or at least for personal protection use a pitch black German Shepherd that's less readily visible—until this little tempest in einem Tee Kessel blows itself out.

23. THE STAR OF BETHLEHEM   Valley Vistas column, Brandon Sun, December 22/73

So far I haven't experienced that once in a thousand life-times opportunity of seeing Kohoutek. Elsie and I tried hard one morning: set the alarm for 6, drove out of town and valley to minimize interference from trees, houses and street lights. The sky was beautifully clear with countless stars—except for light cloud covering the eastern horizon where the comet was supposed to show.

After parking on Highway 4 some 45 minutes with little activity except half a dozen meteors, several giant transfers almost demolishing us, I remarked, "Look, it is getting light in the east. The sun's about to rise." "Those are Neepawa lights", my better and wiser half corrected. Fortunately the Wise Men didn't have to rely on my astronomical astuteness to find and follow their Star of Bethlehem.

As yet I've heard of only one Minnedosan who's located Kohoutek. But he's an excellent photographer and amateur astronomer whereas guys like me have trouble identifying the Big Dipper. Luckily the comet's to be around for a while yet; eventually will be brighter, higher above the horizon, visible early evenings, in westerly direction where I can search in comfort of my rocking chair.

Looking for Kohoutek reminds me of Hubert Darrell, the Klondiker from Birtle. In 1910, the year he mysteriously vanished in northern Yukon and the year Halley's comet last visited us, Hubert wrote his mother in England from Dawson, "I have been watching very closely for Halley's comet and I must say after all the talk from the world's greatest astronomers I am disappointed. They have all diasagreed about its appearance; some have said that good eyes (without telescope) should pick it up last December and that all winter it would be sweeping the sky and be a sight such as never seen before, I've got different cuttings from the press by great astronomers and have closely watched according to their directions and here it is April 25 and not a sign of it, not even with powerful glasses. The comet is a fraud." Perhaps we'll have more success when it reappears in 1986.

"Behold, wise men from the East came to Jerusalem, saying, 'Where is he who has been born king of the Jews? For we have seen his star in the East, and have come to worship him.' ... When they had heard the king they went their way; and lo, the star which they had seen in the East went before them, till it came to rest over the place where the child was," wites Matthew—alias Levi—a former despised tax collector for Rome, about 37 A.D.

The best account I've come across regarding possible scientific explanation of the Magi's 'star in the East' is Fred Bodsworth's article in Dec. 20, 1958 edition of Maclean's. "To many," he contends, "it is a miracle that neither needs nor permits scientific explanation. Others regard it as myth that existed only in vivid imaginations of a people who were always diligently seeking religious signs and symbols in the sky. But a majority of both religious skeptics and believers accept the Bible story as evidence that there probably was a Star of Bethlehem."

Meteors, astronomers immediately eliminated as contenders for the star because of their brief duration. As most theologians concur the Magi were educated Persian astrologers, routine movements of planets also were out, but double or triple conjunctions (two or three planets lined up to appear from earth to have collided) were seriously considered. Pioneer German astronomer Johann Kepler's theory of a conjunction of Jupiter, Saturn and Mars having occurred 7 B.C. was long accepted as best explanation. Subsequent research found it wasn't a true conjunction; added to the fact early astrologers feared planets and considered them evil signs.

For years Halley's comet supplanted Kepler's triple-conjunction explanation of the

Star of Bethlehem and "11 B.C. became widely accepted as the year of Christ's birth" but has since been rejected on historical grounds. Another comet, recorded for 4 or 3 B.C. by Chinese astronomers, was next considered but later also rejected. Nevertheless, comets haven't been ruled out because many possess extremely long orbits (Kohoutek won't be back for 80,000 years) and the one the Wise Men might have witnessed may well be unknown yet. However, when Halley's comet appeared in 66 A.D., shortly before the Romans destroyed Jerusalem, the Jewish historian Josephus described it as the "Sword of God"; certainly not a good omen.

Many today believe a nova (exploding star) may have been what the Magi saw. To some, the drawback here is that novae don't move; at least not in relation to earth.

Conjunction of planets? Nova? Comet? Some other yet-to-be-discovered unique heavenly phenomenon? Matthew's Star of Bethlehem story remains fascinating. Merry Christmas!

24. GLEN CAMPBELL RIDES A MOOSE   Valley Vistas column, Brandon Sun, Dec. 29/73

In October, 1972, I mentioned our centennial book MANITOBA picturing a team of moose at Brandon Fair in 1905 hitched to a sulky, the driver of which was a NWMP officer in plain clothes, and requested information about team and driver.

I never did receive a direct answer, but as many of you probably read in the Co-operative Consumer two months later Maureen Simpson wrote about this in her article "Moose Story Unravelled After 67 Years". With assistance from persons like John S. Robertson of Brandon, Western Producer magazine editor Dorothy Hall and Tom Hoy--formerly of Makinak, Man., and now of Lethbridge, Alta.--she produced a fascinating tale.

Driver Dougall McKinnon broke and trained the two moose owned by Walter Arthur Anderson on a Riding Mountain farm near Makinak. During the early 1900s the moose team was a common sight on Brandon streets for Dougall was courting a girl who lived near the Brandon Hills. In 1905 the moose were 2½ years old.

I can't help wondering whether these animals had any connection with a couple of baby moose owned by Glen Campbell in 1902. 'Cowboy' Campbell was that ubiquitous West-Manite who made international history with a two-year expedition to Yukon during gold rush days, undoubtedly Manitoba's most colorful MLA during 1902 to 1907 and MP from 1908 to 1911, recruiting the 78th Battalion and later the 107th Canadian Pioneer Battalion -- both of which distinguished themselves exceptionally in battle--in the First World War.

Glen owned a ranch on Riding Mountain for a number of years--which he sold to finance his Klondike expedition; another one not far away near Gilbert Plains. Historian J.L. Parker of the latter district recently showed me a photograph taken in 1902 at a Campbell picnic portraying Glen, his two pet baby moose and wife Harriet with friends.

Some time before the picnic Glen had executed a feat that was marvelled at throughout Canada for years. Even Hansard mentions it. Hiding in a tree he'd mounted a full grown bull moose that passed underneath and ridden the frantic, plunging, enraged beast for many miles through the Riding Mountains until finally it fell to earth exhausted.

Training Canadian moose for transportation purposes had first been achieved two decades earlier by another Manitoban. Col. Samuel Lawrence Bedson, who came west with Wolseley's expedition to quell the first Riel Rebellion, was the man placed in command of Lower Fort Garry and later became warden of Stony Mountain penitentiary.

Menotah, one of four Bedson children, in a newspaper interview in 1957 when she was in her mid-80s describes her father's moose team. "Moose took to the business of giving rides to humans better than buffalo. As a child I had long drives with the moose, always tandem--one behind the other--in a low cariole. The driver would take them across the open prairie to within four or five miles of Winnipeg, then turn for home. They trotted very fast, no matter how deep the snow or high the drifts." That these domestigated moose of Bedson's probably inspired the later training of the McKinnon-Anderson(-Campbell?) team is quite conceivable.

25. S.L. TAYLOR, PHARMACIST   Quoted portion in Dec./73 issue of Parkland Bottle Collectors Magazine; complete article in Feb. 9/74 edition Brandon Sun, Valley Vistas column.

At a recent meeting of Parkland Bottle Collectors, that national organization which stresses a bottle's history as much as the antique itself, Cardale's George Crighton exhibited an interesting item. An Underwood's ink bottle with embossed N in INKS reversed, this rare bottle is aqua, 3 inches tall and 2 in diameter at base with the side containing the original blue Underwood's label and the bottom a red, white and yellow label with

S.L. TAYLOR, CHEMIST AND DRUGGIST, MINNEDOSA on it.

A month before George had asked me about this Taylor and because historical research the group does deeply interests me I managed to dig up the following for them:

'Samuel Lucas Taylor, called Sam in early days but known affectionately later as Uncle Lu by nieces and nephews, and Lucas, S.L. or Lu by others, was born the youngest of a family of eight in Hashwaite, Yorkshire. His parents emigrated to Clinton, Ont., when he was a youngster.

Lu's mother had studied medicine in England and when she saw her youngest possessed high aptitude and deep interest for that discipline, taught him all she knew. This paid off well for in 1891, after studying only a year at Ontario College of Pharmacy, Lucas graduated as fully qualified druggist--winning a coveted gold medal besides. The young pharmacist headed west to Minnedosa where brothers Stephen and John (father of Mrs. Olive M. Moir of this district who supplied me with valuable information) had settled some years previous as cattle buyers.

S.L. Taylor opened a drug store in Minnedosa, which operated for two decades. His clerk was George Fairbairn. The Taylor establishment featured a pharmacy on main floor and telephone office above. By June 14, 1900, some 33 subscribers were served by the Bell Telephone Co. switchboard, sold to Manitoba government in 1908. In 1911 Lu sold his store to R.T. Butchart; today known as Alexander Pharmacy. Sept Taylor remembers Lucas well as a fine man who was superintendent of the Methodist Sunday school for many years.

Because of his wife Jessie's ill health, S.L. Taylor moved back East, settling in London, Ont. He became associated with Imperial Life of which an older brother was district manager. There he was a member of Metropolitan United Church, Masonic Order, Thistle Bowling Club. Following a brief illness he died in Toronto at the age of 81, his wife having predeceased him two years earlier. One daughter, Mrs. G.E. (Winifred) Mason, and a son Ross L. Taylor--both of Toronto--survived him.'

A recent letter from John Taylor's daughter Mrs. Moir indicates, "After Father's death my mother, who had emigrated to Birtle, took great delight in spending her summers with us. Her family had come to Manitoba in 1880. Having shown an aptitude for music her father had bought an organ for her, which came out with them. Although only 11 years of age Mother could play her organ quite nicely and the minister, who had three charges, conducted services where an organ was available. At 11, Mother was his organist. Then Grandfather located a lady from England who could give Mother further training. Transportation to this lady's home was a problem and Grandfather overcame this by having a side-saddle made for Mother. At first she rode an ox, but later a pony. That saddle is here on the farm among my relics."

S.L. Taylor's brother H.S. (Stephen), who preceded him to West-Man, became a prominent pioneer an old Manitoba encyclopedia reveals. Parents are listed as William and Anne (Horsey) Taylor of Clinton, preeminent in commercial circles as boot and shoe merchants. At 18, H.S. homesteaded at Birtle where he "had to borrow $2 to make up the $20 which was the homestead and preemption fee; and he also had to borrow postage in order to send a letter back to his people. For his first six months' labor in this province he had to take a yoke of oxen. As opportunity permitted he began the development and improvement of his claim and when he had brought it under a high state of cultivation he sold out". H.S. then joined brother John (E.J.) to establish a very successful meat market at Birtle; then one in Minnedosa they operated seven years. In 1900 they built a profitable general store here, as well as a real estate-fire and life insurance business. H.S. having "passed his examination before Judge Cumberland of Brandon with a record of 100 per cent." The venerable Taylor Building is still very much in use today as Allan James' law office and J.J.'s Salon of Beauty.

26. 1973 MINNEDOSA & DISTRICT HIGHLIGHTS   Valley Vistas column, Brandon Sun,
Jan. 5/74

Across the nation RCMP centennial celebrations created headlines. Our own detachment, which includes a major highway patrol making it one of the largest rural ones on the Prairies, played a significant role in the life and news of this community. With an enviable crime-solving record of 65% this detachment's commanding officer Jim Horn started a popular column 'RCMP Report' in local weeklies, continued by successor Clare Mealing who transferred from Amaranth when the former left for The Pas. Constable Rob Gomes won several marksmanship awards in handgun tournaments in Manitoba and Saskatchewan with Brian Runnalls also scoring high. Our detachment was involved in at least one murder trial and start of an alleged second. For increased efficiency it became computerized by connecting to Canadian Police Information Centre, assisted farmers to organize night patrols to combat rustling. Policemen like Geoff Bunckle, Rick Cole, Paul Currie, Dave Gillis were involved in several news or newsworthy events.

Sports always plays an important role here. Hockey star Ron Chipperfield made news repeatedly; as did other Wheat Kings (includes Travellers) players like Frank Taylor, Peter Wurster, Doug Hedly, Dave Leboutellier, Mike Bradbury (who also won a major golf award). Glennis Scott, Manitoba's entry in Canada Games, won a silver medal, co-managed Canada's national baseball team for which he pitched in Italy. The Clanwilliam Greys captured the Manitoba Senior C softball championship. Golfer Bob Graham won Neepawa's Rose Bowl while Arnold Nicholls the local golf tournament. Bill Campbell set a new provincial jump record in water ski championships held here. Teresa Hoffman and Gordon Smith of Minnedosa and Barbie Bayes of Rapid City won figure skating honors.

A few major appointments and awards included: Honorary life membership in Manitoba Horticultural Society for initiating organized horticultural efforts across Manitoba to former provincial president Stan Gugin. A Manitoba Bar Association 50 year medallion to former crown attorney and current legal aider Bill Burgess Q.C. Albert Moad as Minnedosa constituency Liberals' president. Rapid City's Donald Sharpe director of Dairy Farmers of Canada. Basswood's Joan McDonald an Oddfellow-Rebekah sponsored trip to UN. Harold Averill an IODE scholarship for doctoral studies in Commonwealth history at University of Rhodesia. Sid Paler Rotary president and director of Western Manitoba Regional Laboratory. Favorite wine-maker Bob Dixon managing recently completed high rise Townview Manor, with former MLA Bunty Hutton returning from Estevan as custodian. First prize for local home grounds to the Art Latimers with Graves trophy for best Manitoba farm grounds to the Donald Grahams of Newdale. A $500 University of Winnipeg entrance scholarship to Lois Hymers. Grace Godmaire chairman of housing authority. Cliff Gray Wildlife Association president. Toronto Royal reserve championship for butter to Minnedosa creamery. Full accreditation to our hospital. Grant Johnson president of Chamber of Commerce. Mrs. John Jury president of Red Cross Society. Ernie Delmage president of Manitoba Trout Farmers Association. Roy Munro president of agricultural society. Calla Carrothers won Neepawa Lions Club Rose Bowl and a vocal training scholarship. Garth Carrick achieved his MD, Gerard Murray an OD.

The two biggest battles fought here involved Marquette constituency and Rolling River SD. MP Craig Stewart and journalists led the fight against destroying the historic seat in proposed redistribution, resulting in Bill C-208 suspending the Electoral Boundaries Readjustment Act until Jan. 1/75. Former Rolling River SD chairman Emil Shellborn resigned in protest when the board refused to order those responsible for a large grant overpayment to report to the board and carried the fight to Winnipeg, the board held another in-camera meeting issuing a press release criticizing Shellborn's actions, Education minister Ben Hanuschak skillfully passed the buck, a subsequent by-election returned Emil.

In other political news Conservative Dave Blake was re-elected MLA over NDP Lawrence Bell and Liberal Ed Turner. MP Craig Stewart attended Western Economic Opportunities Conference in Calgary and North Atlantic Assembly in Turkey. Rolling River SD chairman Dr. R.O. Hinch retired, Garry Grant defeated Grant Johnson to succeed him as Minnedosa member while Les Dyer of Rivers became chairman.

In church news Key '73 had a successful year. Father Murray visited us. Anglican rector Murray Ames left for further training and was succeeded by Ralph Jacobs. The late Hannah Sangster left $60,000 to the local United Church, which engaged ministers Robert Werry and Douglas Graves. Newdale's United Church minister G.E. Waddell retired after 30 years of service.

In other news an Erickson dog saved the life of his mistress Wendy Spraggs during a fire. We acquired attractive home economist Lynne Williams--a Souris product. The science fair was more popular than ever; Marvin Frederickson--an original fair enthusiast--graduated to bigger projects like supervising construction of Manitoba's largest building outside of Winnipeg, Brandon's Rosenman building. Former editor of Manitoba Business Journal and Winnipeg Free Press and Tribune columnist Bob Hainstock opened a public relations-free lance writing firm in Winnipeg. Agristeel entered a multi-million dollar contract with John Deere to manufacture arid land seeding and tillage equipment. Minnedosa began major sewer and water expansion, paving, finalized plans for a large golf-curling complex. Anna Laskowsky and Andy Sandstrom celebrated 100th birthdays. Optometrist Tom Lowres retired after 52 years service. Don Taylor's voice was heard on new radio CJRB at Boissevain. AI users protested strongly to Hon. Sam Uskiw against **Bill 120** and Manitoba Breeders' Co-op. Disgust increased with on-and-off-again operations of Canada's Manitoba Distillery. Arnold and Pat Delbridge remodelled Patricia Cafe, renaming it Lin-Dels. Wasagaming Guide became part of Mid West News as the column Wasagaming Roundup while excellent photos by former Brandonite Rick Leach (in process of opening photo studio The Gallery here) began appearing in Minnedosa Tribune. Greg Holden of Clear Lake arrived safely by raft in Australia from Ecuador as part of Balsa Expedition.

27. TEN BOOKS   Valley Vistas column, Brandon Sun, January 12 & May 18/74

Sir William Osler once said, "Money invested in a library gives much better returns than mining stock." I sincerely hope he's right for somehow I've accumulated tons of books but nary a stock or bond. Especially historical books about Manitoba interest me. Whenever possible I get books autographed by authors. Christmas is ideal for acquiring those books you normally hesitate to spend the week's grocery or kids' clothing budget on, and this time of year made-to-order for reading. Robert Barr's harsh commentary in 1899, "The bald truth is that Canada has the money, but would rather spend it on whiskey than on books" I try reasonably hard to avoid. The following are historical books that came my way recently with which I haven't bored readers of this column yet.

Local historian George Harland came out with an interesting 51-page booklet MINNEDOSA AND HER NEIGHBORS in September. I never realized author J.F.C. Wright, who won a governor-general's medal for the highly acclaimed book SLAVA BOHU about Doukhobors, grew up here and was a son of a former Minnedosa postmaster about whom I've written before.

A real old-timer I hadn't read previously was A MANITOBA CHORE BOY by E.A. Wharton Gill—author of books like LOVE IN MANITOBA and AN IRISHMAN'S LUCK—set on "The Hoe Farm six miles from Minnedosa in 1911-'12. This 83 page hardback with 10 photos has become an historical classic of this era. Rev. Gill was Anglican rector here for many years following 1889, eventually canon of St. John's Cathedral in Winnipeg.

Although I seldom read poetry, P.J. Peters' THIS LAND OF OURS is interesting. A 144 page paperback it reflects deep feelings; especially of Manitoba and Canada. "Let us build for the tomorrow, Build a nation strong and free; And the Lord who dwells above us, He will bless our destiny" seems to embody his attitude to life and homeland. Pete, who's well known to horticulturists across Manitoba, grew up in Gretna district, taught school 7½ years in southern Manitoba, joined the RCAF at outbreak of war and immediately after served as interpreter on Canadian war crimes trials, studied agriculture graduating with gold medal from University of Manitoba in 1954.

A fascinating local history is Hazel McDonald Parkinson's A MERE LIVING—A BIOGRAPHY OF THE HARTNEY DISTRICT. Hartney's Henry families, it would seem have a somewhat similar heritage as do the Tanners of this area, their ancestor Cpt. James Henry having been captured by Indians at 14 about 1770 while travelling over the Allegheny Mountains with his father in search of land for their family, lived with them until he escaped in 1774 across the Niagara River and stayed with Col. Butler until old enough to homestead.

Mary McCarthy Ferguson's recent THE HONORABLE JAMES McKAY OF DEER LODGE, E.S. Russenholt's THE HEART OF THE CONTINENT, Edith Paterson's TALES OF EARLY MANITOBA and Elsie McKay's THE STONE FORT are all interesting; especially to people interested in Red River history, or of Manitoba a century ago. James McKay—the 300 pound dynamo of Scots and Indian descent whom Indians, whites, Metis loved and trusted and who became first lieutenant-governor of Manitoba—played a major role in events like saving bison from extinction and preventing the first Riel Rebellion from erupting into a blood bath. I doubt if a better history of Winnipeg and area exists than Ed Russenholt's book. With Winnipeg's centennial celebrations in progress his book will undoubtedly prove invaluable to many. Ed, a popular television personality, grew up in Hartney and Swan River districts. Edith Paterson—a 1969 Manitoba Historical Society Margaret McWilliams award winner—is a household name to Winnipeg Free Press readers. Her book's a collection of historical articles gleaned from that and other newspapers. Elsie McKay's booklet's a fine account of Lower Fort Garry, and it seems historians (including me) often confuse events that occurred in Upper and Lower Fort Garrys as to precise location.

"To Fellow Scribe Peter Neufeld, with best wishes Bill Robinson" reads the autograph in the copy of RATHER FISH THAN EAT my wife presented me with this Christmas. Although

I'm anything but a good fisherman (about 250 fish caught in 42 years, with never one over 4½ pounds) this book will always be a deeply treasured part of my collection. I understand the first printing by popular outdoor and 'Neepawa and Nearby' columnist is almost sold out. Fortunately Prairie Books (Western Producer) of Saskatoon's taking over future publication. Bill's book includes an interesting description and photo of the fishing exploits of two Minnedosans, Theresa Mazerolle and (Mayor) Joyce Stevenson.

Recently read Roy Brown's interesting new book THE FORT BRANDON STORY and was surprised to learn Terry McLean, who did the exceptionally fine cover design, was a Virden resident. Often I've wondered who the Terry McLean was who painted those life-like wildlife scenes on S.I.R. sporting goods catalogue covers that remind me of Ernest Thompson Seton's work. This fascinating 62-page well illustrated booklet is certainly worth reading. If not available in your favorite bookstore or library, it can be purchased directly from publisher Tourism Unlimited of Brandon.

28. ANNE LAMONT   Valley Vistas column, Brandon Sun, January 19/74

I'd come to interview Anne Lamont about her half century career at Minnedosa Courthouse; we spent most of 90 minutes talking baseball, hockey, tennis, football. Though I once participated a fair amount in sports and even taught phys. ed. on occasion, I'm not what you'd call a sports buff. Ron Chipperfield can vouch for the fact that three months I coached a peewee team on which he played back in '62 when the regular coach was away set his hockey career back six months. Anne lives--eats, sleeps, breathes-- sports. Ever since she tossed her first horseshoe at four ("Father got me a set of small ones") on their farm in Westhope district "a number of years ago". I tried to discover just when that was, got nowhere, and being a gentleman in the finest Southern (Manitoba, that is) tradition didn't press the point. I don't anticipate much static from Anne regarding what I say about her in this column for unless by some fluke it appears in the Sports Section today she'll never see it.

At 28 Anne's father John Lamont came from Aberdeen, Scotland in 1870 and following a brief stay in Ontario arrived at Minnedosa. His wife Margaret Alice had come from Ireland as infant with parents, the Hugh Kellys. Aside from homesteading in nearby Westhope district--where his farm quickly became the local sports centre for baseball ("Everyone played: grandmas, grandpas"), football, tennis, curling ("Father made excellent rocks from logs")--John was bookkeeper for Manitoba and North West Railway then being built through this district and later for pioneer Minnedosa merchant P.J. McDermott. For a while he was a property assessor.

Anne had six siblings: Christina, a nurse who died at 31; George, a carpenter; Margaret, a teacher; Katherine, also a teacher, who died at 21; John, a farmer - highways superintendent-school board member; James, clerk of Minnedosa and secretary - treasurer of RM of Odanah and later an oil company executive in Toronto. All are gone now. Fortunately John Lamont Sr. was a pioneer of such note his accomplishments rate a lengthy description in the long out-of-print STORY OF MANITOBA encyclopedia and Anne's niece Mrs. Clair (Jean Lamont) Jardine was visiting her for Anne's mind was occupied with more exciting things like what hockey team was currently playing which and with several unforgiveable managing errors in the last World Series.

Somehow or other I gathered that after graduating from Dominion (Business) College in Winnipeg in 1920 Anne entered Minnedosa Courthouse as stenographer and has just retired as law librarian. For many years she was also court clerk and issued car licences. Judges like Maulson, Simpson, Lindal, Kerr she knew and liked well, worked side-by-side with; F.W. Coward, "I worked with as lawyer and later as magistrate." Occasionally she experienced the personal satisfaction of besting a noted legal individual. "One judge ruled as legal a will completed on carbon copy only. I argued it wouldn't stand up. Later a higher court proved me right." Her annual salary in 1937 amounted to the grand total of $616.03. Now she's completely retired. From law work, certainly not sports. At last she can devote all her time to her most beloved avocation.

As teen-ager Anne longed desperately to play tennis in a regular league in Minnedosa five miles away. Although permission was readily forthcoming and transportation eventually arranged, "I just didn't know where to get $10 for a sweater for the required uniform. But I baked pies, cookies and made butter to be sold at fairs and bought that sweater." Numerous subsequent tennis trophies attest to her proficiency. That she donated heavily to the tennis court completed at Minnedosa Beach recently and sponsors a hockey trophy for youngsters comes as no surprise.

There are two past honors Anne Gertrude Lamont particularly cherishes. One's a scroll "In appreciation of the years of pleasant association, in recognition of devotion to duty" from the Bar Association of this judicial district. The other was being voted 'Lady of the Season' by the Minnedosa hockey players and officials in about 1958. I have a strong feeling the latter gave this remarkable, friendly, vivacious lady the greater gratification.

29. SOME WILDLIFE EXPERIENCES   Valley Vistas column, Brandon Sun, January 26/74

Commenting on a recent article John E. Fardoe of Brandon, who grew up in Little Souris district, writes, "I remember well the two moose Dugald McKinnon drove. I went to school with his future wife Mary McLean. A brother and sister of hers are still living. My father Wm. Fardoe homesteaded SE¼ 10-9-19 in 1879. This farm is still operated by son William."

One of eight wildlife experiences I especially treasure since moving to Minnedosa 12½ years ago following a decade of city life was watching a giant bull moose contentedly munching water plants beside a road to Lake Audy in Riding Mountain. Another memorable one in that park was viewing a large bobcat (or lynx) saunter across a trail in front of our car.

During the past five summers I have on occasion helped a friend David Comrie with farm work. Dave operates several farms adjacent to or near Minnedosa Valley. Four experiences there in particular I wouldn't exchange for as many months' wages.

The only woodchucks (ground hogs) I've run across in West-Man lived near a bush in a grain field. One exceptionally agressive fellow used to make furious charges towards the tractor as though trying to scare it away from his home and only at the last moment would he back off.

Not far from the woodchuck burrow lived a pair of bluebirds. They returned to the same little bluff three consecutive summers. North America owes John Lane of Brandon a debt of gratitude for helping preserve these beautiful song birds. Met this remarkable ornithologist once servicing one of his 3700 nestboxes near property we own on Highway 10, have also corresponded with him. Dr. Lane's father Robert was one of many West-Manites who fought in the second Riel Rebellion as a Boulton Scout.

The only silver fox I've ever seen was a kit who sat watching me swathe some wheat one day. I mentioned it to a teen-aged friend of my son's, Randy Instance, who hunted a lot. He told me he'd seen a parent and several young on occasion in and near Minnedosa Valley. Randy, unfortunately, was killed in 1970 in a most tragic hunting accident; he would, I feel certain, have developed into the type of sportsman this country needs desperately.

Dave owns a female German Shepherd called Cindy of similar size and color as a coyote. One morning I was repairing fence about a mile from the farmyard. Fields were extremely muddy and because I didn't trust my friend's prize bull had brought a rifle along 'just in case'. Finished, I called Cindy who had tagged along and apparently was lying about 10 yards away watching me work. To my surprise she came bounding out of the bushes from the opposite direction while a coyote, which I'd mistaken for her and talked to several times during the past half hour, loped away. I was much too confused to shoot.

The past two summers have seen a pair of loons frequent a pond on our 50 acre 'farm'. The Gordon and Keith Vidals and we were canoeing one afternoon and were amazed at how tame these gorgeous birds of the haunting cry and attractive 'necklace' were. You could paddle almost up to them, and even then they wouldn't fly away—simply dive and pop up nearby.

But by far the most unforgetable moment occurred in March/65. Son Lory and I were taking a Welsh mare to Mrs. Gladys Iverson of Oak Lake district to be bred to her excellent palomino-colored Welsh stallion Golden Star. Star had been imported in dam from Wales by the famous Cambrian Pony Farms of High River, Alberta; later purchased by Gladys for a high price. We'd been down to see him and the Iversons but decided to take a shortcut.

By the time we got to Rivers a sharp wind had sprung up and it was drifting. We made a wrong turn and for a while were lost. Somewhere between Rivers Airforce Base and Assiniboine Valley we crossed a ravine with stream or river—probably Oak River.

Leaping down the side of the slope came two deer with a cougar in hot pursuit. I slammed on the brakes and we watched the chase until finally the deer swerved into a bluff. The snow was soft and deep; all three animals laboring heavily. The cougar would have been an easy shot and though I had a .303 with me I was much too astounded to even consider whether or not to shoot. I was teaching Biology at Minnedosa Collegiate then and several boys who hunted had mentioned recent cougar sightings. I'd laughed and indicated they were probably bobcats or lynx, that there were definitely no cougars east of the Rockies. Next day, to their huge enjoyment, I ate crow.

Last fall when I read Robert Nero's article in Conservation Comment magazine 'But Nobody Believed Me' involving cougar research in Manitoba I immediately wrote him about the incident. Robert's also author of the excellent Dept. of Mines and Resources booklet THE GREAT WHITE BEARS. That I found Dr. Best's article about the cougar shot recently in Stead district and Nero's subsequent involvement of interest is an understatement. Golden Star, by the way, was sold soon after; changed hands repeatedly. I met one of the last owners in Portage recently. He had no idea that the animal he'd known as Popcorn was registered or the finest Welsh stallion this province has seen and had sold him to a stranger whose name he couldn't recall for a song. Star's daughter—one of his very few registered Welsh offspring—which we raised is now owned by Joe Wilson who ranches near Whitewater Marsh.

30. RIVERBOATS, LANDINGS, CROSSINGS Valley Vistas column, Brandon Sun, Feb. 2/74

Though Minnedosa River served as highway for Indian canoes, supported pioneer logging operations by turning sawmills and floating log booms to Brandon-Portage-Winnipeg districts plus furnished power for Manitoba's first major hydro electric plant near Brandon, I don't think it played a role in what's come to be known as the Prairie Navy as did the Red, Assiniboine, Souris with whose waters it mixes enroute to Lake Winnipeg.

Stern- and side-wheelers like the Anson Northrup, Dakota, Selkirk, Minnesota, Manitoba made lasting Red River history. The Prince Rupert, Marquette, North-West, Alpha, Mary Ann Roe, Cheyenne, City of Winnipeg, Assiniboine Queen, Manitoba, Minnesota figure prominently in Assiniboine history. The Empress of Ireland (later the Assiniboine Queen) which plied the Souris 1908-10 immortalized that river in Prairie history.

Historians frequently commend the role riverboats played in Manitoba history. MacDonald Coleman in THE FACE OF YESTERDAY quotes a letter of appreciation to Cpt. Hancock of steamer Marquette on behalf of 21 persons who arrived at Grand Valley in 1881; the same book includes Peter Parker's sketch of the North-West. MINNEDOSA MEMORIES describes 'Aunt Mary' Rose's trip West on the 170-foot Minnesota. Birtle historian J.L. Swainson mentions "the Marquette and Alpha made trips once every two weeks" to Birtle (Wattsview) Landing with settlers and supplies.

Two riverboat captains who achieved a degree of fame were Swedish-born Charles Daniel 'Flatboat' Anderson of Fort Garry who operated boats on the Red from Breckenridge in Minnesota to Winnipeg 1872-75 and William Robinson who sailed the Red, Assiniboine, Saskatchewan and Lake Winnipeg for Northwest Navigation Co. So did Robert Sutherland of Kildonan in 1830, who married Jane Henderson in 1850. One of the first riverboat captains, he homesteaded south of Griswold in 1882, served as reeve of RM of Sifton and died at the home of his daughter Mrs. W.J. McComb of Brandon on April 17, 1907, being survived by three daughters and seven sons. And there was H.J. Rolston Large of Coulter-Brandon-Waskada whose interesting tale Roy Brown and Garth Stouffer expound in THE CAPTAIN LARGE STORY.

Two riverboats that were much in the news during and since Manitoba centennial are the Assiniboine Queen and Alpha. The former, which lay rotting in the Assiniboine just east of Brandon, was salvaged thanks to people like Roy, Garth, Brandon Jaycees. The history of the latter—suffering a similar fate downstream in Spruce Woods Forest—was preserved through efforts of Roy, Garth and others like Reg Forbes. Roy Brown, recipient of Manitoba Historical Society's 1971 Margaret McWilliams award for his untiring efforts on riverboat history, is author of the recent most fascinating booklet with many photos THE MYSTERY SHIP OF SPRUCE WOODS FOREST, published by Tourism Unlimited of Brandon—which incidently also published THE CAPTAIN LARGE STORY.

There are several dozen river landings and crossings in West-Man that played major historic roles; both before and after the coming of white men. I feel strongly they should be marked with cairns, plaques, etc. Not only would these attract tourists, more important might interest our young people in Prairie history—which I feel does not receive nearly enough emphasis in many schools. Sometimes all that's needed is for an organization to point the way. Last year, for example, Erickson Women's Institute suggested to RM of Clanwilliam that permanent markers be erected in that municipality to designate the sites of former country schools of Scandinavia, Tales, Hilltop, Nor-land, Lund, Westmount, Nedrob, Otter Lake and immediate action followed.

A major Assiniboine River landing I've mentioned before that played a most im-portant part in settling much of West-Man north of Brandon which should definitely be marked immediately is Wattsview Landing. Nothing reveals this historic site today but a simple wooden CNR 'Wattsview' sign. CN must have a sense of history. Hudson Bay Co., who owned the dock and warehouse long gone, might possibly be induced to mark it if approached by an organization.

CPR, which certainly has an historical conscience as shown here recently through invaluable assistance in building Tanner's Crossing Park and in Brandon by helping salvage the Assiniboine Queen, would I feel give assistance where their lines pass near historic crossings or landings. Too often we think of CP as merely a railway and ignore countless ocean steamers (many named after West-Man centres) she once sailed; numerous inland lake barges. Though she didn't play a direct role in our Prairie navy, CP nonetheless has an equally fascinating riverboat history herself.

CP boats once plied Canadian rivers like the Columbia and Kootenay. Her first ri-ver steamer, the Aberdeen, was launched May 22, 1892. During the Klondike gold rush CP operated the Constantine, Dalton, Schwatka, Dawson, Duchesny, Hamlin, McConnel, Ogilvie. Of these, the Dawson sailed until 1926 when she was wrecked on Tache Reef, Rink Rapids on the Yukon. That I personally have some compassion for this oft ma-ligned monolithic Canadian institution is undoubtedly obvious; but I know that were it not for CP most of my relatives, many friends, myself would either be dead or liv-ing in Siberia instead of West-Man today.

31. LAST OF THE WILD BISON   Valley Vistas column, Brandon Sun, Feb. 16 & March 16, 1974

"I was here at this Crossing 30 years ago, about 1848, and I saw the buffalo cros-sing over the Little Saskatchewan (Minnedosa) River at the ford just east of this Crossing. It took the main herd that year three days to go south in the spring, and three days to go north up into the bush in the late fall when winter came on!" John Tanner is to have told pioneer Norman Shuttleworth according to George H. Hambley's recent book THE LAST OF THE PIONEERS. Perhaps it was this memorable experience of a young lad of nine which 20 years later induced the war-weary American Civil War vet-eran to settle at Tanner's Crossing soon after his 1869 marriage at Portage. For the next 12 years, besides serving as the settlement's first postmaster, John with "sort of a coracle shaped, circular boat made of buffalo hide" helped ladies cross while the men "would either walk or swim with the oxen or horses and cart or buckboard" o-ver the very river his grandfather John 'Falcon' Tanner plied fur-laden canoes six decades before.

Wildlife historian Frank Gilbert Roe records Cpt. John Schott telling of numerous bison still freely roaming West-Man plains in 1852 where Carberry now stands. "The last buffalo band seen in Manitoba by Schott," he indicates, "was in 1861, when an immense herd was discovered in Grand Valley. They completely covered the site of the present town of Brandon." Most of this herd was slaughtered near Carberry during 1860-65, Trader J.L. Lagare mentions sighting what must have been the last major remnant of this fine herd in Oak Lake district in 1867.

From that point on only rare sightings of plains bison occurred in West-Man. Rev. Hambley, a United Church minister in Basswood-Cadurcis-Fairmount near Minnedosa 1954-60, tells of a Mr. Titus of Napinka seeing "a huge lonely old bull making his way sad-ly toward the west" in 1874. Dr. F.W. Shaw of Carberry tells of travelling to Rapid City in 1879 and seeing tracks of three buffalo about four miles north of Brandon, sighted crossing the Assiniboine travelling north. C.C. Helliwell of Brandon obser-ved eight in Souris region in 1882 while A.S. Barton of Boissevain sighted an old bull crossing Souris plain heading for Plum Creek. H.W.O. Boyer saw the same animal cross his farm--the last bison seen in that region; duly "recorded in all the newspapers."

By mid 1880s wild bison in Manitoba were virtually extinct. A couple were seen passing through Brandon Hills; perhaps once part of a large herd that wintered regu-larly on Little Souris River. Mrs. Alice McKay, born about 1881, is reported in BRID-GING THE YEARS as young girl of five helping her mother tan the hide of a buffalo shot by her father John Wakpa near Melita.

That destruction of our great northern herd of plains bison was greatly accelerated by deliberate US government policy following her last 'Indian War' which grew out of the Civil War is certain. Following the revolt of Sitting Bull evidence reveals the American government of 1878 did with soldiers and hired Indians and Metis deliberately create a corydon just south of the border to destroy migrating bison and thus starve Sitting Bull's Sioux hoping to force them to return to US reserves, which most eventually did. A consequent 2550 ton pile of buffalo bones on Souris River at west shore of Devil's Lake and 2125 ton pile on south side plus 5000 ton pile at Minot help substantiate this. Westward advance of white civilization and the many American Sioux refugees made short work of any plains bison remaining on Canada's western prairies. An August, 1890 photo of a pile of buffalo bones at Saskatoon representing some 25,000 animals in Hewitt's CONSERVATION OF THE WILD LIFE OF CANADA, Regina's first name of Pile O'Bones, Hambley's report of Basswood's Joe Girling plowing "into a remarkable accumulation of bones which extended for hundreds of yards" attest mutely to this heavy over-hunting. Fortunately a handful of conservationists--notable among them Manitobans like Alloway, Bedson, Smith, Eaton, McKay, Ayotte--saved them from annihilation.

Due to their northern habitat the larger wood bison fared much better for a while but eventually also were almost wiped out. E.A. Preble, a close friend of Hubert Darrell's, is recorded by RNWMP Inspector Jarvis having sighted a herd about 45 miles south of Lake Athabasca as late as 1907. American 'sportsman' Harry V. Radford, who repeatedly urged Darrell to guide him on a wood bison hunt but was sharply rejected, proudly killed a giant trophy bull in 1909 weighing 2460 pounds with longest recorded horns-- still standing mounted in Calgary museum; was himself killed the following year by an Eskimo whose life he'd threatened.

In reading about Manitoba's animal emblem one often comes across references to 'buffalo stones.' For a long time such references puzzled me because obviously they didn't all mean the same. It's not until quite recently that I've solved (I think) this riddle. There seem to have existed at least three distinctly different kinds of buffalo stones.

The most common of these rocks are buffalo rubbing stones; which were scattered over much of the Prairies when the first white men arrived. H.H. Marshall, in the 1970 edition of PRAIRIE GARDEN, describes these in detail. Because much of the Prairie was once treeless suitable rubbing places were rare and thus large verticle-sided rocks, often weighing two tons and more, were used by bison to remove heavy winter coats -- frequently infested with lice, ticks and assorted vermin. Depressions up to two feet deep near verticle rock sides where soil was trampled to dust and blown away and edges worn smooth and stained with oil attest to this a century later. Unfortunately, many such rocks were removed by settlers who saw no significance in these boulders, and consequently only the odd one's still to be seen in a few neglected areas. Portage historian Anne M. Collier tells of one such symbol of early Prairie history being "shipped to Charlottetown and given a place of honor on the grounds of the Fathers of Confederation complex; a tangible link between the prairies and the birthplace of Confederation."

The history of North America's great Sioux nation was inextricably interwoven with plains bison. Sioux utilized buffalo stones as sort of good luck charm. Milton Lott deals repeatedly with these. They were in effect naturally smooth and polished flattened unshaped-by-man rocks resembling bison. The shape of head--preferably with suggestion of a curved horn--and hump were especially important. Such buffalo stones were usually small enough to carry easily in the hand. To find one was Wakan--a very good sign that a benevolent spirit was with the finder and bison hunting for him would be favorable. These talismen were invariably given a high place of honor--such as in the owner's medicine bundle, which held items like fossil shells and redstone pipes of particular religious significance to him.

Chad Oliver describes a third type of buffalo stone. "And there--a small smooth and white stone. A buffalo stone from the stomach of the buffalo! He had seen many such in his lifetime." Oliver mentions them several times.

32. HOSPITALS AND DOCTORS   Valley Vistas column, Brandon Sun, February 23/74

With Mother-in-law in Brandon General and Father plus a brother-in-law in Victoria hospital in Winnipeg, my past week seems to have been spent in hospitals.

Chugging along merrily in the old bolt bucket I'd just remarked to my wife on the exceptional merits of '62 Comets when all Hades broke loose under the hood. Fortunately we were near a garage and the friendly Gulf fellows on Highway 10 North and Trans-Canada replaced the water pump-fan bearing and we continued our merry way. If all strangers in jalopies that've have seen better days get similar treatment then one service station at least reflects well on Brandon and West-Man.

Though visiting hours were by then over we weren't really too worried because the people at Brandon General are well known for their compassion. In mid '50s I spent two of the most pleasant weeks of my life there following a knee operation by Dr. F.J.E. Purdie. Several years ago our youngest son Rod had an eye muscle operation there by Dr. James Rooney after two other doctors had played around for 18 months with poor results. Now he's got 20/20 vision and just shot a 95 in a rifle club after only three lessons. The pleasant attractive receptionist-switchboard operator was as understanding as past experience had led us to expect.

As many of you probably know Brandon General now allows children to visit patients twice weekly. It's high time a hospital took this vital step and Brandon's to be commended for a progressive policy. It seems through well-intentioned though misguided motives North American youngsters have for two decades been virtually shut off from illness and death of loved ones. I'm not advocating children live through a Vietnam; but natural sickness and death are integral aspects of life and growing up with which no child should be denied contact.

Decided to give the Comet a rest and hitched a ride to Winnipeg with friends whose daughter's training as nurse in St. Boniface hospital. My earliest impressions of Winnipeg revolve around that hospital which I'd visited as teen-ager when an older sister Sarah trained there and I first struck out on my own for the 'big city' on weekends. I suddenly realized this country actually was bilingual when trying to register in a St. Boniface hotel and the clerk and I were forced to resort to sign language to communicate. Later a younger sister Jo also trained there and I learned gradually to like and respect that hospital and city.

Dad's doctor at Victoria's Dan Bigelow. Boy, what a hard man to get hold of! Staff members tried repeatedly on four occasions to reach him for me with no luck. Jo says he's one of the best; guess that's why he's so busy. I get the impression he's a lot like his older brother whom many West-Manites knew and liked well.

Had just finished reading the fascinating 1969 book FORCEPS, FIN & FEATHERS; memoirs written at 85 just two years before Dr. W.A. Bigelow's death. Souris, Hartney and Brandon residents especially will remember this remarkable medical practitioner. Many sportsmen too will remember him as an excellent fisherman and hunter. A book well worth reading. Victoria has an innovation I found intriguing—continuous visiting hours all afternoon and evening.

After 15 years' absence, riding city buses can be unnerving. After a frustrating 90 minutes locating my daughter at University of Manitoba it took a hectic 45 minutes to get by bus to Victoria hospital about a mile away simply because most are through buses there now. Could easily have walked it in 15 minutes.

Our parents' family doctor's Don McPhail of Boissevain, who's recently been much in the news over his fight with former health minister Rene Toupin for "reducing Manitoba Health Services Commission to a 'nine-man rubber stamp' for the provincial government" and eventual resignation from MHSC. Recall well when Drs. Don and Ethel McPhail first came to Boissevain in the late 1940s. A finer medical team can't be found in West-Man. That many people admire Don's stand goes without saying. Our oldest two were brought into this troubled world by Dr. Ethel; one while she was in the middle of a curling game. Recall vividly as teen-ager being kicked in the face by a horse, fear of being disfigured for life, Don sewing me up with nine stitches so that only a tiny scar remains. And one slightly drooping moustache takes care of that.

33. JURY DUTY   Valley Vistas, Brandon Sun, March 2 & 9/74

Your doorbell rings, the sheriff or some such officer courteously hands you a court document which reads: "You are hereby summoned to serve as a Juror at the sittings of Her Majesty's Court of Queen's Bench, for Manitoba, for the trial of criminal matters and proceedings ... HEREIN FAIL NOT AT YOUR PERIL." You're informed that if you plan to claim exemption under Sec. 63 (1) of the Jury Act you must produce an affidavit establishing suitable grounds within five juridicial days. This I experienced last fall ---as many of you no doubt have in past years, some are about to in connection with the spring assizes.

The only type of jury I'd ever served on before was a local coroner's jury some eight years ago. I wouldn't have served on that one if I'd attended church like I had been regularly then. That particular Sunday morning the family had gone without me. Our church's located on a main street that doubles as provincial highway on which the congregation park their cars. Like numerous other fathers in similar circumstances I'd just double parked in front of the church waiting for the wife and kids to emerge. Our RCMP corporal 'just happened' to be cheerily passing among double parked fathers selecting jurors. One doesn't argue overly with the police detachment's commanding officer when one's incorrectly parked on a busy thoroughfare alive with holiday traffic heading to and from Clear Lake.

Three factors regarding selection of the type of jury on which I recently served in Brandon particularly intrigued me:

To begin with you're just a prospective juror (talisman); in our case there were 50, out of which 12 were selected for the first trial and another 12 for the second. TV programs, usually American, about court proceedings and books like Bill Trent's THE STEVEN TRUSCOTT STORY and John Belliveau's THE COFFIN MURDER CASE had led me to expect numerous questions fired at me to determine my objectivity concerning the case at hand. Not so! Each talisman, after being selected by random ballot in court, was asked to look at the accused and then either crown attorney A.G. Bowering or defense counsel A.A. Hirschfield did--if so inclined--simply challenge you and you were thereby rejected. Despite my rather depraved looking face, I was immediately accepted.

Second, the fact there were far more male prospective jurors than female astonished me. I recalled reading somewhere women had recently been liberated in this respect and were no longer (since Aug., 1972, I learned later) exempt from jury duty on basis of sex alone. A conversation later with Sheriff W.J.D. Stuart convinced me such phenomenon was certainly not the result of jury roll selections made by Brandon court officials from jury lists submitted each October by rural municipalities, villages, towns, cities—such jury lists comprising about 1/20 of the voters' lists and being the responsibility of the clerk (secretary-treasurer) and mayor (reeve). This suggested male dominated jury lists. Our particular jury eventually consisted of two ladies and ten men; roughly the same ratio as in the larger group.

After obtaining a copy of the Jury Act, I conducted a somewhat biased mini survey by contacting municipalities with which I'd been most involved in the past—Minnedosa, Minto (RM), Boissevain, Brandon, Morton, Odanah. Minto and Odanah secretary-treasurers Arla Gowing and Margery Halpenny, who share the same office, assured me their selections were both compiled completely at random from voters' lists--which would produce roughly equal numbers of men and women. Boissevain and Morton secretary-treasurer Gerald May's figures revealed almost perfect 50/50 ratios--suggesting random, or deliberate fair, selection as regards sex. Brandon's clerk I.L. Thomson indicated their last list contained "86 female names out of a total of 495. There really is no reason for such a difference, other than not paying particular attention to ensure that names submitted are better apportioned." Minnedosa secretary-treasurer Keith Wishart, who doubles as Justice of Peace, requested Council's permission be obtained before this data be released--which was readily forthcoming. Females totalled 42% on this jury list, males 58. Joyce Stevenson, West-Man's only woman mayor, indicated she and Keith utilize mostly random selection but avoid husbands and wives being listed the same year.

I can readily understand compassion shown mothers with small babies, etc. But any ratio exceeding 2 women to 3 men seems unwarranted. Or are West-Man women "in the opinion of the selectors ...from the integrity of their character, the soundness of their judgment, and the extent of their information, the most discreet and competent for the performance of the duties of jurors" inferior to men in this regard?

Section 5(u) of the Act exempts from jury duty all "persons who profess the faith and are members of the religious society known as: 'Mennonites'." No part of this act needs revision more than this clause.

For the record, having left that church 16 years ago I'm only of Mennonite ETHNIC origin myself. Thus, in no way do I profess to be a spokesman for Mennonite church members. However, I did grow up in and did belong to that church for a while, most of my relatives and in-laws and several friends do belong, my only brother's a minister in it.

When I recently first saw this exemption clause, to say I was astounded is an understatement. I venture to bet also that at least 99% of all Manitoba Mennonites don't realize it's on the books. A letter from Rev. A.J. Redekopp of Boissevain Mennonite Brethren church, one of West-Man's two major Mennonite congregations, suggests not even the Mennonite clergy's aware of the clause. "No doubt," he writes, "you are aware of the fact that all Canadian citizens are required to sit on a jury when elected by courts, but provision is made for a Christian to appeal his appearance in the case of murder, for conscience sake." If legislation exists to this effect I don't know of it. The Jury Act makes no reference to Christians generally--specifically 'Mennonites'. The only other religious-oriented exemptions are: 5(a) "the clergy of all denominations" and 5(b) "every woman who is a vowed member of a religious order and who lives in a convent or other religious community".

A conversation with kid brother Rev. Jake Neufeld of Whitewater Mennonite church-- West-Man's major Mennonite church embracing congregations like Boissevain, Crystal City, Mather, Lena, Killarney, Manitou, Ninga, Rivers, Brandon--revealed he too was completely unaware of the exemption. True, he's relatively young and possibly some of the older ministers know of its existence. (True also, such a serious matter should perhaps not be discussed while sitting among Boissevain rooters while cheering Minnedosa players at a crucial hockey game in which a young nephew played for Boissevain, the adults becoming even more emotionally involved than the players.)

Raymonde Vermette of the Provincial Library did some checking for me on the history of this particular exemption. It dates back to the 4th session of Manitoba's 5th legislature, having been passed as ammendment to the Jury Act on April 19, 1886, and reading word-for-word as it does today. It was introduced by attorney-general Charles Edward Hamilton QC, Liberal-Conservative MLA for Shoal Lake; a former Winnipeg mayor and Winnipeg South MLA who introduced the Torrens system of land transfer to this province. Because Manitoba Gazette apparently wasn't yet used to record debates there seems to be no record existing to explain the background of this clause.

That the exemption may somehow relate to the Mennonite pacifism tenet is concievable. If so, why then aren't other pacifistic churches like Salvation Army and Hutterites exempt? Regardless, as my brother suggested and I fully concur, each member should then be considered on an INDIVIDUAL basis. Just like Mennonite church members were considered individually during the Second World War. Then, despite the fact members usually were pacifists, despite the fact cultural ties existed between members and Germany, despite the fact some Mennonite genealogical heredity's German (Prussian), despite the fact parents of many Mennonite boys faced with the decision of fighting had experienced a German occupation in the Ukraine in the First World War and had found most of the German soldiers very pleasant, 50% of Mennonite males in the age group involved did enlist in Canadian Armed Forces and most of the remainder served in non-combat capacities like medical corps etc.

The exemption from jury duty's probably part of a promise by the Canadian government made the 1874-76 Mennonite immigrants who settled in southeastern Manitoba on 'Mennonite Reserves', then almost self-governing. This they no longer are; haven't been for many decades. Also, descendants of those Mennonites today don't compose more than one third of the Manitoba Mennonite population (virtually none in West-Man) due to large subsequent migrations in 1924-26 and 1945-50.

Gerald May is in my opinion one Anglo-Saxon who understands Mennonites better than many. Not only did he grow up in a district where about a third are of this faith and daily works with them, this popular secretary-treasurer's himself married to a fine ethnic Mennonite woman and has numerous Mennonite in-laws. In a recent letter he indicates, "In Morton, as you well know, we have a number of persons who profess the faith known as 'Mennonite' which the Act states are exempt. I appreciate this fact and I also appreciate the changing attitudes of each generation. I know that if jury duty was explained to some, or if they were asked, they would have no qualms about serving. Time and experience change many things." I agree wholeheartedly. "I used at least two last year," he adds, "and I will continue to do so. If by chance someone of the Mennonite faith were called to serve and they had strong feelings against serving, then all they have to do is stand down under sub-section (u). I believe that we all must take our turn on a jury, if called, as this is a vital part of our democratic process and legal system." Right!

Mr. Howard Pawley, if you plan to leave a better legacy for the people of this province than did your attorney-general predecessor Al Mackling, you might perhaps begin by taking a long, hard look at those exemptions from jury duty in the Jury Act—especially 5(u). In 1886 that clause may perhaps have had some validity. In today's multi-ethnic, multi-religious Manitoba society it smacks only of second class citizenship.

The rapidly approaching Royal Manitoba Winter Fair calls to mind a pioneer horseman who played a major role in that and other Canadian fairs for almost half a century. That person was Charlie Rear of Minnedosa and Saskatoon.

Charlie was born a son of Reuben and Hannah Rear about 1881 in Barrie, Ontario. He had a brother Melvin and sisters Flossie and Myrtle. In early 1890s the family moved to Cordova district southeast of Minnedosa. As young girl Myrtle punctured an eye with a pair of scissors and died of subsequent infection. Her twin brother Melvin developed diabetes, for which there was no cure then, and also died as youngster.

According to Mrs. May Funnell of Minnedosa--one of the pioneer Shuttleworths who trace their family tree back 700 years to wealthy English Lancashire landowner Henry de Shuttleworth--who knew the Rears well, Charlie's mother was "a dear old soul." Minnedosa veterinarian Dr. W.F. Sirett "claimed he could always depend on Mrs. Rear to look after the horses at horse sales."

Local historians list Reuben Rear as one of the early settlers of Lorndale SD near Cordova. Brothers Joe and Clark (or Alf) operated a confectionary-bake shop in Minnedosa. Nellie and Alma, two of the Joe Rear daughters, were well known West-Man school teachers. Reuben stabled his calves in a sod-covered shanty-type barn. One morning when he went to feed them the flimsy structure collapsed killing him and the animals. Daughter Flossie married Charles Loader of Rapid City, where they long operated a store. Most of the Rears are buried in Minnedosa cemetery.

Blonde and blue-eyed Charles Milton Rear became interested in horses at an early age. As young man he already owned excellent Percherons with which he broke a section of land and seeded it to grain; without a dime in his pocket--all on speculation and against the strong advice of his father who felt the ambitious young farmer was overreaching himself--and thus 'got his start'. By early 1930s he was winning grand championships left and right at Toronto Royal.

Grant MacEwen--originally of Forrest, author of the 1964 book HOOFPRINTS AND HITCHINGPOSTS which pays high tribute to Charlie and today lieutenant-governor of Alberta, in a recent letter to Mrs. Funnell states, "I think of Charlie Rear as the most dedicated horseman that I have ever encountered, so dedicated that he had little interest in anything else and very little time for humans. He seemed to live in a world of his own and consequently appeared odd and extremely absent minded to people around him. Nevertheless, he was a great person to know. I encountered him very frequently in the show ring, and sometimes I was judging when he was showing. I recall one occasion when he seemed to forget what he was in the ring for, and I asked him what was on his mind. He replied that he had just remembered he was supposed to be delivering a horse to North Battleford that day. His room at the Empire Hotel presented a picture I never expect to see again; horse pictures, halter shanks, bridles and the like."

In about 1925 Charlie managed to find time to marry Betty Oxenham. They had a daughter Elaine. However, a family just couldn't compete with Percheron and Belgian horses in Charlie's scheme of things and wife with child left him moving to BC. Later, Charlie lived with the Rapid City Loaders when in Manitoba and at Saskatoon's Empire Hotel when in Saskatchewan.

In THEY CALLED IT ODANAH George Harland tells of attending an Elks' Grand Lodge convention at Kamloops, BC, in 1945, and when it became known that he was from Minnedosa area "one of the first questions asked was: 'Do you know Charlie Rear?' I had to confess that I had not known the man personally, but that I had been on the farm at Cordova where Mr. Rear's horse breeding business had started. I soon found that these people had a high regard for Mr. Rear's ability to raise well-bred animals."

Fred Charles of Minnedosa remembers Charlie well during the 1920s and early '30s when the latter operated an adjacent farm. Their farmyards adjoined; but the Charlie Rear farm site "was bulldozed away about six years ago." Fred recalls particularly one fall when winter closed early, catching most farmers with harvesting unfinished. "Charlie hitched his fine Percheron teams to chains to pull the stooks out of the deep snow and then threshed them; because of the bitter cold let his steam engine run all night so it would be ready to continue threshing next morning."

"Charlie Rear was a man of tremendous color," writes Canadian Percheron Association secretary-treasurer Bruce Roy. "A school teacher in the first instance, on his way to Edmonton in the 1930s he made periodic stops collecting stallion fees. Arriving at Edmonton 'Scratching Charlie' rushed straight to the showring to attend to the judging task, for which he had arrived somewhat late. Having no time to stop at his hotel he arrived at ringside, laid his coat on the rail, set his satchel and briefcase down beside it and quickly moved into the ring, completely absorbed in the horses that were arrayed before him. After several hours of work, the showing for the day completed, Mr. Rear moved back to the ringside to fetch his possessions. His coat, suitcase and briefcase, untouched by hundreds that had passed by during the course of the day, were reclaimed. Within the suitcase was a sum of several thousands of dollars in cash from stallion fees. This was typical of the luck that surrounded this man, who was most absent minded, or perhaps one should say engrossed, when placed in the premise of a heavy horse."

Mrs. Funnell recalls Charlie received his nick-name from a chronic disorder, then known as 'barber's itch', for which there was no cure. She disagrees he was ever a teacher; "did all his bookkeeping on the back of a barn door."

That Charlie was lucky in some horse dealings is borne out in MacEwan's writings. His two best Percherons, the great stallion Dean and famous mare Blanche Kesako, were discovered almost by accident and both in North America. Dean was acquired from farmer A.T. Worsley of Kent, Iowa, at whose farm Rear casually stopped one morning. Blanche he found on a back country road in Moyronne district of Saskatchewan hitched to farmer H.W. Bell's grain wagon. Undefeated many years at western fairs Dean was shown to grand championship by Charlie at Toronto Royal in 1930 and '31. A daughter Crocadon Katisha was senior champion and grand champion for George Fraser of Semans, Sask., in 1936. Blanche took Toronto reserve senior champion in 1929 and grand champion awards for Charlie in 1930, '31, '33. Sold to Carl Roberts of St. Adolphe she was exported in 1934 to New South Wales in Australia for breed improvement there. Both Blanche and Dean easily made CPA's 'blue book', which deals at length with the merits of North America's top 25 Percheron stallions and best 25 mares.

Following his remarkable success at Toronto Royal, Rear is reported to have received an honorary degree from National Breweries and when asked what the HC following his name designated, quipped, "Horse Crazy". "But horse crazy or not," says MacEwan, "he was one of the great horsemen of his generation." Harry Moore of Rapid City, half brother to Charlie's brother-in-law, recalls a heavy horse trophy in Charlie's honor being long in competition; doesn't know whether it's still circulating.

In a recent letter to me George Fraser adds that "I judged Charlie Rear's horses several times at the big shows. I bought a stallion from him which he imported from Scotland, a wonderful draft and stud horse." "One of the greatest men I have known," writes long time Percheron breeder-exhibitor Jonathan Fox of Lloydminster, "and one who did more for more people that I ever knew. I could talk to you for hours about him. He made 22 trips across the Atlantic with Percherons; was the first Canadian to export Percherons to New Zealand. He's done more for the horse industry than anyone I know of."

Mrs. Funnell recalls vividly Flossie helping her brother transport horses by tying long lines of them single file halter-to-tail behind her buggy to load in boxcars at Minnedosa. In March, 1945, Charlie had just returned from selling a carload of stallions in Prince Edward Island. "I saw him at Brandon Winter Fair sitting on a bale of hay watching the teams of heavy horses. He looked extremely tired and worn out." Charles Loader had recently taken him to Dr. Bruser for medical examination and that doctor had strongly admonished him to slow down or he would die within six months. But 'taking it easy' was never for Charlie Rear. Arriving dead-on-his-feet at his hotel room in Saskatoon after the fair, Charlie quietly passed away early next morning and was buried in that city.

And in the May 18/74, Brandon Sun edition:

Former Minnedosa mayor Ed Taylor commented recently to me on the Charlie Rear article. Ed knew Charlie well and worked for him as treasurer of the Manitoba division of his Percheron stud operation. Part of Ed's duties involved recruiting new members; for which he received $1 per member "which during the Dirty Thirties was a most respectable figure." He and Charles Loader annually collected Mr. Rear's stallion fees in this province. Ed found Charlie Rear not only a scrupulously honest man but an equally "great gambler."

35. GLENDOSA ARA-WELS   Free lance article, Manitoba Welsh Pony News '74

This is my fourth article on Ara-Wel Ponies to this magazine, the last two involving mostly negotiations with our federal department of agriculture as regards Canadian registry. The previous articles were also included in my recent book PRAIRIE VISTAS and have generated interest.

As indicated last year there are basically three avenues currently open to breeders of this remarkable Welsh-Arab cross in process of being established as a pure breed. 1. Continue registering our ponies with the American registry in Chico, Cal. 2. Organize our own registry without incorporation in Ottawa; as do cat breeders, for example. 3. Organize as an incorporated Canadian Ara-Wel Pony Association and submit to the chief registration officer, Dept. of Agriculture, Ottawa a list of Canadian breeders raising Ara-Wels--along with number of first, second, third generation animals presently owned-- and request recordation in the General Stud Book until such time as either the Canadian Pony Society accepts them as fully registered or our own association decides to and is permitted to register them.

Although there now are at least half a dozen Manitobans involved in raising Ara-Wels and this province is the logical one to initiate formal organization there hasn't been enough interest to date in creating an association. The major reason probably involves our antiquated federal legislation which makes it virtually impossible to develop a new breed of horse, pony or dog from scratch; a foreign registry for such breed must already exist and even then only animals whose "percentage of blood of the new breed reaches an established level" in that foreign registry are accepted for registration here. I suppose that's why there's never been a new breed of horse, pony or dog ever developed in Canada throughout our history. That's why the closest thing, the Kanata Pony, is currently being developed under provincial (BC) rather than federal jurisdiction.

Because of our out-dated federal agricultural legislation and the fact that particular department is most depressing to deal with (in sharp contrast to its provincial counterpart), I refuse to try to SELL breeders on the idea of forming an association. Whenever there are "any number of persons, not less than five, who desire to form an association ...Canadian citizens of the full age of twenty-one years" who aren't afraid to fight governmental apathy and hostility I'll be most happy to do everything in my power to help organize such association.

We have raised four Ara-Wels to date: one mare and two stallions from scratch (Welsh mares bred to Arab stallions) and a filly last summer from registered Ara-Wel parents. I believe little Blitz was the first second generation Ara-Wel in Canada. We sold the stallion, Glendosa Silver Beau No. 141, last fall because we now had a filly from him and re-bred her mother, Abi, to him. Although we were most impressed with the young cowboy, Harold J. Park of Kerrobert, Saskatchewan, who bought Beau, we would much have preferred to have sold him to someone involved in raising Ara-Wels for now this exceptionally fine stallion is being used on grade mares and as such is likely lost to the Ara-Wel movement forever. Everyone who saw Beau last year agreed they'd never seen a finer show-type pony stallion and with better temperament. Two full sisters exist but I don't know who currently owns them for I believe they were sold by public auction when the Olav Shellborns (Silver Spring Ranch) of Erickson recently sold out and moved to BC.

We hope to have another second generation foal from Abi and Beau in about mid July. We plan to breed a mare to our five year old light silver-grey stallion Arrow (son of the well known popular Arabian stallion Tabra of Kassar Nabal ranch at Hamiota) and sell him in August.

36. TEACHER TRAINING/OPEN EDUCATION FOLLOW-UP   Valley Vistas, Brandon Sun, April 6/74

In November I described Brandon University's experimental five month on-the-job student teacher training program underway in Minnedosa and promised some sort of follow-up. Prof. Jerry Christensen, a proponent of the new-yet-old educational philosophy Open Education to which most of the 11 prospective teachers subscribed to varying degrees, supervised the project.

Some feelings and philosophy of supervisor and student teachers are reflected in a recent written evaluation from which the following comments are derived:

Prof. Christensen: "I've spent too many years as a student trying to digest information that was carefully strained, overcooked and served in jello moulds. I've spent too many years as a teacher straining, cooking and serving. I envisioned an environment in which individuals would be essentially responsible for themselves; actively pursue alternative, individualized ways to gather ideas and experiences that THEY determined would be meaningful to them. In varying degrees, all of these things have happened."

Al R.: "The experiences of the past five months have been part of the greatest learning opportunity I've ever been offered in the name of institutionalized education."

Lory: "I believe that the Minnedosa project is one of the best student teaching projects in Manitoba. I felt FREE to learn and experience areas of my interest."

Judy: "To have experienced this project and to have known the people involved in this project is something I will never regret."

Zelda: "I really like the project because it's so small and we are treated as individuals—with individual problems, concerns, and needs."

Al H.: "As a member of the Minnedosa project my experiences are thus far the most valuable in my entire education."

Ken: "The Minnedosa project has something unique to offer the Education student."

Marilyn: "As far as I'm concerned the Minnedosa project's the program to be in this year."

Grace: "The Minnedosa project's OK. I can't say that it's just great or that it's lousy."

Jo-Anne: "I guess what I'm really trying to say is that I feel the Minnedosa project is the best thing that has happened to the faculty of education and me since I started university."

Helen: "I'm glad that I'm part of this program but agree there should be changes made."

All warmly commended Jerry as supervising, co-ordinating professor.

A letter from a class to one student teacher summarizes well small town grapevine feedback I've received from youngsters 'being experimented on'; two being my own. "We hope you have a good time. Hopefully you will teach next time in Minnedosa. Do you really have to go? You were a good student teacher. We hope you like the present we gave you. Mrs. (X) really likes you for a great student teacher. We're very sorry talking back to you. The minute we saw you we liked you, and don't think we are kidding."

Chatted for a while with Tanner's Crossing school principal John Monteith. He readily admits ANY teacher training project disrupts classes to some degree, but strongly prefers this type to former short term ones. Nor does he believe it hurts youngsters to encounter prospective teachers whose teaching methods may differ radically with those of their regular teachers; may well benefit them. The school itself benefits because teachers acquire more time to work with small groups and individuals requiring extra attention. He found Jerry most co-operative and the student teachers, perhaps because he was able to get to know them better as persons, much more honest and open in their views than previous ones. The longer period allowed student teachers to experiment and if they found a particular age group or classroom teacher hard to work with had time to switch to another. He (and most of this community) found the swimming instruction program conducted by two student teachers at a local pool valuable.

Thirteen years teaching convinced me school secretaries often learn to know teachers better than do other staff members. Mimi Temple feels BU student teachers "will be missed a lot around here." She found them most considerate and co-operative at all times, always giving plenty of notice when they required something, said she knew two resource teachers already missed them.

But not all's rosy in any new project and discussion with regular teachers revealed some problems that developed. One felt having a student teacher with you so long demanded much extra time from her, that often it prevented her from "being myself" with her youngsters at a more personal level, indicated she wouldn't want another one next year. Another felt that although there may have been sufficient communication between BU staff members and school board and principal there was none DIRECTLY with teachers involved and it took most of the five months to understand what was hoped to be accomplished. This wasted class time, and hers. It took one student teacher four months to get her bearings, eventually established excellent rapport with students.

My own feelings about this type of project are: It's most worthwhile and should definitely be repeated somewhere next year; preferably with Prof. Christensen in charge because he now knows where its greatest strengths and weaknesses lie. I think it's excellent policy to throw student teachers into very difficult situations and let them agonize, soul search, experiment. The good ones will prevail and emerge better and stronger as result; a few will fall by the wayside—and it's much better for ALL concerned this occur early. The same school shouldn't be asked to participate two consecutive years, unless the request originates there. Unless they themselves express the wish the same classroom teachers shouldn't be asked to participate in such project more often than once every five or more years; in no way should they be made to feel guilty or non-professional for not participating immediately again. On the other hand, it 'goes with the profession' to take your turn. BU staff should spend more time with each regular teacher helping with a project, preparing them somewhat for a specific project being implemented. All student teachers should definitely 'live in' the community they're teaching—not commute. Brandon University, Rolling River SD, Tanner's Crossing school are to be commended for a worthy and interesting undertaking.

* * *

Several days after this article was published I received a letter from Prof. Christensen, a portion of which reads:

"I just had to take a moment to let you know that your efforts to alalyze, and to communicate about, the project haven't gone unnoticed. I read your recent article with a great deal of interest, and appreciation for your kind words.

"Not everyone, however, is as enthusiastic about the concept as you and I might be. As a concept it is almost dead in this faculty. In fact—in my judgement—there is a great deal of philosophical belt-tightening and giant-stepping-to-the-rear going on here. A bit discouraging for me. Although I suspect that it is a sign of the times, I'll not be content to wait for the carousel to go 'round again. I've got to find another route to the brass ring, if there is one."   (Jerry left BU at the end of the school year)

37. MESSIAHS   Valley Vistas column, Brandon Sun, April 13/74

Mark and Matthew both record that Jesus Christ, whose death and resurrection are still commemorated throughout the world by his followers, predicted "false Messiahs and false prophets will appear" in years to come. Historians don't need to look far away or far back in time for examples.

Isabel M. Reekie in ALONG THE OLD MELITA TRAIL quotes Mrs. William MacPherson describing a fanatic religious group called Adamites crossing the border from United States to Melita district about June of 1908. The group was led by a venerable old man claiming to be Jesus Christ, leader of the tribe of Judah, and his wife the Virgin Mary. A woman with six children was Eve. All carried guns. From Melita they moved to a Doukhobor settlement near Yorkton, but that group refused to have anything to do with them. Later, Mrs. MacPherson read of a real western type gun battle between Kansas City police and the Adamites. One man and two children were shot, 'Jesus Christ' and 'Mary' imprisoned.

Manitoba-born Vilhjalmur Stefansson, to whom Farley Mowat refers as "the most active, successful and many-faceted explorer of the Canadian Arctic in modern times" spending a lifetime trying to persuade Canada to look northward, was as interested in religion of native Canadians as exploring. A Harvard theology and anthropology graduate, his studies of Eskimo religion and Christianity's effect on it are second to none.

"In the matter of Christianity," Stefansson wrote in 1913 in MY LIFE WITH THE ESKIMO," they concede that we introduced it, but they do not concede that we know more about it than they do; just as many Christians concede that Christianity spread from Rome, but do not concede that Rome is nowadays the highest authority in religious matters. A striking way in which this shows itself is in the belief in special revelations which come directly to the Eskimo, and the belief in the rebirth of the Savior among them." He goes on to cite cases on record "of Immaculate Conception and the birth of heralded saviors of the race," cites Greenland's Knud Rasmussen as having found similar cases. A number of these rebirths of Christ floundered because "the child born happened to be a female," negating the prophesies.

American novelist Milton Lott and historian Paul Bailey have researched a most tragic event in North American history involving one Messiah, an event in which Canada played an indirect but supportive role. It concerns the Paiute Indian Jack Wovoka.

The 1870s and '80s were a sad time for Indians in Northern United States. Forced to live on small reserves, hated by most whites, partially Christianized and being admonshed by both white and Indian ministers to quietly accept their fate as true Christians the Sioux (many of who had recently been pressurized to return from Canada where they had fled following the Sioux revolt) and several other tribes were ripe for a Messiah.

Wovoka worked for a white rancher preaching the message, "I saw the great Father, who showed me all and told me to return and make a road for my people, a road of love and peace. Civilization is doomed, the white man is doomed to burn ineverlastingly in the hell of his own making, the unending fire with no ashes and no rebirth." His converts believed they could bring back the buffalo by means of the new Spirit Dance. "The earth is old and worn-out, destroyed by the white men. She will be young, and all the dead Indians live again."

The 'Ghost Dance' movement, as it was dubbed by whites, spread like wildfire among the Sioux and other northern US tribes. Sitting Bull himself became deeply involved in it, and his tragic death is attributed by most historians to his involvement. The American cavalry was ordered to disarm all Indians planning to dance the new Spirit Dance, arrest all actively participating dancers and take them to the nearest military posts until the Indian Christ cease his preaching and the movement die down. These orders were carried out; at Wounded Knee Creek with great brutality when machine gunners and mounted soldiers of the Seventh Cavalry with rifles and swords all but wiped out Big Foot's band of over 300 peacefully dancing men, women and children. May your Easter be a meaningful one.

38. CATHERINE WIENS GROVE   Valley Vistas column, Brandon Sun, April 20 & 27/74

Last summer, like many West-Manites, we visited the newly opened Rapid City museum housed in the old high school in which famous Canadian writer Frederick Philip Grove once taught and to whom a plaque's dedicated on the grounds, viewed the house on Minnedosa River nearby in which he with wife Catherine and daughter May lived seven years. Later, visiting the grave of Elsie's grandmother Susanna Fast (1884-1938) in Rapid City cemetery we saw that author's gravestone (1872-1948) and that of Phyllis May (1915-1927) with inscription 'She is a portion of the loveliness which once she made more lovely.' I'd read some of the recent controversial research on this complex novelist and was intrigued, not so much with the man himself--whose writings other than a few like OVER PRAIRIE TRAILS and OUR DAILY BREAD don't greatly interest me--but with the young woman half his age this author-teacher married.

Mrs. Catherine Wiens Grove (Tena until later years when she began calling herself Catherine), I soon learned, never remarried but continued to live in their farm house teaching near Simcoe, Ont. until her death in January, 1972. Although her husband had also died at Simcoe almost a quarter century earlier, she was however not buried at Rapid City as he'd been.

"I am not sure why she was not buried at Rapid City," Dr. Desmond Pacey of University of New Brunswick, a former Brandon College professor and author of at least two books on Grove, wrote me recently, "but her son Leonard of Toronto could tell you." Unfortunately Leonard, who was born after the Groves left West-Man in 1928, is not co-operating with newsmen these days of vicious controversy involving his renowned father's early European years as alleged German ex-convict Felix Paul Greve; and I don't blame him. Presumably she's buried at Simcoe.

Although Mrs. Grove later became an Anglican she originally was a Mennonite and is of that ethnic origin. Dr. Margaret Stobie of University of Manitoba (where the Grove collection's housed), in her recent book on Grove, states Tena was born at Plum Coulee, Man. This seems to tally with a recent letter I received from Winkler historian Frank Brown who indicates, "The parents at one time resided at Reinland, a Mennonite village south of Winkler and at Plum Coulee. It seems that while they lived at Reinland, Mr. Wiens was involved in the mill at that village. Later they moved to Lowe Farm, Man., and OUR DAILY BREAD is the story of Mrs. Grove's family, the Lowe Farm Wienses, called Elliotts in the novel which has a setting in southern Saskatchewan."

Most writers simply list Catherine as coming from Rush Lake, Sask., where the family later lived. When she taught in Winkler, where she met and married Grove who also taught there, she was really living in the same district she grew up. This year, together with Winnipeg and Steinbach, her people are celebrating their centennial anniversary of arrival in Canada.

Countless critics have commented on OUR DAILY BREAD. I feel it's about as good a portrayal as any son- and brother-in-law could write of in-laws. As my own experiences and ethnic background closely parallel his wife's, I really feel he portrayed quite accurately the immense upheaval then taking place in Mennonite families; except in case of the 1874-'76 immigrants it occurred in early 1900s and in the 1924-26 ones from which I descend, in 1940s and '50s. Although Grove was not a Mennonite like his wife he was nevertheless a strong pacifist and spoke fluently the same language his wife's people had spoken for centuries.

Frederick's outspoken views on pacifism and Germany during the First World War created untold problems for him in western Manitoba, whereas Catherine remained popular throughout those turbulent years. If he actually was Felix Paul Greve, married in Germany and later in the US before coming to Canada and born Feb. 14, 1879 to Charles Edward and Bertha Greve at Radommo on the Polish-Russian border while on journey from Schwerin, then he coincidently grew up in the same area his wife's ancestors lived several centuries until about 1800.

"I know," Prof. Pacey wrote me, "Mrs. Grove maintained to the end that the story of Grove's life which he himself told in IN SEARCH OF MYSELF was essentially true, for that reason it is probably a mercy that she did not live to see (Douglas O.) Spettigue's most recent book with its almost conclusive proof that Grove was originally a German called Felix Paul Greve who was imprisoned for fraud in Bonn in 1903." Their marriage certificate lists Grove's parents as Charles Edward and Bertha Rutherford Grove and birthplace as Moscow.

Grove describes his early relationship with his future wife as, "It was this duty (principal) which made me formally acquainted with Miss Wiens, the primary teacher. For fully eight or nine months our relation remained official and quite as impersonal as it could be. There was no opportunity for us to become intimate; and perhaps neither of us had any desire for such an opportunity. We never met except officially." Brown wrote me, "One of Mr. Grove's students at Winkler told me that before Mr. and Mrs. Grove were married, Mr. Grove took his classes out on a picnic to Walhalla, N.D., and Miss Catherine Wiens was along too. Local teachers used to take their classes out to the sand slides on the Pembina River at Walhalla. It happened then that Mr. Grove and Miss Wiens wandered away from the student body. The students were left alone for quite a long time and had to shift for themselves. When the two lovers finally returned, the picnic promptly ended and they all returned to Winkler." In fact, Stobie learned that as early as in December Grove wrote his close friend I.J. Warkentin, a U. of M. graduate then studying at Leipzig, "I am going to get married soon" but that by February Catherine was rejecting him.

Manitoba centres like Virden, Gladstone, Eden, Falmouth, Selkirk, Rapid City, once all knew the Groves well; Brandon and Haskett the novelist before his marriage to Catherine Wiens.

Grove describes his wife "good to look at. She had an extraordinarily striking figure, tall and slender like my own, yet well modelled. Her appearance, I said to myself, was aesthetically satisfying; she dressed simply but in excellent taste." Frank Brown told me, "Some of Mr. Grove's former students maintain Mrs. Grove was a pretty woman." "I only met Mrs. Grove twice," Dr. Pacey wrote me, "though I corresponded with her from time to time over a thirty year period. My last meeting with her was in Caledonia, Ont., in November of 1967, when I went to that town to give a Centennial lecture at the High School. Mrs. Grove and her son Leonard and his wife Mary came down from Simcoe to have dinner with me, and to hear my lecture. By that time Mrs. Grove was a woman over seventy with grey hair, but she was still perfectly straight of back and a very commanding figure. She was a woman of great dignity and self-control, something of the 'grande dame'."

Catherine's war-time experiences in West-Man as wife of a controversial writer and person dubbed 'the hippie dropout' of his era, caused her much anguish. Both Gladstone and Virden gave her husband a terrible time. Even in Rapid City, where she'd started a wolf cub pack and most people liked, or at least condoned, her 'Manitoba Thoreau' husband and loved her, Dr. Stobie tells us, a small group of pseudo-patriots tried to get her fired in June of 1925 because the Groves were believed to be Mennonites whose "ideals and mode of living do not conform to what a Canadian's should." Ironical treatment when Haskett residents had all but tarred and feathered Grove for allegedly corrupting Mennonite youngsters with non-Mennonite doctrine. Fortunately the school board, students, and most parents refused to be intimidated and sanity prevailed. One of several similar petitions read: "We, the pupils, ex-pupils and intending pupils of Mrs. Grove's room, humbly beg the School Board to maintain Mrs. Grove's services for another year." Following her visit to Rapid City in summer of 1964 Catherine wrote, "It all looked so bleak and lonely. And yet the people were all so wonderfully, honestly happy to see me. It was quite an experience." Writers agree that of all places the Groves lived "the little town of Rapid City had the loveliest setting."

Catherine and Frederick Grove deeply loved their young daughter May; who some writers claim died in Minnedosa Hospital of ruptured appendix. Stobie states she died after the operation. Grove claimed she died under ether. In checking with our hospital's administrator and records clerk I learned that no record exists here of such operation, was informed this wasn't unusual for the operation (if performed here) must have occurred in old Lady Minto Hospital (now an apartment block) from which records are most incomplete.

Kaye Rowe, writing in Manitoba Arts Review in spring of 1949, described May as "a pale, sweet child" who "played in the tangled garden" of their home on Minnedosa River and "could talk French and Latin at an age when her schoolmates were beginning to learn long division." Upon May's untimely death Tom Saunders of Winnipeg Free Press quoted Grove writing, "Sleep without fear, my child, not long alone: For there is room for me too in that throng. Some quarry even now grows my stone. Here will I come, nor will I tarry long. Now am I anchored; and forever now Must here I tarry. For a woman gave A child to me; and to the ground I bow; My roots are growing down into a grave."

In his recent article On Editing the Letters of F.P. Grove, Pacey says, "Grove's most common term of endearment for his wife in letters addressed to her was 'Tee' which, Mrs. Grove reported he had told her, meant 'mistress' in Chinese. What evidence we have suggests that his marriage to Mrs. Grove was the most prized event in his life, and she his mainstay throughout his Canadian years."

At Grove's Rapid City funeral, Kaye Rowe quotes one resident saying, "His idea of a good time, of a holiday, was to go tramping over the fields with May and Mrs. Grove. They'd bring home a basket full of the derndest things: those little green garter snakes, alive! those orange toadstools, the white fungus that grows in the wounds of old trees, birds' feathers and queer stones from the brook's edge." Perhaps another comment there summed the Groves up best: "Never was any better than Grove—unless it was Mrs. Grove. Anybody around here'll say that."

In the May 18/74 edition of Brandon Sun the following:

"In regards to the death of Phyllis May Grove," Oswald G. Stone who published Rapid City Reporter wrote me recently concerning my article on Catherine Grove—who was his teacher in grades 6 and 8, "may I quote you the following from the Thursday, July 28, 1927, issue of the Reporter. 'This bright and clever girl had been taken to Minnedosa hospital on Wednesday afternoon to undergo an operation for a sudden attack of pendicitis and the same evening had passed away.' She died Wednesday, July 20, and the funeral service was held from the Grove residence Friday, July 22. Pallbearers were: Ernest Birkinshaw (high school student who spent many hours talking with Mr. Grove and now a professor at Brandon University) and three students from Mrs. Grove's room—Emory Rogers of Winnipeg, George Blakeston of Roland and myself. Some of the information Dr. Pacey and Kaye Rowe have used in recent years they got from our newspaper files."

Commenting on this article Dr. Pacey writes, "The case for Grove being Greve is not yet proven, but the circumstancial evidence is overwhelming. Greve did serve a year's sentence for fraud (he borrowed a lot of money from a friend under false pretences), but he appears to have restored his relationship with the man for he again borrowed from the same source for his trip to North America in 1909."

And in the August 17/74 edition:

In April I wrote about Catherine Grove, speculating as to where she was buried. I read with interest an item in the July 18 edition of Minnedosa Tribune of their son A. Leonard Grove of Toronto visiting West-Man and burying the cremated remains of his mother in the Rapid City family plot on July 9.

39. MINNEDOSA RIFLE AND PISTOL CLUBS   Valley Vistas, Brandon Sun, May 4/74

One of Minnedosa's more popular buildings is a long low ugly windowless concrete structure tucked away on a dead end alley. The old shooting range of disbanded world-famous 212th Manitoba Dragoons is today utilized by rifle and pistol enthusiasts to almost equal degree as when that renowned West-Man regiment trained here.

Minnedosa Rifle Club was born 11 years ago due to untiring efforts of people like its first president Ed Howe (deceased), former Dragoon commanding officer Ernie Delmage, Bob Scotland (deceased). Secretary-treasurer for 10 of those years was Mrs. Jessie Hymers of Basswood, who told me recently that though the club doesn't attract as many girls as boys the former—contrary to expectations of us chauvinist males—often shoot better.

On an average about 40 to 50 young people between ages nine and 18 turn up to shoot. Two consistently excellent marksmen Mrs. Hymers recalls vividly were Bruce Burton and Judy Scotland. Current instructors are Fred Harvey and Cliff Gray, who double as president and secretary-treasurer respectively. Annual competitions for ribbons, crests, trophies help keep interest high. That this enthusiasm spills into many homes I don't doubt for a moment for we ourselves get a weekly dose when our nine-year-old gobbles his five o'clock supper so he'll be ready for seven. (A month after I wrote this item Rod won the Bronze trophy)

Though the club's operated only a decade, civilian rifle competitions are hardly new to Minnedosa. During the early part of this century, says MINNEDOSA MEMORIES, "a Rifle Association was formed. Mr. S. Fairbairn was a crack shot, and challenges with him were common, in which he always won. One or two years a team went to England to take part in the Bisley meet."

Chatted with Mr. Fairbairn's grandson Sid Hancock who inherited one of numerous trophies won by this sharpshooter. Not only was Fairbairn a crack rifle shot but also one of Canada's top trap shooters. In competitions in Ontario, for example, he carried off championship trophies three consecutive years while setting one unbelievable record of smashing 200 clay pigeons out of 200. His trophies he gave his five daughters, his many medals his sons. One daughter living here, Mrs. W.J. Burgess, cherishes one of those trophies. Her attorney husband recalls two Bisley sharpshooters from this area were Clarence Kerr of Franklin and Austin Patten of Birtle.

Mrs. Ellen Telford inherited a Minnedosa Rifle Association medal won in 1904 by her father Joe Burgess. It's of stirling silver depicting two crossed rifles and a target. Joseph Burgess, an early encyclopedia reveals, was one of western Manitoba's outstanding pioneers. Born 1865 at Lindsay, Ont. one of 10 children of Samuel and Anne Burgess, he came to Manitoba in 1881, learned butchering in Winnipeg three years and by 1916 "was the proprietor of the oldest meat market in Minnedosa (today Solo Store operated by son Jack and grandson Jim), also owned a furniture store adjoining plus 480 acres farmland and an interest in another 1,000 acres." In 1890 he married Edith Wake. Sixteen years a councillor, he was elected mayor in 1912. A prominent Oddfellow, Anglican church warden and hospital director, he raised 11 children. Both Edith and he died in 1952.

But rifle fire's not the only sound echoing from the old Dragoon range. About 10 years ago Sgt. Earl Wesselman, then the local RCMP commanding officer and now staff sergeant and section NCO in Brandon, furnished the impetus to organize a pistol club. The past three years has seen this club sponsor hand-gun tournaments drawing competitors like Olympic contender Keith Elder of Wawanesa, Regina's RCMP shooting instructor W.R. Phillips, Brandon's W. Romanyszyn and Cam MacPherson, Rounthwaite's Pete Chalanchuk, Minnedosa's Constable Robin Gomes.

Reasons for interest in shooting pistols are no doubt as numerous as participants. Perhaps club president Art Wilson's is typical. "I used to hunt a lot," he told me recently, "but found that as the years went by I liked killing birds and animals less and less yet still enjoyed shooting as much as ever." Age requirement for membership is 16 and over. Currently the club's only female member is Pat (Mrs. Wes) Burton.

Undoubtedly the club's best marksman is RCMP constable Rob Gomes. A native of Windsor and London, Ont., he joined the force seven years ago, and after brief duty in Brandon transferred here. A popular policeman who made national news in competitions last year and has some 25 trophies to his credit, Rob identifies strongly with West-Manites for he met and married his wife, Judy Buchok of Justice, while stationed here. The Gomeses have a two-year-old daughter Pamela. Since 1970 Rob's served as club secretary-treasurer, indicated that though the whole 13-man detachment also keeps in practice in the range one other constable shooting in the club is Brian Runnalls. By the time you read this Rob will have taken up residence in Regina where he'll instruct RCMP recruits in the proper use of pistols, rifles and shotguns. Many will miss this pleasant colorful Mountie, whose exceptional shooting skill and sound philosophy of life will help produce better future policemen.

40. WOMEN'S INSTITUTE AND GOVERNMENT GRANTS   Valley Vistas, Bdn Sun, May 11/74

An organization that's been much in news lately is the Women's Institute. Many and varied pros and cons have been submitted concerning governmental assistance for this historic body.

Recently I spent a pleasant couple of hours drinking tea and chatting with three charming WI members of long standing who've played major roles in this organization here and elsewhere—Mrs. Rebecca Lace, Mrs. Florence Brown, Mrs. Jessie Hutton — and gained some insights into the work of a group I've always deeply respected.

The first WI in the world was founded Feb. 19, 1897, at Stoney Creek, Ont., due to efforts of Mrs. Adelaine Hoodless who'd lost a baby to impure milk and persuaded Hamilton school board to introduce a course on Domestic Science in their schools. This WI was in effect the female counterpart of male-oriented Farmers Institute functioning under Ontario Department of Agriculture. Several men helped write the constitution, and for 29 years even served as superintendents. The organization mushroomed. By 1906 it had spread to Western Canada and 1915 to England; by 1953 to most countries as Associated Country Women of the World.

In Manitoba, the first WI sprang up in Morris in 1910 through inspiration of Mrs. Findlay MacKenzie. Three West-Man groups--Minnedosa, Valley River, Virden--were founded almost simultaneously the same year. Sponsored by male-oriented Agricultural Society, the Home Economics Society (as it was first called) was like its Ontario parent as well as sisters in provinces like Saskatchewan and Alberta under provincial department of agriculture jurisdiction. Even today, indicates Mrs. Lace--who was a member four years in England and 44 in Minnedosa serving on local, district, provincial executives--that department appoints a member to the provincial WI executive (a recent one being former Minnedosa home economist Della May Radcliffe of Cardale) and whenever a group dissolves all remaining treasury monies and property owned are turned over to Manitoba government. Even the previous hiring of the WI provincial secretary by our agriculture department is somewhat misunderstood for she did as much work for that department as for WI. Such historic factors, it would seem, have not been taken into account by persons critical of WI receiving so-called 'preferential' treatment by government.

The ladies I talked with had mixed feelings about Deputy Minister Bill Janssen's recent announcement that in future Manitoba government would instead give WI a $20,000 annual grant "to hire its own executive secretary and run its own affairs. They can make their own arrangements as they please." None were certain whether this new 'no strings attached' deal also included no further governmental appointments to WI executive and no further commitment to turn treasuries and properties of disbanding organizations over to government coffers. Regarding the reduction of home economists in Manitoba (Minnedosa being one wiped out) they felt 4-H activities would suffer greatly but this would have little effect on WI.

The first officers of the historic local here, MINNEDOSA MEMORIES (much of which Mrs. Brown, a WI life member who's been a member 45 years wrote)states, "were Pres. Mrs. Andrew Boyd; sec.-treas. Mrs. W.H. McLean; vice-pres. Mrs. D. Cannon; directors, Mrs. Hugh Dyer, Miss May Ewens, Mrs. J.R. Gugin, Mrs. Charles Meadows, Miss Harrison and Mrs. Robert Woodcock." The current president is Mrs. Bertha Thomson, with Mrs. Mable Jury treasurer and Mrs. Laura Thomson secretary. Membership has dwindled from a peak of almost 100 to about 30 today.

'For Home and Country' reads the motto of this organization, and through the years it's performed invaluable service across Canada. Typical activities of the local club have included: sponsoring boys and girls clubs, aiding the hospital, financing baby clinics, Red Cross work during wartime, initiating short courses like Homemaking, sponsoring a restroom and library, helping during disasters like floods, sponsoring bursaries and worthwhile contests. Frequently it's meant starting some much-needed community project until it becomes self-supporting.

Like many historic organizations, the future of Women's Institute is clouded with uncertainty. The rural-to-urban population shift and emphasis in Canada with subsequent growth of countless new clubs are taking their toll. In Minnedosa's group, for example, most members are of retirement age; 10 over 80. Yet some of the more rural districts nearby, like Cordova and Basswood, constantly attract young women and flourish. In England, which is considerably more urbanized than Canada, WI is growing strongly. Regardless of the ultimate fate of this Canadian-born international organization, it's a poor citizen indeed who'd not doff his hat to an institution that's written some truly remarkable history.

41. ALTERNATE DAYS KINDERGARTEN   Valley Vistas column, Brandon Sun, May 18/74

Attended a lengthy public school meeting at Tanner's Crossing last week, which undoubtedly marks a milestone in parent-teacher-Rolling River SD communications that since late '60s have been lousy at best. Some 200 parents, teachers, school board members and officials met to discuss things like the new credit system to be introduced in high schools here, feasibility of a community library in the collegiate, all day kindergarten alternate days instead of half days daily, field trips, changes in elementary school which may reduce effectiveness of library services and music program. Chaired by new Minnedosa member Garry Grant the meeting was a most encouraging sign of community interest in education of our children with parents and teachers finally expressing feelings openly on issues and trustees and administrators showing sincere willingness to listen—in sharp contrast to general apathy of us parents, reluctance of teachers to jeopardize careers by expressing public opinions, board members operating behind closed doors with press and others frequently barred from meetings through in-camera motions during the 1969-74 era. Garry's invitation to parents and students and press to attend board meetings often will hopefully be accepted by many—and honored by other board members. As one person who's been ejected repeatedly, I'm adopting an optimistic though somewhat cautious 'wait-and-see' attitude.

And in the August 17/74 issue:

Life around here wouldn't seem normal if Rolling River school division weren't in hot water. This time the controversy (public and private) rages over a recent board decision to replace half days daily kindergarten with full alternate days for a year's trial basis. Of 57 Minnedosa homes involved 39 strongly oppose the move, as do most Tanner's Crossing teachers. Local member Garry Grant's been most co-operative.

Personally, I can't see why the compromise suggested by Minnedosa parents and teachers of two classes being regular half days with parents supplying their own noon transportation and one class held alternate full days wouldn't work. As rural Manitobans are discovering more and more lately, the real weakness of large school divisions is solutions to problems seldom take account of individual community wishes. Unless school boards soon learn to respect individual community aspirations and make some attempt to personalize solutions, the rift between boards and public will, in rural areas at least, widen to the point the division concept will flounder.

42. REV. JOHN TANNER   Valley Vistas column, Brandon Sun, May 25 & June 1/74

Minnedosa attracts many American tourists. Occasionally friendships develop between residents and such persons. One Minnedosan whose Canadian hospitality impressed Graham P. Hunt Jr. of Cincinnati, Ohio, is Sept Taylor. A recent letter touched off a chain reaction of additional historical research data on the intriguing Tanner saga of which I've written before.

"Down river from Cincinnati, near Aurora, Indiana," writes Hunt, "is a power station called Tanners Creek. On the Kentucky side of the Ohio River opposite Tanners Creek is Petersburg, which according to Cincinnati district attorney Joseph Bullock used to be known as Tanners Station. Some log buildings, he told me, are still intact though disguised. A John Tanner was captured by Indians there while gathering hickory nuts as a child, later lived near Red River where he had Indian children. It would be interesting if Tanner's Crossing, now Minnedosa, is connected in this way to Tanners Station, now Petersburg."

And so it is! Petersburg founder was Baptist minister John Tanner, whose son John 'Falcon' Tanner lived as Indian many years and whose missionary son Rev. James Tanner of Portage district was Minnedosa founder John Tanner's father.

Through Mr. Hunt I began corresponding with Petersburg historian Mary A. Rector. Petersburg, she writes, is a village of 350 people some 30 miles south of Cincinnati. Local legend claims both John and brother Edward "went to gather walnuts, found a tree about a quarter mile from home and were quietly filling their baskets when fired upon by Indians who wounded the younger John and capturing both, carried the lame boy and made the other walk until night where they encamped a short distance above Miami River. During the night the brothers had a long talk and decided the older would make his escape after the Indians were asleep. They had not been secured too well as the Indians did not think one would leave without the other. After the Indians were asleep, Edward did make his escape, swam the Miami and Ohio rivers and reached home that night. Next morning the father and friends started in pursuit", without success. "Years later Allen Morgan, a boy Mr. Tanner raised, found him in Michigan and brought him home. He was then married to an Indian and had several children. He had become so attached to Indians he could not be persuaded to stay, so he returned to the Indians and his wife and children."

Mrs. Rector put me in touch with Anne Fitzgerald of Florence, Kentucky, whose husband William had over many years researched court documents involving Rev. John Tanner but had died in 1969 before his findings could be properly compiled and published. Fortunately I was able to obtain a photocopy of his 27-page rough manuscript.

Born about 1732, Rev. Tanner was of English and Scotch-Irish descent. In 1770 in Chesterfield, Virginia, he and six other men were jailed, "some whipped and several fined," for ignoring a 1643 Virginia law prohibiting all but Anglicans to preach the gospel. While in prison they continued preaching "through the grates; many people attending their ministry, and many professed faith." Even John Clay, father of the famous statesman Henry Clay, was imprisoned for breaking this law. Three years later Tanner was rearrested by Col. Archibald Carey for again breaking it, released on 200 pounds bail which John Clay co-signed. Until able to raise a heavy fine, he was again jailed.

Following freedom, Rev. Tanner moved to Halifax county, North Carolina, where he served as minister in Rocky Swamp until about 1784 when he moved to Kentucky and founded Tate's Creek church in Madison county, later preached in Fayette county, in 1795 served Clear Creek church in Woodford, then in Shelby county, emigrated to Missouri, where he died in 1812 near Cape Girardeau.

In 1777 while in North Carolina Rev. Tanner baptised a Mrs. Dawson whose husband hated Baptists and had sworn to kill anyone who dared baptise his wife. Enroute to Sandy Run to preach he's ambushed by Mr. Dawson and shot at close range with a large horseman's pistol. "Seventeen shot went into his thigh, one of which was a large buckshot, that went through his thigh and lodged between his breeches and thigh. In this wounded condition Elder Tanner was carried to the house of Mr. Elisha Williams in Scotland Neck where he lay some weeks, and his life was despaired of but through the goodness of God recovered."

In 1872 in Lincoln county he'd become licensed to perform marriages taking the Virginia oath of allegiance. He and several families built the stockade against Indian attack at Tanners Station. In 1797 he served as juror in Fayette county, in 1810 petitioned Congress to permit him to construct a canal from St. Francis River to Mississippi and operate a mail service.

In later years Rev. Tanner became quite wealthy, was a large slave holder with 21 listed on tax rolls. He became involved in all sorts of business deals, several of which resulted in law suits, was a long-winded fiery preacher highly critical of the personal conduct of congregation members. John Clay found him "a powerful preacher, but hard to get along with," who became involved in several fights "but there is no record that he killed anyone." His will was signed in June of 1812, probated that October in Caldwell county, Kentucky.

Following his father's death Falcon returned home, having "forgotten his language and in manner and thinking was an Indian. When he learned that he had not inherited anything from his father, whom he had never seen since his capture, he became violent and brandishing his tomahawk stormed from the room."

Correspondence with Mrs. Fitzgerald led to contact with historian Marguirite Hussey of Walnut Creek in California, a John 'Falcon' Tanner great-granddaughter who's compiled a most scholarly 53-page document on Rev. John Tanner of which only 27 were printed, one of which I was lucky to acquire.

Mrs. Hussey found Rev. Tanner's father was also a John (grandfather Edward, John or Joseph Tanner, great-grandfather Edward Tanner, great-great-grandfather Joseph Tanner) and mother a Dianna who originally lived in Virginia but later in North Carolina. Her research verifies most of Fitzgerald's work, and in a letter to me indicates his notes contained "some new material for me." Rev. Tanner's first wife was Dorcas or Sussanah. By 1780 there were at least four children: Edward, Lucy, Agatha (or Agnes), and John (Falcon). In Tanner's early Kentucky years Indians frequently attacked white settlements due to French and later British instigation during the Indian Wars and Revolution. In one raid Rev. Tanner's uncle killed and scalped an Indian. His brothers David and Edward built a fortified salt works at Blue Licks near Tanners Station. Mrs. Tanner died when Falcon was two, and his father married Rachael Cain.

Hussey quotes eyewitness John Garnet's legal deposition describing Falcon's abduction indicating he was alone when captured. "The following year the Indians returned and captured Edward but he managed to escape in the night and got back safely." Soon after Falcon's kidnapping his stepmother died, "probably in childbirth as the baby was given her name." By that time there were 11 children, the others being Elizabeth, Sarah,

Mildred, Mary (Polly), Dianah and James. In 1792 the 60-year-old minister married 16-year-old Sally Rucker, daughter of distinguished Baptist co-worker James Rucker.

During Rev. Tanner's later years while crippled with rheumatism, his younger sons James and Rucker became involved in notoriety. Arriving in New Orleans without money the dark and swarthy Rucker permits James to sell him as slave. The latter quickly pockets the money and leaves his younger brother to his fate. Only with much "difficulty Rucker obtained his freedom and, penniless, started to walk home." Other children of John and Sally's were Nancy, Pamelia, Polly, Tabitha and Joseph.

Just before he died Rev. Tanner made a new will because he was convinced Edward, who held his power of attorney, was defrauding him. Edward had married Sally Rucker's sister Sooky, and thus strangely was his father's brother-in-law.

Mrs. Hussey devotes nine pages to John 'Falcon' Tanner. He had nine children; a son and two daughters from his first Indian wife Sky Dawn, six children (of whom two died in epidemics) from his second Indian wife Theresa after Sky Dawn deserted him in 1810. His oldest three apparently remained in Indian country, the son becoming "a hunter for an American trader, Norman Ketsou, and he was at Pembina in 1850. He had a son who by 1870 was a renowned trader on the Upper Saskatchewan River; this son was called Kissesoway Tanner." Falcon and Theresa's surviving children were James (of Portage la Prairie) born 1812, Martha Ann 1813, John J. and Mary Elizabeth later.

Martha studied teaching at Catholic St. Vincent's Academy in Cape Girardeau, Missouri, taught there herself many years and later at Mackinac, Mich., but never married. In a letter to Mary E. on Dec. 15, 1878, she states that she and Mary are now "the only two heirs left," is buried on Mackinac Island where a tombstone bears her name. Mary E. (born about 1823) also attended this academy, as did their uncle James Tanner's daughters Mary and Edna; married a La Vogue, sons Joe and George becoming prominent Duluth businessmen, next married Joseph Tall and had a son Joseph and later in life as widow married a Hoffman. John J. was living with his mother in Sault Ste. Marie, Feb. 14, 1848, on the very spot their home had burned in 1846, John claiming he'd married too young and "his wife was led astray and committed adultery," was divorced and remarried. His mother Theresa was still alive in 1860. Falcon was last seen alive heading into the forest with rifle and, social outcast that he'd become, immediately was blamed for the murder of employer Henry Schoolcraft's wild but influential brother James. A year later his remains were discovered in the woods nearby, but not until long after was his name cleared when an army officer confessed to the crime because of jealousy over a girl.

Of Falcon's siblings Edward seems to have tried hardest to find and later help his captured brother. In 1825 he moved to Texas and died in 1839, a son distinguishing himself in the Battle of San Jacinto against Mexico. Descendants live in Cleveland near Houston. Mildred married miller George Martin of Harrisonburg, Louisiana. Following Rev. Tanner's death his wife Sally returned to Kentucky and married James Rutter, a year later Zadock Thomas and had six more children, died of cancer about 1883.

Tanner's Crossing school recently acquired another book dealing with Falcon's exploits—Elliot Arnold's award-winning WHITE FALCON. It mentions the close friendship between Alexander Henry and John Tanner; later with Henry's successor John Harlie. Here his first wife's called Red Sky of Morning, oldest son Little Pheasant, second child being a girl and third being "Martha, which was the name of Harlie's wife in Scotland." Falcon persuades Harlie to build Fort Daer at Pembina, pledges peace and assistance of the Chippewas, Ojibways, Crees and Assiniboines for Selkirk's settlers. When Northwest Co. captures Daer, Falcon guides Cpt. MacLeod's soldiers from Rainy Lake over treacherous Rouseau Swamp to recapture it; later leads a small band of Indians while the soldiers sleep to recapture Fort Douglas (Winnipeg). Selkirk summons Falcon and says, "You have determined the course of history here. How may I repay you for what you have done?" "Bring peace to the valley," replies John Tanner, and Selkirk nodding soberly answers, "I promise you that. On my honor."

43. MONARDA MINNEDOSA & MONARCH SOURIS   Valley Vistas column, Brandon Sun, June 8/74

"The heat of a Prairie sun brings it to full bloom. Look for it on the grasslands and openings of the aspen parklands of southern Manitoba," states our provincial department of mines, resources and environmental management's colorful booklet MANITOBA WILDFLOWERS describing Bergamot, one of our most beautiful native wildflowers. A West-Manite who recognized the potential of Monarda menthoefolia years ago and did something about it was horticulturist H.H. Marshall.

I stumbled onto Marshall's work by accident, and until two weeks ago didn't know of his involvement with two perennial flowers that had caught my eye several months earlier. Hoping for an early spring I'd been leafing through Boughen Nurseries' (Valley River, Dauphin area) catalogue and noticed the heading "New from Brandon Experimental Farm, Monarch Souris and Monarda Minnedosa." As these names refer to favorite towns and valleys of mine I was intrigued and read on. The former, it indicated, form large clumps 2½ to 3½ feet high with numerous large heads of red-purple flowers, the latter similar height with clear white blooms—the lower lip of the flower being broad giving a compact appearance to the heads. And cost is only $1 per plant.

A check with Brandon Research Station director W.N. MacNaughton put me in touch with Henry Marshall, who had since developing these varieties at Brandon in late '60s transferred to Mordon Research Station, and referred me also to an article by this botanist in the 1968 PRAIRIE GARDEN that described the two Monardas—Souris and Minnedosa—in greater detail.

"A breeding program at Brandon Research Station," states the article in part, "using as parents the native lilac-flowered species (commonly called Bergamot) and the scarlet-flowered Monarda didyma from the Eastern United States, is producing many hardy selections in a wide range of colors. Other breeding techniques are creating lines with larger leaves and flowers. Still other lines are sterile, thereby conserving energy for greater flower production. A lavender-scented type has been acquired recently." Both varieties flower in July, Minnedosa a week earlier than Souris.

Monardas belong to the mint family. This family possesses two unusual traits: highly aromatic leaves when crushed, square stems. Most of us are probably more familiar with the wild species we simply call 'mint' (Mentha penardi) which contains small purplish-pink flowers and grows about a foot tall. Minnedosa Valley, for example, abounds with it and often you can smell the pleasant fragrance well before you come upon it. Who hasn't some time or other crushed the leaves in water and flavored home-made soft drinks with them on a hot summer afternoon? Indians used to utilize the Bergamot variety to cure certain ill-defined muscular ailments. The Monardas are named after Nicolas Monardes, a Spanish physician and botanist who way back in 1571 introduced one of the species native to North America into Europe from the United States.

"Henry H. Marshall," writes Prairie Garden's editor, "is doing a lot of bold plant breeding with ornamental plants. His work with Heucheras, Monardas, roses, chrysanthemums, and native flowers is contributing added beauty and enjoyment to Canadian gardening." Two weeks ago Brandon University recognized this man's significant contributions to horticulture and gardening with an honorary doctor of science degree.

In a recent letter to me Dr. Marshall indicates, "we have released two more since I came to Mordon that may be available from Aubin Nurseries at Carman. 'Minnedosa' is a white-flowered form of the wild Monarda found near Brandon. It has quite a good white flower but the stems tend to be rather weak. 'Souris' is a first generation hybrid with Cambridge Scarlet. Souris is hardier than its Scarlet parent but has a red-purple color and grows about 30 inches high. 'Neepawa' is similar to Souris but has a deep pink or light red color. 'Miniota' is white with a pink tip on each flower and grows somewhat shorter than the colored varieties." That many readers will follow with interest this noted horticulturist's future flower research goes without saying.

44. CERAMICS AND KEITH CHORNEYKO   Valley Vistas column, Brandon Sun, June 15/74

Marj Johnson's ornate bookends holding Pierre Berton's KLONDIKE, Jessie Hutton's attractive daisy-decorated teapot, Susan Peters' Euch des Lebens beer stein and Grace McTavish's chess pawns—all depicting the theme January, Winter Snow—greeted visitors; followed by displays like Marg Davidson's graceful flamingos indicating February brings Valentines Day. Janet Ziemanski and Clara Trott's wee folk portraying St. Patrick's Day would have delighted the Irish Rovers, or my colleague from Leprechaun Country. Jean Paulson's crocus design MANITOBA plate, E. Cartwright's bunny with cart or Elaine Chisholm's figurines bestowed happy Easter wishes. By now you know I'm wandering through Minnedosa's popular annual Art and Ceramics show.

May produces Mother's Day suggest two exquisite plaques by Eva Jacobson, while another arrangement implying romance reminds us we're now in the months of brides. July and August bring summer celebrations like our Fun Fest with numerous comical figurines by artists like Lydia McGuirk, Betty Morris, Debbie Amundsen and Inge Kettner alluding to funfilled days to come. Barbara Rochester's mallards and Audrey Lane's bull fight hint at September while Addie Peters' owls reflect Halloween, several fruit bowls Thanksgiving. Christmas trees, Yule logs, bells, candlesticks by persons like Jean Sharpe remind us the year draws to close with pleasant family festivity.

The past decade's seen ceramics become one of Manitoba's fastest-growing avocations. That Prairie people are finding and utilizing more leisure time in creating beautiful art forms to express innermost emotions is undoubtedly one sign we're rapidle leaving behind a raw frontier type culture to embark on a more refined one . Hardly a day passes that our news media doesn't feature one of the fine arts.

But any fine art of high calibre doesn't just happen; regardless of natural aptitude and creative desire of people. Usually there's a special person who helps draw out, direct, fashion creativity. Keith Chorneyko of Minnedosa's well known across the Prairies as such a catalyst.

Keith grew up in Eden near Neepawa and for 23 years taught plus served as principal in Manitoba elementary schools like St. James and Minnedosa, teaching his own unique style of art to countless students. Our own daughter Verna, who's just completed first year fine arts at U of M, is one of many who credit Keith with providing guidance essential to develop inherent aptitude in formative years. Since 1961 he's been instructing the Minnedosa ceramics group, which usually averages about 40 members , and five years ago left school teaching to open KB CERAMICS AND FLOWERS on North Main here. Some 200 different ceramics items are on sale. That his wife Bernice, a Somerset native, helps operate this thriving shop is indicated by the name.

In January of 1971 Ceramics Arts Association of Manitoba was formed to guide the mushrooming art form at provincial level. Keith Chorneyko was a major founder of this organization. Saskatchewan has since followed suit with a similar one. Keith's a popular judge in both Winnipeg and Regina ceramics shows.

But no true artist stops at any one plane to rest on his laurels (or whatever) and vegetate. January found this father of two in Clermont, Florida, studying porcelain and stoneware making. To non-artists like myself, there's no tremendous difference. To real artists the difference is probably not unlike driving the family car to church Sunday morning and competing in the Indianapolis 500 in the afternoon. Kiln temperatures, for example, jump from a 'mere' 1,905 degrees F. for ceramics clay to 2,250 for porcelain, heating time from six hours to eight. Keith, who plans to start advanced members in this medium, had a most attractive display himself at the show illustrating figurines, lockets, busts, small vases of beautiful color schemes and intricate design, is just getting nicely started in stoneware.

I discussed a topic with Mr. Chorneyko that's been close to my heart for years—the indifferent calibre of fine arts as taught in Manitoba elementary and in high schools. We agree that generally city school divisions place considerably more emphasis on courses like art and music and consequently hire better qualified instructors, whereas rural ones stress these only if they happen to acquire a teacher who excells in one such area in addition to the Three Rs type for which he was actually hired. Although appropriate changes in grant structure may be required, we strongly feel a way of equalizing this inequity is to initiate Saturday morning classes for those interested; or even summer school classes as is common in American centres. Oh yeah!

45. CHIEF RED CLOUD   Valley Vistas column, Brandon Sun, June 22 & 29/74

The Mystery of the Red Clouds is what this item might be called. At least, to me it's a real mystery. Of what significance, if any, was there a century ago when two Indian chiefs of same tribe and era had identical names? What kinship; if any, existed between the American Sioux Chief Red Cloud of Wyoming and Dakotas whose many exploits included the wiping out in 1866 of an entire army force second only to the Custer debacle, and the American Sioux Chief Red Cloud who led his band to West-Man to settle and live out his days on Birdtail Creek reserve following the Minnesota uprising of 1862?

I doubt if an American student or adult lives who hasn't heard of Red Cloud. Pick up at random (as I did recently) 10 American western pocket novels dealing with whites fighting Indians and three will probably mention this war lord. E.E. Halleran's WAGON CAPTAIN, Clay Fisher's YELLOWSTONE KELLY, Clair Huffaker's WAR WAGON, all deal with him at length in historical fiction style. Even an Archie comic strip recently showed the school principal all but die of fright when he realized he was about to attend a costume dance as General Custer to which Archie and friends were going as Sitting Bull,

Crazy Horse and Red Cloud.

Near Douglas, Wyoming, stands a cairn that reads: "On this field on the 21st day of December, 1866, three commissioned officers and 76 privates of the 18th US Infantry and of the 2nd US Cavalry, and four civilians, under the command of Captain Brevet-Lieutenant Colonel William J. Fetterman were killed by an overwhelming force of Sioux, under the command of Red Cloud. There were no survivors." The battle's commonly called Fetterman Massacre, the nearby knoll Massacre Hill. During the so-called Indian Wars, major American army forces were annihilated only twice—Fetterman by Red Cloud, Custer 10 years later by Sitting Bull. The Semi-Weekly Boomerang of Laramie, Wyoming, in June 29, 1908 quotes William Murphy, a soldier who came upon the scene moments after the battle, reminiscing, "Red Cloud in after years often talked of the heroism of that massacred band. One man, he said, killed seven Indians and wounded nine more before he was overpowered." The Fetterman plaque ignores more than 65 Sioux warriors also killed in the same battle.

There's an old saying: 'When the Whites won, it was a victory; when the Indians won, it was a massacre'. Our department of Indian affairs indicates, "an armed force in the field may be defeated and wiped out but it cannot be 'massacred'."

The great warrior Red Cloud (Makhpiya-luta, also Makhipiya-sha) was the principal chief of the Ogala Teton Sioux; the largest band of the Sioux nation and probably the most famous and powerful chief in the tribe's history. Historians generally believe the name derives from the way his scarlet-blanketed warriors once covered the hillsides like a red cloud. If so, it was bestowed after he'd won recognition as leader for he didn't inherit chiefship, which rested with another family entirely. Red Cloud's own father died of drunkeness, brought about by introducing liquor wholesale into the tribe since 1821. That the chief's children did use the name Red Cloud as surname later is shown by the fact a son living in South Dakota in 1894 was called Jack Red Cloud. It may well be the Birdtail chief was another son. Descendants of the latter, two of whom I met two years ago, today use the surname Cloude. A Birdtail resident told me recently he knows several of these Cloudes well, but currently none live there.

That Red Cloud's Sioux who fought Fetterman of Fort Phil Kearney in Dakota Territory and those who fought soldiers and civilians in Minnesota were likely allies is suggested in a letter to a friend by the fort's army surgeon C.M. Hines dated Jan. 1, 1867 indicating, "All the Sioux, including those who committed the atrocities in Minnesota, are in our neighborhood." US Indian commissioner Lewis Bogey however disagreed, claiming they were 500 miles away.

Our Indian affairs records show Manitoba Sioux at Portage la Prairie, Birdtail, Oak River and Oak Lake descend from the Medaywakanton and Wahpaykootay bands of the Dakota Sioux who took refuge here following the Minnesota fighting, plus from a handful of Sitting Bull followers who elected to remain here two decades later. Although RCMP closely watched Sitting Bull (at one point Inspector Allen even arrested the famous warrior for riding a stolen police horse) that force doesn't have a file on West-Man's Red Cloud, RCMP historian S.W. Horrall wrote me recently.

Wattsview pioneer W.W. Dodge described Red Cloud's band at Birdtail as follows: "There were about 100 in all, and about 20 of them warriors, most of who had taken part in the earlier wars in southern Minnesota. It would be hard to find a finer bunch of men anywhere. Lithe, supple, alert and straight, several of them six feet or over in moccasins. Pioneers will recall Solomon, Sioux Jack, Big Hunter, Honikaw brothers, Sioux Benn, Thunder Shonkako and Moses Bunn Sr. The women too were active and prepared for every emergency." Two other men were Enoch and Black Face.

Viscount Milton in THE NORTH-WEST PASSAGE describes the terror in Winnipeg when the Minnesota Sioux first arrived there. Had it not been for Manitobans like James McKay and certain HBC officials, the refugees would quickly have been forced to return. As it was, Chiefs Little Six and Medicine Bottle, writes Mary McCarthy Ferguson in THE HON. JAMES McKAY OF DEER LODGE, were tricked and kidnapped by Mr. McKenzie (American), Osime Quigere and Mr. Bannatyne (Canadians) and delivered to Major Hatch at Pembina, to be hanged at Fort Snelling.

That numerous later Sioux refugees in Canada were of the same tribe as Red Cloud of Fetterman battle's borne out in a July 3, 1880, letter from NWMP superintedent J.M. Walsh to our interior minister indicating, "I have this day succeeded in obtaining consent of unconditional surrender to US authorities from Chiefs Broad Tail, Dull Knife, Stone Dog and Little Hawk on behalf of Ogallalla Sioux in Canadian Territory." A letter 11 days later mentions a US reserve being prepared for these bands. On Sept. 11, he refers to a conversation with Sitting Bull in which the latter expressed hatred for Red Cloud and Spotted Tail for selling the Black Hills to the US government, his major objection to returning to America being he might be forced to live "on an agency presided over by either Spotted Tail or Red Cloud, and to pay obedience would be too humiliating."

WANDERING IN WATTSVIEW describes Birdtail's Red Cloud as "a very different Indian. He did not speak English, was a warrior mostly at odds with the white man. He was a good hunter and an expert horseman. He kept a band of horses and rode a black stallion. During the (second) Riel Rebellion, they asked these Indians for help. Chief Red Cloud was willing to go, but Moses Bunn said 'No, the Canadian government has given us this land and we won't rebel'." Presbyterian Rev. John Black of Kildonan's letters reveal Rev. Solomon Tunkansuiciye became Birdtail Creek mission's first minister.

The only conflict between Red Cloud's band and white settlers near Birdtail Sioux reserve involved the chief's horses trampling and eating grain crops. After several horses were impounded, Red Cloud astride his steed met pioneer Albert Bartley out riding one evening and expressed his disgust by striking the settler's mount sharply on the rump with his blacksnake whip.

Because American Sioux living in Canada aren't treaty Indians, Indian affairs has no record of early chiefs and family heads. Today, 1,700 Sioux live on 21,000 acres of Manitoba reserves. Citizenship was granted by Order in Council on April 24, 1873, land appropriation two months earlier. This occurred only after exhaustive research proved our Sioux refugees had always been friendly to the British crown and Canadian government, particularly in the war of 1812.

Though historians concur Sioux warriors seldom tortured prisoners or mutilated enemy corpses the 1862 Minnesota revolt and 1866 Fetterman battle seem to have been exceptions. Manitoba historian Olive Knox describes the uprising at New Ulm, Minn. "The massacre there sparked the rising of other Sioux tribes, who attacked all the white settlers on the Minnesota and Saulk rivers. Men were shot down, women violated and murdered and children tortured, thrust living into stoves or cut down with tomahawks." Fetterman's superior, Col. Henry Carrington, went all out describing 17 different gruesome atrocities like "entrails taken out and exposed, eyes torn out and laid on rocks, punctures upon every sensitive part of the body even to soles of feet and palms of hands" to his superiors. It's generally conceded Fetterman and Capt. Fred Brown (who'd sworn to scalp Red Cloud) shot one another when capture and death were imminent.

That Carrington's report evoked a public outcry across the US precipitating years of harsh Sioux treatment is no surprise. Birdtail's Sioux Benn, interviewed years later by historian J.L. Swainson, indicated his band participated only in a skirmish with American troops at Battle Lake, Minn.; in which "several scalps were taken." US Indian commissioner Bogey concluded at the time that all Sioux attacks on the army were due to "a state of starvation, having made repeated attempts at a conference that they might make peace oand obtain supplies for their families, and the rescinding of the order prohibiting them from obtaining arms and amunition, were rendered desperate."

Reminiscing in the Midwest Review years after what novelists like Tom Curry call Fetterman's Folly, C.W. Bickford--a private at Fort Kearney in 1866, tells of an episode involving the war chief on May 4, 1870. John Richards, a nephew of Red Cloud, murdered two soldiers who'd won the friendship of a Crow maiden he coveted. To save his relative from hanging, Red Cloud with several other chiefs proceeded to Washington and negotiated another peace treaty with President U.S. Grant (army general at time of Fetterman battle) in exchange for a pardon for Richards. An accompanying photo of Red Cloud depicts a sad handsome man with deep-furrowed face and shoulder-length hair.

Born in 1822 at Platte River forks, this Sioux war lord had at least one sister. A niece married Maj. Charles Jordon. He took no direct part in the 1870s Sioux revolt of Sitting Bull-Crazy Horse-Gall fame. As warrior he performed 80 separate deeds of bravery in battle. Unlike many chiefs of his day he had but one wife, with whom he lived from early manhood. This despite, as historian Mari Sandoz writes, in later years her frequent shouting "at the old chief in a most unseemly manner, that would have cost him much of his fine following in the old hunting and warrior days." His immediate band was Iteshicha. The signer of numerous treaties and a frequent delegate to Washington, he was from Indian standpoint a true patriot.

Possibly the most ironic event in the great Sioux's dramatic life occurred in 1894 as revealed in a May 1, 1940 Casper Times article. With son Jack and a friend he revisited his old Wyoming stomping grounds where 28 years earlier he'd declared war on whites for coming into his land and killing his game, was arrested and fined for "hunting game as non-resident without a license." Unable to pay the fine, the old chief's forced to leave his team and wagon in exchange. This episode precipitated swift retaliation by Eagle Feather and Black Kettle leading a hunting foray deep into north-central Wyoming in which at least two whites were killed. For some years before his death at Pine Ridge (Black Hills), S.D., on Dec. 10, 1909, Red Cloud was blind and decrepid, living in a house built for him by the US government.

Chief Red Cloud of Birdtail's buried in a cemetery on a point on Assiniboine Valley facing Scissor Creek on the west side of the De Clare near the CNR tracks. I haven't seen the grave myself but have talked to someone who has. Following the chief's death John Bopha, believed to be a brother of Red Cloud's wife, took over his fine horses. Violet Keel recalled Albert Bartley "made a treaty with Bopha that if the Indian horses got out on the plains he would drive them back, if the Bartley horses went to the reserve, Bopha would do the same. That treaty was kept through the years." I understand one elderly descendant, Sam Bopha, still lives there. I sincerely wish someone could tell us the connection, if any, between Chief Red Cloud of Wyoming and Dakota battles and Birdtail's Chief Red Cloud of Minnesota wars.

46. SEASONS   Minnedosa Collegiate Yearbook, 1973-74

> The fresh green garb of new life now breaks through
>
> And gently, but so definitely, does spread
>
> Into such glowing colors bright with red.
>
> The hopes and dreams of all mankind renew.
>
> The sultry heat brought storms, then skies of blue,
>
> In turn the frost-colored browns and oranges led
>
> To foggy morns and winter's snowy bed.
>
> Thus, one more round, and earth's fulfillment too.
>
> A new-born baby's healthy cry is heard.
>
> The youth's triumphant, well-formed body hurls
>
> Victorious shouts to aging parents' form
>
> Which, surely, like a migratory bird
>
> Prepares itself, and softly, warmly curls
>
> Its toils and dreams against the winter's storm.
>
>   -- Elsie Neufeld

47. CHARLIE ALLOWAY   Valley Vistas column, Brandon Sun, July 6/74

Winnipeg centennial celebrations are in full swing and many are the events and pioneers recalled. A Winnipeger of a century ago who interests me more than most is Charlie Alloway.

Charles Valentine Alloway lived in the shadow of his older brother William Forbes Alloway all his adult life. Much has been written about Bill Alloway, philanthropist and founder of Winnipeg Foundation and of Alloway and Champion Bank that later merged with Canadian Bank of Commerce. Bill's contributions to Manitoba history will no doubt be reviewed this summer, Charlie's likely ignored. Not only did Charlie live in his older brother's shadow but whenever he did make a unique major contribution Bill's name somehow became linked with it and historians later invariably credited the exploit to both brothers.

Of 11 Canadians and half dozen Americans who played some role in saving Manitoba's emblem--the North American buffalo--from extinction, most credit undoubtedly should go to Charlie Alloway. If Bill played any part in this monumental conservation project it must have been a most indirect role; like possibly owning part of the pasture Charlie kept his captured bison on or helping to outfit one of his three bison-capturing expeditions (1873, 1874, 1883) into Saskatchewan and Alberta. All the countless risks, problems, heartbreaks in this massive venture were Charlie's. During the third foray, his widow told Manitoba Historical and Scientific Society years later, her husband almost lost his life crossing Minnedosa River in early spring. An 800-foot torrent of floating ice slabs, the flooding stream stopped his party several days until the daring Charlie "rode the crest of the ice floes for many hours" managing finally to cross and with cod line drag a rope over, create a trolley service to ferry horses, cargo and men across.

In TALES OF EARLY MANITOBA Edith Paterson quotes Charlie reminiscing, "The nearest I ever came to being killed was by a timber wolf. They tell you a timber wolf will not attack a man, I want to say that one will," and describes in detail the attack and hand-to-fang battle near Carrot River between Hudson Bay Junction and Prince Albert. Were someone else making this statement I'd take it with a grain of salt for I'm a writer who's made the same claim.

Bill Alloway came West in the first Wolseley expedition of 1870, Charlie in the second in 1871. Many writers lump the brothers together as coming in the same one—the one in which Bill came of course. Personally I'm glad Charlie came in the second because recently I've dug up some little known information on the first that historians have studiously ignored which places it in a most unfavorable light. Details will follow soon.

Peter Lowe's 1946 article for Manitoba Historical Society helps separate fact from fiction where the Alloway brothers are concerned. Lowe was general manager of Alloway and Champion Bank for 25 years and I thank historian Helen (Champion) Waugh of Winnipeg for locating this particular item for me. Lowe says of Charlie in part: "On several occasions in the early days he visited both Fort Churchill and Port Nelson. He was also well acquainted with the Peace River country, and his visions of its development as an agricultural area have been realized. When the West was being opened up he had the distinction of carrying the first mail between Calgary and Edmonton. He was a lover of nature and became an authority on bird and animal life of the Prairies; president of Winnipeg Bicycle Club in days when that pastime was at its height of popularity. Between 1872 and 1878, Charlie Alloway became acquainted with every trail, stream and lake, throughout the West, and acquired a speaking knowledge of a number of Indian dialects as well as of French. The greater part of his life in this period was spent on the trail." A Winnipeg Tribune item following his death in early September of 1929 carries the appropriate caption "Blazes Trails of Northland". A 1972 Wild West magazine issue refers to him as "the Canadian conservationist."

Mrs. Waugh recently wrote me, "My own memories of Charlie are of a little white haired old man, with a drawly voice. Very kind to us as small children, which Bill never was. Late in life (1902), Charlie married a very attractive woman many years younger than he was, Maud Denholm (daughter of Andrew P. Denholm) by name. She was a niece of Alec McMicken, one of the early magistrates in Winnipeg. They had only one child, a son, who grew up to be a most attractive young man, Hamilton by name. Tragically he was killed in a flying accident in England while on active service with the RCAF. There were no other children, and as far as I know there are no direct descendants of that branch of the Alloway family." Son of Arthur William Alloway, a Queens Own Rifles officer, Charlie was born in Ireland.

Provincial archivist John A. Bovey wrote me, "Very little has been written about Charlie Alloway but there are still quite a few people in Winnipeg who remember him. The late Dr. F.C. Bell of Vancouver knew him well and showed me a number of photographs which Alloway had taken around Fort Chipewyan in the 1890s, and later given to him." Mrs. Cecil (Rosamonde Gagnon) Shannon in a Winnipeg Free Press article said of him, "Charlie Alloway was lots of fun, always laughing." If it were possible to turn back time a century, Charlie Alloway'd be the Winnipeg pioneer with whom I'd most like to chat.

48. CP SHIPS AND U-BOATS   Valley Vistas column, Brandon Sun, July 13/74

In 1972 I wrote several articles on Canadian Pacific ships, which involved the important role they played in both world wars. Some were West-Man namesakes. Most sinkings were by German navy then challenging Allied high seas superiority. Information on individual U-boats and officers involved was most sketchy. My request for additional information to West German armed forces headquarters in Berlin a year ago evoked considerable research on their part, results of which have just been received. Must be my Prussian name that did it. I thank especially officer Sonnenthal for this data.

On Sept. 6/15 the Hesparian was sunk by U20. Commander was Walter Schwieger, born April 7, 1885. He was killed in action aboard U88 July 6/17. Commander Hans Galster of UC51, which laid the mine sinking the Ionian Oct. 20/17 just off St. Gowans Head, was himself killed in action on the same submarine a month later.

Six submarine commanders who sank 6Piships in the First World War not only survived that terrible Krieg but lived to fight in the next one. Commander Degenhart F. von Loe of U100, which sank the Lake Michigan April 16/18 near Eagle Island, became captain of a corvette Aug. 20/40. Helmut Brummer-Patzig of U86, which sank the Medora May 2/18 near Mull of Galloway, was born Oct. 26, 1890 in Danzig, became captain of a frigate Sept. 1/44. Friedrich Strackerjahn of U105, which torpedoed the Milwaukee Aug. 31/18 off Fastnet, was born Aug. 26. 1877 in Luebeck, became naval captain Oct. 1/42. Ernst Hashagen of U62, which destroyed the Miniota Aug. 31/17 off Start Point, was born Aug. 24, 1885 in Leipzig, became a frigate captain July 1/42, died June 12/47. Wilhelm Werner of U55, which sank the Montford Oct. 1/18 off Bishop Rock, was born June 6, 1888 in Apolda, became a high ranking officer Oct. 1/42, died in Luebeck May 14/45. The Calgarian was torpedoed March 1/18 off Rathlin Island by U19 whose commander was Johannes Spiess, born July 25, 1888 in Berlin, becoming a corvette captain Aug. 1/41. First officer then was Hans-Albrecht Liebeskind, born July 20/92 in Koeln.

On Sept. 9/18 the Missinabie was torpedoed off Daunts Rock by UB87; commander until war's end was Karl Petri (April 21, 1887 to April 17/29). The Mount Temple was captured and sunk Dec. 6/16 about 620 miles off Fastnet by the raider Moewe commanded by N. Claus Burggraf, born April 5, 1879, died Aug. 20/56 in Baiersbach at Stephanskirchen. Johannes Ries, born July 8, 1891, commanded UC77, which sank the Pomeranian April 15/18 near Portland Bill, until she herself was sunk in the English Channel on July 26/18.

During the Second World War the Beaverburn was torpedoed Feb. 5/40 in the North Atlantic by U41 whose captain was Gustav-Adolf Mugler, born Oct. 10/12 in Danzig - Langfuhr. The same day HMS Antelope destroyed her nearby. On Aug. 17/42 the Princess Marguerite on voyage from Port Said to Cyprus was torpedoed by U83 whose captain was Hans-Werner Kraus, born July 1/15 in Beulwitz. On March 14/43, U83 was sunk 37-10N, 00-05E by RAF Squadron 500. U32 torpedoed the Empress of Britain Oct. 28/40. Captain was Hans Jenisch, born Oct. 19/13 in Gerdauen. Two days later at 55-37N, 12-20W, HMS Harvesta and HMS Highlander destroyed that submarine.

Captain of U48 which sank the Beaverdale April 1/41, was Herbert Schultze, born July 24/09 in Kiel. He was the highly controversial captain who sank Britain's first merchant ship, SS Royal Sceptre, and three months later the SS Brandon, then a neutral American whaling vessel. U178's captain Hans Ibbeken who sank the Duchess of Atholl Oct. 10/42 off Ascension Isle was born Sept. 20, 1899 in Schleswig. The 'pocket battleship' Admiral Schier destroyed the Beaverford Nov. 5/40 in North Atlantic. Theodor Krancke, born March 30, 1893 in Magdeburg commanded her, was promoted to admiral March 1/43. First officer was Ernst Gruber, born Sept. 19, 1900 in Vacha. Other officers were Wolfgang Huebner, Alfred Schuman, Alexander Ewe.

Records don't agree as to who sank the Niagara off Hauraki Gulf, N.Z., June 18/40. CP historians believe it was a mine. According to German historian Cpt. Bernhard Rogge who commanded his nation's deadliest raider, the Atlantis, she "had been sunk off Aukland by the raider Orion." German naval records reveal the Orion was commanded by Kurt Weyher, born Aug. 30/01 in Graudenz, promoted Jan. 1/45, and first officer was Adalbert von Blanc, born July 11/07 in Wilhelmshaven.

Perhaps most intriguing's the case of Cpt. Otto Kretschmer (born May 1/12 in Heidau) of U99 who torpedoed the Montrose (HMS Forfar during war) off Ireland's west coast Dec. 2/40. Wolfgang Frank, officer on Admiral Doenitz' own personal staff and author of THE SEA WOLVES, and current German naval records agree that U99 was sunk by HMS Walker March 17/41 at 61N, 12W. Frank indicates Kretschmer himself was captured. He was one of Germany's greatest naval aces, being the second U-boat captain to win the oak leaves to his Knight's Cross after sinking 300,000 tons of Allied shipping plus three British destroyers. His capture, says Frank, was such a blow to Hitler's pride he refused to allow it to be acknowledged for two months despite Doenitz' strong insistance. German naval records, on the other hand, list Kretschmer as becoming captain of a corvette just 16 days before Frank claims he was captured aboard the sinking U99, that he went on to become captain of a frigate Sept. 1/44, eventually admiral of a flotilla. Und so geht es!

At an auction in Birtle recently, Parkland Bottle Collectors president, George Crighton of Cardale, purchased a silver-plated serviette ring (holder) which came from the 'CPS Minnedosa' that transported countless immigrants to Western Canada and played a major role in both wars--for the Allies during the First and Italy in the Second. Mr. Crighton's loaning the keepsake to Minnedosa Museum. Perhaps one of our ancestors (several of my own came to Canada on that particular steamer) lifted it from the vessel as souvenir of the voyage. Danke, George.

And in the August 17/74 issue:

"I was very interested in your write-up Saturday, July 13 on the different CPR boats that were sunk in the two world wars," writes Harry Horne of Brentwood Village, Brandon. "I have a great feeling for the Missinabie. My mother, three brothers and two cousins sailed the first week of December, 1914, from Liverpool and landed at St. John, N.B., 10 days later. I remember the trip as if it were just last week. We had to close down at nights just like a floating coffin for submarines. But coming up the Bay of Fundy it was very foggy and we struck a rock, but it did no damage to the hull. The jar broke the hot water pipes and there was boiling water all over the place. No one was injured. This happened about 3 a.m. I understand she was refitted into a hospital ship later." According to CP records this trip was her maiden voyage.

49. REV. JAMES TANNER   Valley Vistas column, Brandon Sun, July 20 & 27/74

As you read this the Second Princess Patricia Canadian Light Infantry, a regiment in which many West-Manites fought in the last war, is probably dragging wearily into their Winnipeg barracks from an historic re-creation of Colonel Wolseley's 1870 march from Thunder Bay as part of our capital's centennial celebrations. I've great respect for the Pats; little for the event they're commemorating.

No doubt the Pats know nothing of several contemptible incidents perpetrated by Wolseley's men when they reached Winnipeg to quell the Riel Rebellion ('Resistance' is more apt, claim some historians). Undoubtedly because most historians ignore them. True, some are critical of the expedition being sent at all; or at least prior to proper Manitoba civil government being established. But I don't fault an army regiment for this because it takes orders from its nation's government and people (us) it represents. On the other hand, I do believe a commanding officer and individual soldiers are responsible for the manner in which they perform a designated task.

Recently I chatted with retired Rev. H. Hambley, United Church minister in this area 1954-60 and author of two historical books, visiting his wife's sister who's our neighbor. Discussing research I've done on the remarkable Tanner family, II deplored the little data available on Minnedosa founder John Tanner's father Rev. James Tanner. Not being overly bright sometimes it hadn't occurred to me to search church records for such information instead of usual historical sources, or that one historian (Olive Knox) had already done just that. Hambley steered me onto the right track, records involving mostly letters written by Rev. John Black now stored in United Church Archives in Toronto.

Rev. Black of Kildonan, first Presbyterian minister to Canada's Prairies, came to Winnipeg in September of 1851 after years of strong urging by Scottish settlers for a minister of their own. One such petitioner was free trader James Sinclair, father-in-law of Catherine Trottier Sinclair whom Minnedosa's founder married in 1869. John Black played a major peace role in the 'Resistance' by persuading settlers, Metis and Indians to refrain from violence and tried in vain to persuade Riel not to shoot Scott. James Tanner was a close friend and occasional co-worker of Black's. In his tragic story lies a bit of Manitoba history worth recording.

Black came to Manitoba via US having travelled by chance with the official party of Gov. Alexander Ramsay of Minnesota enroute to Pembina to negotiate a treaty with the Chippewas, accompanied by newspaper correspondent John Wesley Bond. At Norman Kittson's Pembina trading post he first met Tanner who was to interpret the negotiations. Early Canadian historians like Alexander Ross strongly criticize this treaty which ignored Metis rights and which several major Indian chiefs refused to sign. We tend to forget that the Selkirk Settlement for the preceding third century had included the

Pembina area as much of it lay in what's now North Dakota and Minnesota.

Pembina's Joe Cavileer, who with Kittson hosted the official party and Black, describes James Tanner to the latter as, "before his conversion he was a notorious character. He was a giant in strength and although kind and gentle when sober he would terrorize an entire village when frenzied with rum. But what a changed man he is now. I think the Bible is the only book he reads, and if you ask him for any point of information he can give you chapter and verse and even repeat the entire passage. Last winter he was my neighbor and many a long evening I joined his family for their devotions. He would read a chapter of the Bible, then comment upon it in the most beautiful, simple and sensible language I have ever listened to. And his prayers, well, I've never heard more forcible ones than his. You know at times I was led to feel like the Roman governor before Paul—almost persuaded to be a Christian."

Black and Bond meet Tanner and gaze into his candid black eyes as he towers above them, long black hair brushing his shoulders. They discuss Father Belcourt's mission at St. Joseph, Fort Daer (which Tanner's father 'Falcon' had persuaded HBC to build) and Kittson's post. Pointing east across the Red River Rev. Tanner reminisces, "It's across that country my father led Lord Selkirk's soldiers to retake the HB posts from the Nor-Westers and make Fort Garry safe for settlers. The company paid him $20 a year for the rest of his life for his help." Ed Russenholt and Hartwell Bowsfield are two historians who acknowledge John's important role in that historic event; most credit the action to captains Miles Macdonnell and P.D. Orsonnes who played minor roles.

Rev. Tanner strongly favored Christianizing Indians because of excessive power medicine men held over them which often produced serious problems; like persuading Tanner's tribe to kill all their dogs as Manitou commanded and then almost starving to death. He mentions his Baptist minister grandfather, tells of missionary work he himself has been doing in Minnesota with A.B. Adams, D.B. Spencer, Alonzo Barnard, Frederick Ayers. His older brother, he indicates, "is still a heathen. He's a chief of a big tribe. Still he's an honest and fair man and lives and hunts with his relatives. If I could convert him he would be a great help in our work. I still have hope."

Rev. Black's letters reveal that as he listened to Tanner's sermon to the Red Lake Indians congregating for treaty negotiations, using the Chippewa testament of his father's translation, he became filled with hope of Presbyterian Indian missions blossoming in Western Canada. Bidding Tanner farewell Bond and he travel to Fort Garry with a letter of introduction to Kittson's father-in-law, Narcisse Marion of St. Boniface.

In October Tanner visits Kildonan, speaks to Black's congregation describing the Christianizing and agricultural training of American Indians by Presbyterians, preaches to St. Peter's Mission Indians at mouth of the Red. Together they approach Governor Colville with plans to establish an Indian mission on White Horse Plains. Colville puts them off for there's already a Catholic mission operating and he doesn't want two sects competing for converts and isn't convinced converted Indians have higher morals.

Next April Tanner with assistant Elijah Terry again visits Black, tells of his new mission at St. Joseph. Tanner's been to New York and Washington that winter and interested a Baptist society in the project. The two remain in Winnipeg several weeks, visiting settlers and preaching; Terry becomes engaged to Flora MacDonald and plans to return in fall to marry her. They return to St. Joseph while Selkirk's settlers fight the worst flood the Red's dealt yet. Returning to their desolated homes the settlers learn that Terry's been ambushed by Sioux that June while getting a load of timber for a new school, killed and scalped. His companion had fled to Tanner for help, who had arrived too late with armed men.

During the night of August 13 the Sioux again attack; this time the home of Tanner's neighbor 400 feet away, Congregationalist missionary David Spencer. David, knowing James is sleeping with "his family in the lower room" and "his Indian pupils would be asleep in the loft," tries to attract his attention by firing a gun. Meanwhile, his wife Cornelia dies of two bullet wounds. He hurries for help but the Sioux vanish as quickly as they came. Mrs. Tanner cares for the Spencer children until they can be sent East to grandparents, James conducts funeral services for the mother.

For 10 years Black doesn't mention Tanner. Following the 1862 Minnesota Sioux uprising he worries about Tanner's safety and is relieved to hear the American missionaries fled in time. About two years later he mentions there's still no Presbyterian Indian mission in Western Canada, but serious consideration's being given. James Tanner, who's "been wandering among his people on the plains along the Assiniboine" is cited as most logical choice for missionary. Except for a church built in Headingly in 1865 nothing concrete materializes and Black next mentions Tanner in the summer of 1870. Manitoba's just become a province and Col. Wolseley sent to Fort Garry with a 'peace force'.

Rev. Black has only contempt for Wolseley and his men. This appears due to several incidents for which he holds them responsible. The first involves a plot by Wolseley's men to murder Riel; who's warned in the nick of time and escapes. Wolseley's own feelings toward Riel are expressed in a letter to Lady Wolseley in Begg's journal. "Hope Riel will have bolted, for although I should like to hang him to the highest tree in the place, I have such a horror of rebels and vermin of his kidney, that my treatment of him might not be approved by the civil powers."

Black tells of Wolseley's soldiers ransacking the fort, molesting Metis women and beating their men. So far I haven't found other historical supporting evidence.

Black mentions a Metis stoned to death by Wolseley's soldiers when he tries to swim the Red. Begg quotes Bishop Tache's report of Elzear Goulet (one of the Scott firing squad) attacked in Winnipeg by a group, several of whom at least were his men and stoned as he swam the Red, indicating this "shameful event was one of a number of deeds of violence which followed the end of the resistance." Russenholt indicates investigation traced the crime to two volunteer soldiers.

The incident which angers Black most involved Tanner. "Rev. James Tanner, for the past few years an itinerant preacher to his people on the Prairie, came to Winnipeg for supplies. The soldiers raced around his wagon, whooping and rearing their horses, firing shots into the air, until the horses ran away, overturned the wagon, and James was killed." When Black hears of the tragedy he hurries to claim the body to give it a Christian burial. Tanner's Indian chief brother beats him to it, face stony and eyes scornful, blazes, "Alive, my brother preached your gospel. You killed him. I take him to my people who do not kill their medicine men." Henrietta Black tries to comfort her grief-stricken husband with, "Chief Tanner knows you loved his brother. He will not hold his death against you." Lying awake that night John prays, "James, my brother in God's work, forgive them if you can—but I can't—not yet."

No other historian I know of describes this incident thus. Wolseley himself does mention "individuals fleeing along the Assiniboine from the fort in buggies as the troops advanced." A close Kinosota friend of James Tanner's son John told me recently he'd been told James died at High Bluff "breaking his neck falling from a wagon when a buffalo robe scared the horses." An Alonsa son of James' foster son James heard the death occurred at High Bluff when "the horses bolted while driving over newly-broken land", James falling off and a wheel crushing his head. Portage historian Anne Collier places the 'wagon accident' at Poplar Point, half-way between Portage and Winnipeg.

That Rev. Tanner did not die accidently is certain. The December 10, 1870 edition of The Manitoban describes Dr. Bird's inquest in which David McKenzie and Joseph Pritchin testify two men threw something at the horse and fled. Dr. Lynch, deeply involved in fighting Riel and later Marquette's first MP, testifies he examined the body about "half an hour after the accident. He was quite dead; had him carried to the nearest house and opened a vein but to no purpose. Examined the body and found a fracture of the skull transverse." The coroner jury's verdict read, "the late James Tanner died from a fracture of the skull caused by his being thrown out of a wagon while the horse of the said wagon was running away, and that the said horse was caused to run away wilfully and maliciously by two persons unknown to this jury, thereby causing the death of the said James Tanner."

Whatever the precise circumstances surrounding Rev. Tanner's murder, this case (perhaps because he was both an American citizen and Metis) seems to have evoked no further official interest and was soon forgotten. Col. Garnett Joseph Wolseley, on the other hand, was created C.B. and K.C.M.G. for his Manitoba 'peacekeeping' services, later promoted to commander-in-chief of the British Army and made a viscount.

50. MINNEDOSA KINNETTES & HISTORIC BUILDINGS   Valley Vistas, Brandon Sun, Aug. 3/74

It was a most inspiring open-air church service. The setting, Tanner's Crossing School courtyard on Minnedosa River's north bank, most pleasant. Despite a golf tournament already in full swing, hundreds of persons did come to worship as part of our popular annual Fun Fest. Hymn singing, led by choir director-auctioneer-farmer Dave

Comrie, is even more enjoyable outdoors than in the confines of buildings. Songs like Don't Be A Sunday's Child by a quartet of attractive young ladies added to the agreeable atmosphere; Rev. Graves, Mrs. Ebner, Rev. Stone and Hilding Alex assisting with the service. But the sermon by Rev. Bruce Miles of First Presbyterian Church in Winnipeg especially impressed me. Perhaps because it happened to be the first time I'd heard a sermon by a Presbyterian minister. Perhaps because of research I've been doing lately involving pioneer Manitoba Presbyterians Rev. John Black and Rev. James Tanner. As I listened to Rev. Miles' inspirational message I couldn't help feel that Rev. Tanner especially would have appreciated this sermon on the bank of the very river his father plied fur-laden canoes from Clear Lake to Brandon trading posts in early 1800s when he lived with his Indian foster mother and in the yard of the multi-million dollar new school named after his only son who owned this property and operated historic Tanner's Crossing 200 yards east in the 1870s.

Immediately across the river stands 'The Castle', one of Minnedosa's most attractive historic buildings. Built in 1901 by Judge R.H. Meyers as the Tilston Place and now an apartment block, this old mansion's one of four buildings deeply involved in the Fun Fest as part of an interesting project by the local Kinnettes. Tired of 'Made in Japan' type souvenirs sold tourists each year, they decided to create some with genuine local flavor in the form of hasty notes depicting an artist's sketches of historic buildings of which Minnedosans are justly proud.

"Typical stone home built in 1895" reads one caption. This house was one of several constructed here by stone mason T.D. Taylor, whose sons Ed and Sept and granddaughter Nancy are well known Minnedosa residents. Incidently, Mr. Taylor also built a stone 'castle' for Dr. Ralston (surgeon for Boulton's Scouts) in Miniota area. Bill Crooks, one of our best mechanics, is the lucky person now living in our beautiful 1895 stone house.

One sketch naturally illustrates our old post office-turned civic centre and most widely known landmark about which I've written in the past. The fourth is one people only see about once a year---the wooden pavilion (pagoda) at the fair grounds built in 1905. This old building's earned a permanent niche in Canadian literature because of its description in the delightful book A MANITOBA CHORE BOY by Rev. E.A. Wharton Gill, a former Anglican minister here and local farmhand before that.

The artist who sketched the buildings is no stranger to West-Man. Bill Johnson grew up on his grandparents' homestead east of Erickson, completed part of his high school in Erickson Collegiate and remainder at Carbon near Drumheller, Alberta. Returning to West-Man to obtain a B.A. at Brandon University (where he became a close friend of Minnedosa Collegiate's current principal Harold Gillishammer) he went to Vancouver to acquire a library degree, now works in Calgary and travels often across Canada sketching. Whenever he requires peace and tranquility, as artists (and writers) do from time-to-time, he heads for a little shack at Erickson his grandparents left him.

That the Kinnettes are to be commended for creating more interest in old architecturally beautiful historic buildings goes without saying. Executive Bev Kane, Diane Boyd, Carol Delmage, Wilma Jones with project committee Diana Gillishammer, Leoni Bilcowski, Darlene Bright, Diane Carter are already making plans for a much more ambitious undertaking along similar lines next year. Preserving the old simply for sake of age is stupid; preserving the old because of historic significance and worth is highly commendable. Here's wishing the Kinnettes every success in such a venture!

51. THE JACK BURGESSES   Valley Vistas column, Brandon Sun, August 10/74

When two marriage partners celebrate their 50th wedding anniversary the occasion is one we should take seriously. Perhaps because today so many marriages flounder long before a half century's come and gone. Perhaps because so often one or both of the partners die along the way. In my own family for example, despite an exhaustive study of its genealogy, I've come across no couple that celebrated its golden wedding anniversary.

But people do from time to time achieve that precious milestone. When two persons, whose parents all helped pioneer this district, reach such milestone this intrigues me especially. A Minnedosa couple that recently celebrated a half century of connubial bliss are May and Jack Burgess.

One of 10 children May grew up in Riverdale district southwest of here where parents Kenneth and Emma (Tuttle) Murray farmed. Her father hailed from Scotland and mother from England. She attended Willow Grove school 10 years, Minnedosa Collegiate and then business college. Living half way between Minnedosa and Rapid City she intimately knew the latter, a "thriving centre" those days. For a while she worked in Minnedosa as stenographer for popular Liberal MLA-cabinet minister-high school principal George Allison Grierson, then in Hamilton Bank (now James Building) which merged with Bank of Commerce.

One of 11 children Jack grew up in Minnedosa where parents Joseph and Edith (Wake) Burgess operated a meat market. Jack's mother also came from England; her father John established a lumber yard in Minnedosa. The 1885 stone Wake Block on Main Street commemorates this pioneer family. Joe Burgess, one of West-Man's most prominent pioneers and long time mayor here, has been the subject of several references in this column. Early recollections of Jack's include particularly the old Main Street bridge with steel framework and overhead warning sign to WALK YOUR HORSES, and deep ruts leading into Minnedosa River just southwest of Toovey's warehouse marking the location of historic Tanner's Crossing.

The first Burgess slaughterhouse stood near where Minnedosa Lake spillway today stands. As youngster Jack's education was repeatedly interrupted by the First World War when help was impossible to get. He recalls vividly riding his pony door-to-door taking meat orders and delivering them by cart next day. Nevertheless he eventually made it to Grade 11 plus a short business course. His main hobby was curling.

May and Jack were married July 16, 1924, by Presbyterian Rev. Hodges in what is now Minnedosa United Church. Two of May's siblings still live in West-Man, Allan Murray in Brandon and Glen here, while four of Jack's call West-Man home--Fred and Frank Burgess of Neepawa and Bill Burgess and Ellen Telford of Minnedosa. Their two children, Ken of Brandon and Jim of Minnedosa, are well known in business, education and civic circles. There are seven grandchildren.

Despite a rather violent hail storm in progress the Burgesses and I discussed two topics of concern to many today--weakening and breakdown of marriage; increase in irresponsible behavior, violence, alcohol and lessening of respect for the rights of others and for the law.

Life in Minnedosa during the first decades of their marriage was quiet and generally pleasant. People trusted each other; one's word was one's bond and no one ever signed notes when owing money. Nothing was ever locked. Granted, Minnedosa was only one third its present size and not a tourist resort. Hostility towards police was virtually unknown. The lone constable Charlie Law was loved and respected by young and old. Jack recalls this worthy lawman's favorite expression when some individual did on occasion kick over the traces of, "I getee, I putee in the cooler tomorrow."

May and Jack Burgess 'went steady' eight years before marriage, my own parents too as long. Yet few of my own generation seemed to; myself a bare 20 months. I often wonder whether my children (will takengoing steady as seriously as did their grandparents (or even parents) before rushing into matrimony. Perhaps this is a factor. Perhaps too, as the Burgesses feel, material things are too easily acquired on credit today and young couples miss most of the experience of starting out with nothing and planning, saving, working together in sort of orderly step-by-step sequence to acquire the necessities of creating a home. Commenting on separation of marriage partners by death Jack cites the case of the six councilors with whom he was long associated--all now dead whereas their wives all still living.

May and Jack Burgess have both played significant roles in developing this town and province. Aside from operating a most popular and successful grocery store, in which he still works regularly with son Jim, Mr. Burgess can point to 20 years of public service in civic affairs as councillor, mayor, hospital board chairman. Significantly, whereas his father chaired the board when Minnedosa's first hospital (Lady Minto) was built, Jack chaired it when our present one came into being. May looks back on 53 years of Rebecca (ladies' equivalent of Oddfellows) service, which included a term as provincial president in 1957-'58. Both have been deeply involved in horticultural activities since 1940--as their beautiful yard and greenhouse amply testify.

52. MINNEDOSA RCMP   Valley Vistas column, Brandon Sun, August 17/74

As I've mentioned before, because of a large highway patrol stationed here plus our own detachment, mounties play a significant role in daily life here. Last year, transfers of Sgt. Horn and Cpl. Kohlman with Cpl. Koetke's leaving the force to settle here as a civilian, with Sgt. Mealing and Corporals Durling and Edwards coming here made news. This year it's been various constables involved in transfers.

I've mentioned Rob Gomes going to Regina as arms instructor for recruits. Since then Paul Currie's gone to The Pas to join Sgt. Horn. As part-time detention centre officer I get to know most of the police well and found Paul most personable. Just before he left he demonstrated the RCMP computer system to me about which we have heard so much lately. When he ran both our names and approximate ages through the magic machine I was astounded (and secretly relieved) to learn within seconds that no Peter Neufeld was wanted anywhere in Canada--while a Paul Currie was. (And I always thought the Pauls made more reliable disciples than the Peters!) Was very glad to hear the RCMP computers, unlike their American counterparts, are not available to every Tom, Dick and Jane who wants access to them--lawyers, probation officers and even credit agencies.

An excellent constable who is leaving us to join the RCMP detective division in Toronto is Dave Gillis. "Smiling Dave" is what the fellows he'd arrested called him in jail. Seldom have I come across a prisoner who disliked Dave for arresting him. Dave Toma's got nothing on this guy. He's been here over four years, and like many who pass through here it seems that just when a community really gets to know and like an individual policeman he gets transferred. Oh well, we of Minnedosa who are blessed with so many good things should not begrudge our Toronto brethern one of our bountiful blessings.

Another constable being transferred is Dave Sparrow. Though he hasn't been with us nearly as long as Gillis he's performed several remarkable feats already nevertheless and will be missed. Treherne highway patrol's where you'll find him, so drive especially carefully next time you're in that area. Four other constables who have been here a while we hope won't be affected by the current rash of transfers are Rick Cole, Geoff Bunckle, Peter Tremblay and Brian Runnalls.
(Shortly after this article was published Cst. Bunckle was transferred and several months later Cpl. Durling.)

53. NORMAN KITTSON   Valley Vistas column, Brandon Sun, August 29/74

In researching the Tanners I came across several references by American genealogists of that remarkable family to a "Norman Ketsou" of Pembina, N.D., who supposedly employed Rev. James Tanner for a time. After months of wondering who this man was I eventually realized that the employer in question undoubtedly was none other than Norman Wolfred Kittson who played a major role in Manitoba, Minnesota and North Dakota commercial life of the 1840-70 era.

Born in 1814 at Chambly, Quebec, a son of George and Nancy (Tucker) Kittson, he was a grandson of the famous explorer-North West Co. trader Alexander Henry the elder's second wife. No doubt his stepgrandfather strongly influenced his decision to go West at 16 and enter the fur trade as apprentice to the American Fur Co. By 1843 he'd become agent for that company at Pembina, having been placed in charge of the valleys of the upper Minnesota River and the Red. He was HBC's main competition in the Red River Valley during that era.

Of the three major oxcart trails linking St. Paul to Pembina, and thence to Pembina Trail (now Pembina Highway) into Fort Garry, one was the Woods Trail (also called Crow Wing or Otter Tail). Countless Manitoba settlers travelled this trail when emigrating from Ontario. Historian Edith Paterson indicates that contrary to general belief that this trail was cut through the forest in 1844 "a letter by early furtrader R.M. Probstfield states that Norman Kittson travelled the trail in the late 1830s." In 1844 he took six carts loaded with $1,200 worth of goods along this trail to St. Paul and returned to Pembina with supplies retailing at 10 times that amount. No doubt some of these goods were purchased by Selkirk Settlers in Fort Garry for he frequently traded there and early historian Alexander Ross lists 1844 as one such trip.

On one of his many trips to Fort Garry, Kittson married a daughter of Narcisse Marion, one of the oldest and still most prominent St. Boniface families. A rather prominent brother-in-law was Roger Marion (1846 - 1920). A daughter, Annie Jane Kittson (later Mrs. Horace Chevrier), is according to Nan Shipley "reputed to have been the proud owner of the first mink coat in Fort Garry." During some of these early fur trading years, a reliable Manitoba source recently verified, he employed James Tanner as freighter-trader. "An astonishing revelation made by one of Lord Selkirk's close friends," writes Shipley, "was the amazing ability of James' father John 'Falcon' Tanner "to unobtrusively take down conversations in shorthand--writing on his fingernails, kept long for this purpose."

In 1854 Kittson withdrew from the fur trade and entered the general supply business for Indian and Metis trade. "Such men as Joe Rolette, Norman Kittson and James McKay," says Shipley, "grew wealthy in the tough but rewarding freighting business along the Pembina Trail in the 1850s and '60s."

Much Manitoba history of 1860s and '70s revolves around riverboat and rail transportation. Norman Kittson's name is synonomous with much of it. At first he quietly built one steamer and barge after another to ply the Red between Fort Garry and St. Paul. Also operating a boat enterprise then was former Canadian James J. Hill of St. Paul who owned such boats as the Selkirk. During the winter of 1871-72 Kittson, Hill and Donald A. (Lord Strathcona) Smith--whose photo depicting the last CPR spike being driven every Canadian's seen--created a steamship monopoly by forming Red River Transportation Co. The first boat, one which transported many settlers to Manitoba, this new corporation built was the small but luxurious Dakota.

Ed Russenholt terms the river freighting monopoly "an incredibly profitable partnership" which "by rate-cutting, political and 'legal' skullduggery they ruin--and take over--competition, then fix rates as they choose. River steamboats operate on leisurely schedules. Vessels tie up every 40 miles, to take on cordwood, collected by local traders. Often passengers go ashore--to hunt, or stroll across short-cuts. The wood-yards become town-sites."

In 1874, says Paterson, a group of St. Paul and Winnipeg citizens formed an opposition line called Merchants International and operated the Manitoba and the Minnesota in an effort to lower freight rates. On May 8, 1875, the Free Press was reporting 11 steamers and tugs (excluding countless flatboats) operating along the Red into Winnipeg. "However, in 1876 the new line was taken over by Kittson's, which again reigned unopposed." During high water these boats frequently plied the Assiniboine as well; to Portage, and often to Brandon and beyond.

In 1877 the railway building boom hit Minnesota and saw Kittson, Smith, Hill and another Canadian George (Lord Mountstephen) Stephen "grab the St. Paul and Pacific Railway--bankrupt, mortgaged, foreclosed, remortgaged--from Dutch bondholders," invest only $300,000 of their own cash to acquire equity of $28,000,000 (much of it at expense of American taxpayers), link it to Pembina and Winnipeg and rename it Great Northern Railway. Kittson died in 1888--a vastly richer and more prominent though less popular man than when he came West more than a half century earlier.

54. DARRELL, FORGOTTEN GIANT OF THE NORTH   Free lance, Canadian Frontier, Fall/74

"There's gold, and it's haunting and haunting; It's luring me on as of old; Yet it isn't the gold that I'm wanting, So much as just finding the gold." Thus Canada's colorful poet Robert Service penned in Dawson City when the frantic Klondike gold rush had become but a trickle. That these immortal lines may well refer to a specific sourdough then living in Dawson whom the poet knew well personally is not only conceivable, but intriguing. The man in question was Hubert Darrell. Like Service, Darrell didn't reach the Klondike until the legendary gold rush of '98 was no longer a stampede. And, like Service, he staked permanent claim to Arctic immortality as did few others. Yet Canadians know virtually nothing of this outstanding pioneer who wrote 10 years of incredible Arctic history--a saga unmatched by any peer of his decade, white or native.

As boy of 15, Hubert, one of seven children of Lily Elizabeth and Charles Darrell of Worthing, Kent, England, dreamt daily of Canada's exotic West for which his 17-year-old brother Charlie had sailed recently. The year was 1890. By the thousand, European settlers were pouring onto the Canadian Prairies. Periodic trips by their father, a life insurance executive, to his company's branch office in Montreal had magnified in the two brothers the spirit for adventure in the New World. Charlie duly arrived at Shoal Lake, Manitoba, on the historic Carleton Trail and obtained employment at the Robert Collis farm while searching for land to buy as most homesteads had already been snapped up and he was but a minor. Within a year Charlie managed a down payment on a picturesque farm in nearby Warleigh district about 10 miles southeast of Birtle and built his log cabin.

Stephen B.W. North, son of William Ivor Wolseley North of Warleigh, who became Hubert's closest friend in Manitoba, told me recently that Hubert's parents "had a tough time making him stay another year in school, so anxious was he to come to the wild west. He left England at 16 and joined his brother. Hubert farmed with his brother until the Klondike Gold Rush, went up north to improve their joint fortunes and help pay for the farm, but undoubtedly the love of wilderness and adventure played an important role."

Dr. Margaret Dudley of Winnipeg, a retired teacher and university professor whose older sister Agnes Dudley was engaged to Hubert, and whose father was then postmaster at Warleigh, told me, "As a child I liked both the Darrells and can vaguely recall what Hubert looked like--but very vaguely. I was six when Hubert courted Agnes. He wanted her to go North with him."

Arriving at Great Slave Lake in fall of 1897, with winter rapidly closing in, Hubert decided to prospect in that area for a while before continuing on to Yukon. March 8, 1899 found him still there. Writing his mother from Fort Resolution (original letters owned by Scott Polar Research and microfilm by Glenbow-Alberta Institute) he told of much red granite there, but no gold. Five months later he wrote his father, "Not a trace of gold on Great Slave Lake. Stopped there this summer in order to prospect around the east shore; 250 men from Mackenzie were there prospecting. Lots of lead and copper and white iron. A friend, Mr. Potts of Chicago, was fooled with 'salted gold'."

A chance meeting with explorer David T. Hanbury, who brought him a letter from England, dramatically altered Darrell's destiny in the Arctic--which, aside from a lengthy winter muskox hunt deep into the Barrens with 25 Yellowknife Indians under Chief Yinto, had hitherto been mostly cold, often hungry, and comparatively uneventful. In July of 1901 he agreed to guide Hanbury's second fact-finding expedition into the Arctic; a project which lasted 16 months, spanned much of the North, and uncovered invaluable data.

Characteristically, Hubert made light of this immense undertaking in letters to parents who worried readily. Always, during those long months, he'd been--secretly--looking for gold. Hanbury wrote a long detailed book with numerous photos called SPORT AND TRAVEL IN THE NORTHLAND OF CANADA, published in 1904 by Macmillan of New York and London. World-famous Arctic explorer Vilhjalmur Stefansson, who knew Darrell well, paid high tribute to the Hanbury-Darrell expedition.

Once during the expedition, Stephen North said, "Hubert left the party and climbed a ridge of hills and noted a river on the far side. Returning, he mentioned this fact to the explorer and Hanbury subsequently named the discovery after himself. Other members of the party were unanimous that it should have been the Darrell River."

Renowned Arctic explorer Roald Amundsen, who also knew Darrell well, said of him, "With a crew of men like that, I could go to the moon. He would certainly have been a member of that (South Pole) expedition had not fate intervened. One of the finest men of the northern breed that it has ever been my good fortune to meet."

Stefansson commended a later, lone exploration trip by Darrell across the Endicott Mountains as a vastly greater achievement than one performed by Amundsen and acclaimed by the world. In a letter to Hubert's fiancee Agnes Dudley, Sept. 30, 1912, (original owned by Dartmouth College) he exclaimed, "Darrell had to his credit more real achievement than many who are famous for their work in the North. It does the world good to know about such men, men who quietly and unostentatiously do remarkable things." In his book MY LIFE WITH THE ESKIMO he devoted four pages to extolling Darrell's Arctic exploits.

On Banks Island in 1917 Stefansson discovered Sir Robert McLure's cache recording that explorer's April, 1851 illfated North West Passage voyage--at a location predicted by Darrell to his sister Kathleen on September 8, 1908, in which he eagerly described plans for locating the cache--plans which fate rudely cut short.

In letters to his parents, Darrell praised the elderly Hanbury's abilities for coping with harsh Arctic conditions. "I want to see Carnegie," he wrote from Fort Resolution upon returning from the mission after hearing that the Frances Allyn--which carried most of the expedition's scientific specimens--had just sunk in Hudson Bay, (according to New Bedford Whaling Museum curator Philip F. Purrington the "Schooner Francis Allyn, Captain Santos, burned at sea near Cape Fullerton July 15, 1902. A Scotch steamer Active was in the vicinity bringing the shipwrecked men to Era.")"about the copper in the North as no one yet saw or knew where they were. Geologists have bothered their heads for the last 125 years and have never yet found the copper and it has been left to a mere traveller to discover it. The copper deposits are most valuable, of wonderful richness. I've shown samples to a man from Lake Superior, a shrewd man who says they're better than any he's seen in Lower Canada. If any party sets out to seek copper without me I shall go right back there and stake it before them. I have no intention of letting a good thing slip out of my hand. You don't need to be told copper is not as valuable now as it will be in the future." Neither he nor Hanbury lived to stake claims to these copper deposits that later made men rich. Hanbury died in San Francisco in 1910; Darrell mysteriously disappeared later the same year in Anderson River country on a gold prospecting-exploration trip.

In 1904 Hubert returned to Warleigh to farm while Charlie visited family in England. "My father and Hubert hit it off very well from the start," recalled Mr. North. "On Hubert's last visit south they spent most of autumn and winter together on Charlie's place. There was a heavy crop that year and they stooked it together, had a thoroughly enjoyable time. He loved the Arctic; as so many do who've once lived there. He left shortly before his brother's return and actually they never met again, which was a source of great distress for Charlie."

Dr. Dudley added, "He came back once, and wanted my sister to go back North with him, but she was teaching school at that time and thought they should wait until Hubert had a home, and a much less precarious mode of existence." Wrote Darrell to his parents: "I've had many good times on that farm and often regret leaving it; but what's one to do if there's no profit? I enjoyed putting the crop in immensely; sowed in depth according to moisture and the result was justified. I was my own boss and could go out in the field just when I saw fit." He then shifted operations to northwestern Mackenzie, northern Yukon and eastern Alaska--places like Fort McPherson, Arctic Red River, Fort Yukon, Dawson, Peel River, Fort Good Hope, Rampart House, Herschel Island serving as home base at different times.

For several years Darrell's search for the elusive pot of gold took a back seat to two other historic Arctic events; both revolving around American whaling fleets which, since the mid-1890s, had been wintering in the Bailey-Herschel islands region of Beaufort Sea.

When funds ran low Darrell sometimes did odd jobs at HBC posts--operating these in absence of managers, accompanying traders on fur-buying excursions, and carrying mail to outlying posts. It was as a mail carrier that Amundsen first met him in February, 1906, his "face black with smoke accompanied not even by a dog, and dragging his toboggan behind him", loaded with mail from Fort McPherson for posts in northwestern Yukon and across Richardson Mountains--"hundreds of miles from the nearest human being, cheerfully trudging through the Arctic winter across an unblazed wilderness."

Added Stefansson: "To travel alone without dogs is an unheard of thing even among Eskimo." When Darrell contracted to bring the beleagured whaling fleet their mail some ships had already been frozen in shifting Arctic ice for three years, with supplies running dangerously low and the lives of 500 men depending upon word being brought out in time to summon a relief ship. With customary nonchalance, Darrell embarked upon the hazardous venture, and joked about it afterward to his parents.

John A. Cook, American whaler and author of THAR SHE BLOWS, then in charge of the ship Bowhead, recounted Darrell's dead-on-his-feet April 22, 1906 arrival. Stefansson has recorded the finish of that amazing feat: "Although he travelled alone he had no adventures and no mishaps (adventures and mishaps seldom happen to a competent man), and when he arrived on the Yukon the telegraph dispatches recorded the simple fact that mail had arrived from the imprisoned whalers in the Beaufort Sea, and not a word of who had brought it or how it had been brought." Saving the lives of 500 fellowmen was one of Darrell's routine all-in-the-day's-work achievements!

That spring, Darrell was asked to join the Leffingwell-Mikkelsen expedition aboard the Duchess of Bedford. He refused, confiding to his parents that the main reasons against joining were the exceptionally low salary and the ship being without motor power, predicted failure. Stefansson, slated as ethnologist for the same mission, also recognized the latter drawback in negotiating Arctic ice and agreed instead to join the vessel at Herschel Island should she get there. She didn't! Darrell, exploring alone on foot in the vicinity, was the first to bring news of the expedition's failure to the outside world.

The Mackenzie-Yukon RNWMP quickly recognized Darrell's unique talents and vied for his services. In short order he became in frontier Arctic Canada what the invaluable Metis guide Jerry Potts had been to Mounties in frontier southwestern Canada three decades before.

In 1903-04, Sgt. Francis Fitzgerald and Cst. Sutherland had brought law and order to Herschel Island harbor where many whalers now wintered annually and had for a decade created havoc among Cogmollick and Nunamiut Eskimo by bootlegging whiskey and seducing wives. The real problem confronting Mounties then wasn't furnishing isolated outposts like Herschel with supplies, for this was readily accomplished in summer by ship or riverboat. In that pre-wireless era, the major obstacle was the developing of an adequate overland communication and mail system between Dawson or Fort McPherson and outlying detachments, hundreds of miles away. As a special constable who quickly became their best guide, this was where Darrell fitted in.

Postponing plans to prospect for gold in Alaska, Darrell guided Corporal Haylow from Fort McPherson to gale-blasted Herschel Island, across 300 miles of treeless and trackless Arctic wilderness. Commenting on the harrowing experience to his father upon return he concluded with, "Cpl. Haylow is a most excellent man and if any of the other police had gone in place of Haylow there would, I really believe, have been a funeral with no service or mourners." Added Stefansson, "He was about as new to that country as the policemen were, but still he was a competent guide, for he never lost his head!" RCMP records of that period agree.

Writing his father from Dawson on June 17, 1908, Darrell admitted that he almost did make that long-dreamed-of gold strike. "Last spring I met a miner called Fred Smith, an Englishman. He was interested in what I had to tell him; especially as I was able to show him rock I had taken out the year before. This spring he went out and struck it rich."

Dawson, he found to be exceedingly dull and disease-ridden; he himself was confined to the Good Samaritan Hospital. Worse, everyone was broke. "A number of men have received help from the government and have shipped out of the country because there was no work for them. The fellows had no money to buy grub so the government sent them out on the road to work so many days and receive a free ticket to the outside."

That winter saw Darrell guide a five-man police patrol 500 miles from Dawson to Fort McPherson, and 500 back—and repeat this the following winter. In the spring of 1910, he guided his last patrol when Minister of Interior and Superintendent General of Indian Affairs Frank Oliver toured the Yukon. That December, Hubert Darrell vanished.

Francis Fitzgerald (then Inspector) with Constables Carter, Kinney and Taylor, attempted the Dawson-McPherson run without Darrell; all perished from extreme cold, blizzards and starvation. Ironically, wrote Darrell's trader friend Joseph Jacquot (with whom he'd prospected until September 21 and was to meet at a pre-arranged spot after freeze-up) in the Dawson News of July 6, 1911, had his companion not vanished, the four policemen would have lived, for the partners planned to follow the identical route to Dawson and would have reached the police before death occurred. Stunned, Canadians mourned the Mountie tragedy—a tragedy which completely overshadowed Hubert Darrell's mysterious disappearance.

55. CANADIANS SAVE BUFFALO   Free lance article, Western Producer, Nov. 7/74

Several recent magazine articles have dealt with saving our North American bison from extinction. The impression is left that virtually alone a small handful of Americans conducted this important conservation project, with Canadians playing but a negligible role. As former high school biology teacher in Manitoba centres like Winnipeg, Brandon, Minnedosa, Portage la Prairie, who frequently came face-to-face with this question in lessons and class discussions, I strongly resent the insinuation. That magazines and writers involved often are Canadian simply adds insult to injury. Some journalists haven't been doing their homework.

At least 11 Canadians, mostly Manitobans, played highly significant roles in saving the plains bison from extermination. And even of the half dozen Americans usually credited with saving the bison, one is referred to by writers of his era as a "French Canadian"; a second was an American Indian living in Canada. Let's keep the record straight.

In 1870-71 two young brothers, William F. and Charles V. Alloway, came to Winnipeg as privates in the Wolseley expedition from Hamilton where their father was a captain in the Queen's Own Rifles. Charlie, the more sporting one, became a keen hunter and horseman. Frequently he roamed the Prairies trading and hunting with Metis and Indians.

Wild West magazine tells of one such trip in Qu'Appelle Valley where his party was warned by Indians to move camp, which minutes later was plowed to pulp by a "brown river of buffalo" while "for 24 hours the men watched the steadily loping herd go by at the rate of about 10 a second". Alloway said that he believed that more than a million buffalo passed by in that time.

Charlie, who took over the amateur veterinary practice William started and added a trading post, saw the handwriting on his wall in 1873 when he bought over 21,000 buffalo hides at $3-$4 each from a single Indian brigade and turned his attention instead to trying to stop the slaughter of these fine animals.

Nan Shipley rightly calls James McKay "Manitoba's most outstanding citizen." Val Werier describes him as "a man of great girth and reputation, a buffalo hunter who weighed 350 pounds and was first speaker of the House"; Edith Paterson as "a noted trader and hunter."

In spring of 1873 Alloway and McKay travelled west to capture buffalo calves. Taking a domestic cow with them to serve as foster mother they joined a Metis brigade and spent the whole summer capturing three young calves in Prince Albert region and bringing them to Winnipeg. Next spring the two men captured three more but one died. One writer credits John McKay, James' brother, with those two trips indicating John turned his share in the five calves over to his brother. Colonel Bedson's son, interviewed many years later agrees. Charlie himself in about 1925 stated it was James.

The bison calves were placed in an enclosure near James McKay's home in Silver Heights where Deer Lodge hospital now stands. By 1878 the herd had grown to 13. James died in 1879 and Charlie sold the animals to Bedson for $1000 because he was joining William--founder of Winnipeg Foundation--in banking, Alloway and Champion.

Long after Charlie Alloway's death his widow, Maude, told Manitoba's Historical and Scientific Society of her husband leading a third bison-capturing expedition. In late winter of 1883 the party set out. Aside from "capture of a number of fine specimens made with assistance of several Indian buffalo hunters" in the Battle River region about 100 miles from Edmonton, their greatest problem occurred crossing the Minnedosa (then Little Saskatchewan) River between Minnedosa and Rapid City.

These calves too were corralled in the recently-vacated 30-acre Deer Lodge pasture and "as with the other herds, these few multiplied to quite large proportions. A number of the buffalo in Assiniboine Park today are the progeny of this herd." At least three calves from that expedition seem to have been acquired by Howard Eaton.

Maude Alloway concludes her account with, "It has been said that to Charlie Alloway should go the credit for the preservation of the buffalo in Manitoba for if it had not been for his foresight years ago the American bison would be but a misty vision." I concur wholeheartedly.

Like the Alloways, Samuel Lawrence Bedson came West with Wolseley to quell the Riel Resistance. Born the son of a Montreal army officer in 1849, Colonel Bedson was in charge of Lower Fort Garry. When the federal government established a penitentiary-mental hospital there in 1871 he became its first warden. Later he selected the Stony Mountain site for a new prison and upon its completion in 1877 continued in charge.

A popular sportsman always surrounded by friends and full of life, Sam proved a kindly but just warden. A lover of wildlife, he kept a menagerie of bears, badgers, wolves, deer, moose, geese and other game birds on his farm nearby.

The same morning the 13 Alloway-McKay bison were moved to Stony Mountain, one cow had a calf. That night the herd escaped and returned to Silver Heights tramping through deep snow. The following day they were herded back to the prison--a total of 62 miles for the newborn calf.

Under Bedson's tender care the bison multiplied rapidly totalling 125 by 1888. In 1928 the colonel's son, K.C. Bedson, told a reporter he had as young boy 40 years previous helped herd his father's bison on the prairie near Stony Mountain, the herd never totalling more than 94 at any one time.

The apparent contradiction is explained by the fact that a few cattalo (bison-domestic cattle crosses) were involved and that the herd was disposed of over a period of years during which young ones were still being born.

By 1888 the settler influx forced Bedson to conclude it was no longer practical to keep his bison. About six were donated to New York and London zoos. At least 27 were given to Donald A. Smith (later Lord Strathcona) to repay a loan.

The bulk of Sam Bedson's remaining herd--listed as high as 98 by some researchers and low as 56 by others--was eventually sold to C.J. (Buffalo) Jones, manager of Garden City (Kansas) Buffalo company. Jones was no conservationist, had hunted with Teddy Roosevelt in Africa and dreamed of establishing a big game preserve for hunters to hunt bison for a fat fee.

In November of 1889 when Jones was in Winnipeg negotiating details of the transaction, he had a standing offer of $60 each for all hides he could produce, $.50 per pound for meat to restaurants in big American cities and a further $100-$500 per head for trophies. Also he was besieged with telegrams from persons in Minnesota and the Dakotas anxious to purchase the herd at $500-$1000 per head.

The sale was delayed briefly when a group of Winnipegers tried to form a company to buy the bison to propogate them commercially. Two years later Bedson retired, accepted a position on the Alaska Boundary Commission but died suddenly in Ottawa.

Sir Donald Smith donated all but five of his buffalo to the Canadian government who installed them at Banff National Park where they flourished under Superintendent Douglas' care. Winnipeg's street railway company purchased the five from Smith and a further three from Howard Eaton, donating them to Assiniboine Zoo.

Much has been written of the role played in preserving the plains bison by the Montana Pend d'Oreille Indian, Sam Walking Coyote (known also as Sam Weld). Some writers hail him as a devoted conservationist. Others laud his action as a "ray of light in all the ruthless killing" of these noble beasts. Most have him capturing bison calves in Montana. Again it's high time the record be set straight.

We can thank the Historical Society of Montana where George Coder of Ohio State University recently conducted in-depth studies on buffalo history for separating fact from fiction here. For a detailed account of who caught Sam's bison where and why he points to a story in the Rocky Mountain Husbandman of November, 1923, as most accurate.

It all began in 1873 at a Piegan camp on Montana's Milk River where lived Sam Walking Coyote "who had a sharp tongue, a swift temper and son-in-law" (whose name historians to date have failed to uncover) who "cheated his wife's irascible father in a horse swap" arousing Sam's ire.

Life quickly became too hot around camp that winter for the young horse-trader because "every time the old man thought about him he reached for something to throw; and his aim was good." Dixon Craig of Edmonton Journal, who's also done good bison research, calls Sam "a renegade Indian."

The young Pend d'Oreille left his father and mother-in-law and bride, headed north into Saskatchewan where he became an honest hunter of what remained of the southern half of the great bison herd. One day he was lucky enough to capture two calves, a bull and a heifer. A Canadian Press story datelined Wainwright, Alta., gives the number as four, two bulls and two heifers.

Because he missed his young wife considerably he decided perhaps her cantankerous father might forgive him if he brought the calves as a gift. He herded his peace offering across the Canada-US border into Montana where his father-in-law eagerly accepted it. Presumably the young brave lived happily ever after with his loved one.

Sam trailed his calves to the Flathead reservation and by 1884 had 13 bison on his range. Old age and difficulty in financing his wards caused him to sell.

Charles A. Allard is frequently called a "French Canadian". His father was a white man, mother an Oregon Indian, wife a daughter of Louis Brown--first settler of Frenchtown, Montana. Allard and his Mexican-Blackfoot friend and ranching partner Michel Pablo decided to buy Sam's herd; or at least 10 of the 13 animals. Gene Telpner describes the transaction.

Walking Coyote refused to accept a "white man's cheque" so the two ranchers had to dig up $2500 cash. As the trio counted out the money, dividing it into 25 piles, a mink ran by. "With the instinct of the hunter strong in their spirits, they immediately gave chase--forgetting temporarily all about the buffalo herd and the large sum of money left lying on the ground." Fortunately it was still there upon their return.

A 1948 item in the Canadian Cattleman indicates that following the sale Walking Coyote "immediately hit for town and after a few weeks of city life was found dead under Missoula Bridge."

By 1893 the bison herd on the Allard-Pablo ranch on Pend d' Oreille reserve near St. Ignatius Mission had increased to 100. Meanwhile, Buffalo Jones' grandiose dream faded when intense Texas heat and ticks killed off most of his herd, selling the remnant of 35 (one source says 26) to Allard and Pablo in 1893. Charles died in 1896 and many bison were sold to eastern zoos. Despite this the herd totalled 250 in 1899.

In 1899 the owners of the buffalo herd, most of which originated from calves captured in Canada, were Charles Allard Jr. and brother Joseph, Michel Pablo and Andrew Stinger. By 1906 it numbered almost 800 and was then the main herd of plains buffalo in North America, the only other one of note being Canada's Banff herd.

Four Canadians, two of them Manitobans, played major roles in returning the Montana bison herd to Canada: Norman Luxton, son of famous journalist (Toronto Globe, Winnipeg Free Press, Nor'Wester) W.F. Luxton, was the progressive publisher of Crag and Canyon Weekly in Banff; Alex Ayotte, a huge man weighing 240 pounds, had served with Canada's department of immigration in Montana for years and now lived in St. Jean, Manitoba; Hon. Frank Oliver, former journalist of Toronto Globe and Mail and of Winnipeg Free Press and founder of Alberta's first newspaper—Edmonton Bulletin—was minister of interior, married to Harriet Dunlop of Prairie Grove, Man., and Howard Douglas who was superintendent of Banff National Park for a long time.

To Luxton, a close friend of Oliver's, goes the credit of convincing his politician friend the Allard-Pablo buffalo herd should be purchased by Canada and re-established here.

To Oliver goes credit for quick action in 1906 in persuading Parliament that Luxton's idea had merit and upon receiving approval setting necessary wheels in motion to advance what's often been described as "the greatest animal comeback in the history of the world."

Ayotte (with a little assistance from Howard Eaton) negotiated the purchase of about 716 animals at $245 each, supervised three hazardous roundups and drives to Canada which took several years and continued to supervise five annual roundups in Alberta.

To Douglas fell the immense task of making the whole project succeed, helping also to disperse bison to Canadian zoos and other parks—like Riding Mountain National Park in Manitoba where for years the second largest captive herd in existence has been proving a popular tourist attraction.

An interesting sequel to the bison conservation project was research conducted from 1894 to 1914 by Mossom Boyd, Big Island Stock Farm at Bobcaygeon, Ont. in crossing plains bison with domestic cattle. In 1915 his bison and cattalo were also purchased by the Canadian government, taken to Wainwright, with the cattalo project later transferred to Manyberries were it continued until 1964.

Buffalo ranching today is becoming increasinly popular; as are cattle-bison crossing projects by individual ranchers (e.g. Beefalo). In recent years buffalo have multiplied to the extent that even limited hunting seasons have become necessary to contain the rapidly-expanding herds.

(Our fine arts daughter Verna illustrated this article with sketches, the captions for which read: 'As Manitobans played the greatest role in conserving the buffalo it is most fitting their province's emblem is one.' 'Manitoba Dragoons with symbol of buffalo charging on prairie, became world-famous in Canada's Northwest Rebellion, Boer War, France and Flanders in 1914-18 and France-Normandy-Northwest Europe in 1939-45.' 'Our Mounties, who a century ago selected a buffalo as their symbol, have become the world's best known police force.')

56. TREATY FOUR CENTENNIAL   Free lance article, Birtle Eye-Witness, Dec. 4-11-18/74

With numerous centennials we've been celebrating since our national one of 1967 it's easy to skip one. In 1971 the signing of Treaties One and Two was commemorated with much ceromony at Lower Fort Garry. Yet the centennial of the September 15, 1874 signing of Treaty Four, a treaty involving more land than the first two treaties combined, has created hardly a ripple in this province.

Granted, Treaty Four involved Saskatchewanians much more than it did Manitobans. Nonetheless, interesting bits of Manitoba history revolve around this treaty.

Indian names, especially those of chieftans, were infinitely more expressive and interesting than those of Caucasians. Thirteen Saulteaux (called Ojibway in Ontario and Chippewa in America), Assiniboine (Stony) and Cree chiefs signed this historic document at Qu'Appelle Lakes that day as representatives of their respective bands. They were: Ka-Ki-shi-way (Loud Voice), Wa-pii-moose-too-sus (White Calf) and Cha-ca-chas of Qu'Appelle River; Kea-we-zauce (Little Boy) and Pis-qua (The Plain) of Leech Lake; Ka-kee-na-wup (One That Sits Like an Eagle) of Upper Qu'Appelle Lakes; Kus-kee-tew-mus-coo-musqua (Little Black Bear) of Cypress Hills; Ka-ne-on-us-ka-tew (One That Walks on Four Claws) of Little Touchwood Hills; Can-ah-ha-cha-pew (Making Ready the Bow) and Kii-si-caw-ah-chuck (Day Star) from south of the South Saskatchewan River; Ka-wa-ca-toose (Poor Man) of Touchwood Hills and Qu'Appelle Lakes; Ka-kii-wis-ta-haw (He That Flies Around) from near Cypress Hills; Mee-may (The Pigeon) or Gabriel Cote, of Fort Pelly area.

Some Canadian officials involved in negotiations and the signing were: Manitoba Lt.-Gov. Alexander Morris, Canadian Minister of Interior David Laird, Indian Commissioner William J. Christie, Lt. Col. W. Osborne Smith and Capt. A. McDonald, as well as 19 other white and native civilian and military witnesses. Two signatories were women: Helen H. McLean and Flora Garrioch.

The original negotiations and signing of this treaty triggered acceptance of the same agreement by 14 other bands. Two Manitoba bands in the St. Lazare-Binscarth area led by Chiefs Wa-wa-se-ca-pow (The Man Proud of Standing Upright) and Ota-ma-koo-ewin (The Man Who Stands on the Earth) signed six days later at Fort Ellice. Two of several witnesses were Archibald and Ellen McDonald, Mr McDonald being the HBC's last chief factor at Fort Ellice. A descendant, Ed McDonald, whom I interviewed recently, still farms in that area.

Canada Archives documents reveal that one band at least wasn't overjoyed with provisions of the treaty. A lengthy letter to the Interior minister by Lt. Gov. Morris from Government House in Fort Garry on October 23, 1875, explains. It seems that Chief Wa-wa-se-ca-pow felt annuities per head should be increased from $5 to $12, a store for the sale of goods be established on his reserve by the government, that his band receive an extra supply of provisions for the coming winter, that cattle be given to them immediately for they'd already cut hay for feed. An experienced diplomat, Morris managed to satisfy The Man Proud of Standing Upright without committing his government to anything drastic by granting him "an order on the Honorable James McKay, for a small quantity of the surplus stock of provisions, which remain from those provided for Treaty No. 5 and he left expressing himself satisfied with his interview."

Chief Wa-wa-se-ca-pow's people settled on Silver Creek Reserve No. 63 on the Assiniboine River south of Binscarth. However, most band members were unhappy with the location. Some withdrew from treaty entirely, others formed a new band at Valley River between Grandview and Roblin, still there today. On January 14, 1898, the abandoned portions of Silver Creek were thrown open to settlement with the stipulation that any treaty families remaining on this reserve could do so. The only resident members left were John Tanner's family of Gambler band. This tiny 860 acre reserve, now called Gambler, is still farmed by Tanners today--several of whom I know well. Much of Silver Creek developed into the Metis settlement of Madeline.

Chief John Tanner's relatives had played major roles in Manitoba history. His grandfather, John 'Falcon' Tanner, was the white Baptist minister's son captured by Indians with whom he lived 30 years and about whom much has been written. He's noted for achievements like helping Lord Selkirk negotiate treaties necessary to permit establishing the Selkirk Settlement and to recapture Forts Daer (Pembina) and Douglas (Winnipeg) from the Northwest Co. during the 'Pemmican War', with Rev. Dr. Edwin James translating the Bible into Saulteaux. Chief John Tanner's uncle, Rev. James Tanner, had been a popular Metis Presbyterian missionary in the Pembina, Winnipeg, Portage la Prairie region between 1850 and 1870, murdered between Winnipeg and Portage during the aftermath of the Riel Resistance--upon which he'd exerted a powerful influence to prevent its becoming a major conflagration. John's father, Picheito (abbreviated or nick-name) Tanner, had been a major Saulteaux chief in the Portage-White Horse Plains-Delta region, had generated most of the native hostility against the Medaywakanton, Wahpaykootay and Santee Sioux refugees who fled to Manitoba after the Minnesota uprising, had died in retirement with Chief Wa-wa-se-ca-pow's people in the early or mid 1870s. John's cousin, John Tanner, had founded Tanner's Crossing, now Minnedosa.

On September 8, 1875, Christie concluded negotiations at Fort Ellice with Chief

Chee-cuck of Qu'Appelle Lakes, one witness again being McDonald. The next day Chiefs Okanes (Bone), Wah-pee-mak-wa (The White Bear), Payepot, Le Croup de Pheasant, Kee-si-koo-we-nin of Qu'Appelle Lakes, Duck and Riding Mountains area also signed, chief factor McDonald again witnessing.

Of these bands many members located on two reserves, one in the Clear Lake-Lake Audy area of what's now Riding Mountain National Park and the other between the Turtle and Valley rivers on Lake Dauphin. Both reserves had already been in existence since Treaties One and Two and both are gone now. At about the same time, Chief Kee-si-koo-we-nin, who'd been in charge of the Lake Dauphin reserve previously, exchanged it for one in Elphinstone area south of the park—named Keeseekoowenin in his honor and still there today.

This chief, whose descendants use the name Burns, had succeeded famous old Chief Mekis (The Eagle) who had signed Treaty Two on August 21, 1871 (one source claims he signed on Mekis' behalf as the latter had just died). Three of his children became involved, directly or indirectly, in a famous most fascinating venture whose 75th anniversary was celebrated last year—the Klondike Gold Rush. Harriet Burns married the prominent historical figure, Glenlyon Archibald Campbell, who as a Boulton Scout had commanded attention by becoming the only soldier promoted to captain during the 1885 Rebellion and later by having ridden a full grown bull moose to exhaustian in the Riding Mountains for fun, with brothers-in-law David Burns and Walter Scott, made national headlines by completing a two year expedition to deliver horses and guide prospectors via a new route through northern Alberta to the Klondike gold fields. Later an MLA and MP, Glen recruited both the 78th and 107th battalions during the First World War, died as Lt.-Col. on active duty in France where he is buried. Harriet had predeceased him May 17, 1910. (Some researchers refer to 'Bone' as the original source of the name 'Burns', suggesting a relationship with Chief O-kanes rather than Chief Kee-si-koo-we-nin). Burns, Campbell, Scott descendants continue to play major roles in Manitoba.

I could be completely off base but I have a strong hunch that Chief Croup de Pheasant, Chief Picheito Tanner and Chief Na-ha-wa-nanan (who signed Treaty One on August 3, 1871) are really one and the same person. Involved are two languages, all referring to virtually the same thing. Picheito moved west shortly after the signing of Treaty One and could have been involved in the signing of two treaties; Yellow Quill was, Kee-si-koo-we-nin may well have been. Further, Picheito's name as youngster was Little Pheasant.

Of numerous reserves established in the late 1800s, perhaps most Manitobans know best one that disappeared 44 years ago—Okanesse in Riding Mountain Park, named after Chief Okanes. Located near a highly popular tourist resort, Okanesse Cemetery reminds people annually visiting the buffalo compound that "This cemetery is the remnant of a once active Indian village. It is named Okanesse, an Indian family name meaning Bone in English. Buried here are 44 people. Is it too late to preserve their ancient skills, customs, and legends?" One of the more recent graves has a headstone reading: "Michel, son of Mr. and Mrs. G. Bone, died June 1, 1915, 22 years old." When the park was created in 1930, the band relocated to Keeseekoowenin reserve.

On January 21, 1876, Chiefs Kii-shi-konse and Cu-tuk-ee-ka-kan of Swan Lake in Lake Winnipegosis-Porcupine Provincial Forest area entered the treaty, Archibald McDonald again acting as one witness. To accomodate their people, five reserves were established in that area. On August 4 of the same year Chiefs Oo-za-wee-koo-quin-ape (Yellow Quill, also spelled Oo-za-we-kwun), Kenisten (The Cree) and Ne-pin-awa (Summer Fur) brought their bands under that treaty at Fort Pelly, west of Duck Mountain Provincial Park just inside Saskatchewan. Last bands to accept the treaty were Assiniboins, who'd originally lived in West-Man south of the Assiniboine River in Brandon, Souris, Deloraine, Boissevain, Killarney, Wawanesa region and later migrated westward when the Saulteaux, Sioux and whites moved into their territory. At Fort Walsh, Te-pee Hoska (Long Lodge), Throne That Catches The Coat and Nich-a-ur-taka (Poor Man) signed for their people while NWMP Inspector J.W. Walsh and Sub Inspector John H. McIllree represented the Canadian government. McIllree had been one of three senior Mountie officers in charge of policing West-Man when the force was created three years earlier.

The eastern boundary of Treaty Four coincided exactly with the western boundary of Treaty Two. Commemorating the memory of one native signatory, Yellow Quill, is the current unique project operating in the former Rivers RCAF base called Oo-ze-we-kwun. In sharp contrast to the agriculturally oriented treaty, it trains native people to fit into a rapidly urbanizing industry oriented society. Powder, shot, ball and twine up to $750 annually per band; two hoes, a scythe and axe plus seed wheat, barley, oats and potatoes for each family that farmed; a plow and two harrows for every ten such families; a yoke of oxen, one bull and four cows, chest of carpentry tools, various saws and augers, files and grindstone per farming band were some such treaty provisions. Major West-Man towns and villages within the actual treaty boundaries are Swan River, St. Lazare, Roblin, Minitonas, Birch River, Benito, Bowsman, Mafeking, Pelican Rapids.

The excellent new book A VIEW OF THE BIRDTAIL by Marion Abra, dealing with the history of Birtle municipality, tells of the tragic tale of one band whose chief signed Treaty Four. Dealing with the severe winter of 1879 she writes: "Fifteen families of starving Indians were brought to Fort Ellice (where St. Lazare is now) by a relief party sent out after White Bear made his way there. They were cared for, then pitched their tents in the valley. In the spring they contracted a fatal disease--perhaps small pox--and all died except the stalwart White Bear. Spring floods swept away the bodies, and the tribe vanished."

As indicated, not all the reserves established under Treaty Four were located within the precise bounds described by this document nor were all the bands party to the treaty living solely within its boundaries then. Nor were all reserves established a century ago related to Treaty Four. In fact, four major Manitoba reserves provided for in 1873 and created soon after didn't involve any treaty at all for they concerned American Sioux refugees. These are: Birdtail Creek near Miniota; Sioux Valley near Oak River; Oak Lake near Oak Lake; and Long Plain Sioux near Portage la Prairie. It would seem that these Manitobans too are due recognition on making this province their home a century ago.

57. TREATMENT OF COSSACKS   Free lance article, Winnipeg Tribune, January 11/75

With deep consternation I read the Tribune's series of articles based on Lord Nicholas Bethell's recent book THE LAST SECRET. If we who fought as Allies in the Second World War have anything comparable to Nazi Germany's 'Final Jewish Solution' for which to answer, this treatment of the Cossack soldiers and their families must rank in that category.

That Winston Churchill and Franklin D. Roosevelt at Yalta would secretly agree to turn over to Russia--by force if necessary--all Soviet citizens who fell into Allied hands in the closing days of the Second World War is incomprehensible. That Churchill and Eisenhower tried at least to differentiate between Cossacks who had fought against the Allies (in this case, strictly Russia) and those who hadn't is of slight solace. That Allied commanders like Lt.-Gen. Charles Keightly and Brig. Geoffrey Musson placed their own interpretations on the Yalta agreement to include many thousands of Cossacks who had left Russia a full quarter century earlier is most reprehensible. (Since this article was published I learned this brutal act was but a small part of a vastly larger one--the forced return to Russia of some two million anti-Communist Russian citizens who'd fled to the West, including many Mennonites))

No doubt THE LAST SECRET has shocked many Canadians. Undoubtedly it nay shock even deeper if our action as Allies is placed in true perspective. This was not simply 'just another war atrocity' we can shrug off with a sympathetic comment or two. Of the 35,000 Cossacks returned to Russia (those who didn't commit suicide first or were shot trying to escape) to what we well knew was certain death for most, and brutal slave labor camps in Siberia for the rest, many had been our own comrades-in-arms before.

The Cossacks were pre-Communist Russia's best soldiers. During the First World War many Russian soldiers who fought side-by-side with British, American and Canadian soldiers against Germany were Cossacks. In short, had they emigrated to Britain, the US or Canada they would have been welcomed with open arms as Legion members. And Legion color parties would have attended their funerals, Legion crosses today mark their graves.

Unbelievable? Not really. Though I don't know personally of Cossack soldiers having become such Legion members (no doubt there were some), I do know of Mennonite soldiers who fought for Russia in the First World War being granted this consideration here. One such soldier, who later lived in the village of Whitewater in southwestern Manitoba near where I grew up, Jacob Fast, was honored by Boissevain's Legion color party upon his death and a Legion cross today marks his grave in Boissevain Cemetery. First World War veterans especially must sorrow over the tragedy of their Cossack comrades.

No doubt many Manitobans of Mennonite descent are particularly horrified to learn of this revolting treatment of Cossack soldiers and their families by some of our own Allied commanders. Being of such descent myself, as my parents and relatives grew up in the Cossack (Don and Dnieper rivers) region of Russia which they left at similar time as did most Cossacks, I too feel deep revulsion. A favorite uncle, Cornelius Neufeld (deceased) of Killarney district, fought shoulder-to-shoulder (as did many other Mennonites) with Cossacks as 'White' soldier in the Russian Civil War.

Granted, Cossacks were more military-oriented than most ethnic groups, Mennonites somewhat less. Despite this, some 50% of Canadian Mennonite youths enlisted and fought as Allied soldiers in the last war; and of the remainder a large number served in non-combat military units like Medical corps.

One of Manitoba's most well-known war heroes came from Boissevain district, the older brother of a close friend those years and now brother-in-law; Pete Engbrecht shot down some eight German planes, served in NATO longer than any other Canadian. Recently retired he lives in Beausejour. That these particular Legionaires must feel deep disgust for Allied commanders like Musson and Keightley goes without saying. No doubt many Canadian Legionaires of Ukranian descent do also.

Much has been written recently of the deep involvement of Allies, including 600 Canadians, in the final stages of the Russian Civil War. The international force, which following Armistice entered Russia via Murmansk to fight on the side of White Russia against the Bolsheviks well into 1919, included many Cossack soldiers. The 16th Brigade of Canadian Field Artillery was one Canadian unit participating in the final vicious fighting of that bloody revolution; a unit composed of RCMP recruits, another. Some British commanding officers were General Edmond Ironside, Major F.F. Arnoldi, Colonel C.C.M. Maynard; our senior Canadian officer, Colonel John Leckie. (Since writing this article I learned the book OPERATION KEELHAUL cites Field Marshal Alexander, later Canada's governor-general, as the man in charge of the forced repatriation of those two million persons--many his former friends and comrades.)

Captain R.D. Adams was awarded the Military Cross for valour to become the first Canadian soldier ever decorated in North Russia. Another decorated Canadian, awarded the Cross of Siberia, was Colonel John Stoughton Dennis Jr.--a man who later did more to help settle Canada's Prairies than any other single person. Many of his settlers were emigrants from the Cossack region of Russia. Our ready assistance to the Cossacks in the Russian Civil War undeniably played a major role in their willingness to surrender peacefully to us in the Second World War. Betraying this trust (not to mention direct promises they would not be sent to Russia) makes the action of those Allied commanders involved even more deplorable.

No doubt numerous Canadians today experience sorrow over the Cossack tragedy because of deep feelings many of us have developed over the years for the highly popular Don Cossack choir and dancers. This remarkable group originated from Cossack soldiers who fought as Allied soldiers in the First World War and as White soldiers in the Russian Civil War. Some of my people listened to their melodious singing several years before they became organized.

Certainly, the despicable action of a handful of our Allied commanders, which resulted in the virtual annihilation of the whole ethnic people these performers represent, will rouse deep guilt feelings within us whenever we see and hear this magnificent group perform in years ahead.

58. THE TANNERS OF TANNER'S CROSSING   Free lance, Minnedosa Tribune, Jan. 16 & 23/75

The old man sat beside his log cabin watching the sun rise slowly over the vast expanse of water he loved deeply. Manitou-Waba, the Voice of the Great Spirit, his three Indian grandparents called it. Maybe even his white grandfather who'd lived long with Shawnee and Saulteaux tribes as Shaw-shaw-a-be-nase, The Falcon, called it that more often than Manitoba.

They were all gone: grandparents, father, mother, Maggie, Catherine. Who would remember a simple Metis when he too had gone to meet The Great Spirit? Except for one stepson far away he had no one to love and remember him now. He was 93; it was time to pass on.

He would never live as long as Mother. Poopie, her Saulteaux people had called her, lived to 108. That was indeed old, but not unknown among her people. Eighteen years ago she'd died, the year the Great War had started. How well he knew about war! He had buried her in little St. Bedes cemetery just a mile north along the shore of this very lake. Soon after, he'd buried Sister Maggie beside Mother. Now it was his turn. Sometimes it worried him that Father wasn't buried here too. His Metis father rested in an Indian burial ground far south near Portage la Prairie where Father's half brother Saulteaux chief buried him according to the old ways that year of race trouble some called the First Riel Rebellion.

He, John Tanner, had been born August 17, 1839, at Torch Lake (Lac du Flambeau many called it) in Wisconsin. His father James Tanner had been a strong mountain of a man who took after Grandfather John Falcon Tanner who'd been captured at eight by Shawnees and lived 30 years with Indian people—hunting, fishing, trapping, starving, fighting the Sioux. At five and a half feet he himself resembled more his mother who was small, slender. Only his grey-blue eyes and sandy hair betrayed white blood.

Grandfather Tanner had lived on the shore of Lake Superior at Sault Ste. Marie to the north then. How old he'd seemed—gnarled as oak branches, skin wrinkled and bark-like. Sad. Bitter. He never smiled. His eyes bored through you. People said he had a terrible temper, that the white government took Aunt Martha away because he beat her, that Grandmother Theresa no longer lived with him because he bullied her also. But he had loved that old man.

Later, when Grandfather vanished, white people claimed he murdered one of their most noted men, James Schoolcraft. Lt. Tilden had organized a huge man-hunt for "that white Indian". The 'Tanner Summer' it had become known as far and wide. A year later, Grandfather's skeleton had been discovered in nearby bush, and it had been impossible to tell how he died. How happy John had been years later to hear of Tilden's death-bed confession to the Schoolcraft murder! Often he'd wondered if threatening hints by Sault Indians that it was Tilden himself who had also murdered their friend to make it seem he had run away after committing murder were true. At least Grandmother had returned to live out her days in a new house Uncle John had built her on the same land Grandfather had lived his latter years.

Poor Grandfather came to such tragic end after living so remarkable a life. He'd learned the ways of Indian people, and told of them in books as had few whites. He'd helped Hudson Bay Company build Fort Daer at Pembina and persuaded his Indian foster people to trade there instead of with the American Fur and Northwest companies. He'd negotiated treaties with Red River Valley Indians for Lord Selkirk so that Scottish settlers could come to Manitoba. When Alexander Henry the Younger's Indian wife and father-in-law were slaughtered by the Sioux, he was one of only 20 men brave enough to avenge their death after 1400 would-be-avengers fled at first hint of battle. He had guided Capt. P.D. Orsonnes with Selkirk's soldiers from Rainy River across treacherous Rouseau Swamp and helped them recapture Daer from the Northwest Company during the Pemmican War, virtually single-handed recaptured Ft. Douglas in bloodless coup because Uncle Picheito, then called Little Pheasant, was being held hostage there. Later he'd helped Rev. Edwin James translate the Bible into Saulteaux.

What a beautiful fall day. Mallards, canvasbacks, Canadas flocking to migrate. If only the Kinosota people weren't so poor. A stock market crash in New York caused it, they said. Well, at least he had a good pension now and could help a few live better.

Father had freighted for Norman Kittson between Pembina, St. Paul and Winnipeg. It was then he'd married Poopie, a pretty Red Lake Saulteaux maid.

Pembina's Joe Cavilier had aptly described Father like John remembered him then as "a notorious character. He was a giant in strength and although kind and gentle when sober he would terrorize an entire village when frenzied with rum. But what a changed man he is now." Yes, Father had become converted to the white man's Great Spirit. There at Pembina they'd continued to live two years while Father preached to his Saulteaux people as Presbyterian missionary.

When he was twelve, The Great Gathering took place of all his Saulteaux uncles and aunts, cousins and friends for a treaty they made with the governor. Next year Father had been away many months in New York and Washington persuading the Baptists (Great Grandfather John Tanner had been a Baptist minister) to open a mission at St. Joseph after the Presbyterians refused. He'd never forget that nice Elijah Terry who'd come back with Father to teach at the new mission, how the two built the new school and church until one day some Sioux ambushed and scalped Mr. Terry. Father, so gentle and peace-loving since he'd found the white man's religion, quickly rallied the men and with guns rode after the Sioux killers. Soon after, the Sioux had returned. In dead of night while he and Maggie, their parents and some Saulteaux children come to study at the new school had slept, Rev. Spencer's wife had been shot close by while her husband had tried desperately to attract Father's attention by firing over their house. Father sadly conducted funeral services next day and the Spencer children lived with them until they were sent East to live with grandparents. For a number of years, except for fear of Sioux attacks, life had been good for Father, Mother, Maggie and himself. Then came The War.

John always remembered this as The War. Historians called it the American Civil War, coinciding with so-called Indian Wars. He'd just started farming in Sterns County near their St. Joseph home. In August of 1862, he'd headed into St. Cloud to enlist as private in the Union Army's Ninth Regiment of Minnesota Voluntary Infantry. For three long bloody years he'd fought and scouted and starved with that regiment until honorably discharged at Fort Snelling near St. Paul. Meanwhile, his family and people had all moved across the border and were living near Portage la Prairie, Father a missionary without a church there. Father's half brother, Uncle Picheito Tanner, was an important chief of the Red Lake tribe there on the Portage-Delta-White Horse plains.

While scouting at Fort Abercrombie in 1863 he'd sustained a rupture that developed serious complications and prevented him from ever fathering children. How that used to shame and worry him! During October of 1864 especially he'd seen enough blood to last him a lifetime. And Uncle John had died fighting in The War; in the second Battle of Manasses, he'd learned later.

Soon after discharge he too had headed for St. Mary's la Portage. This was country where Grandfather Tanner'd lived and hunted once. Here Step Grandmother Mis-kwa-bun-o-kwa, Dawn Sky, had lived much of her life; even after she'd left Grandfather and taken Uncle Picheito along.

Those short years near Manitou-Waba Lake had been good years. Except, that is, for losing his right arm from a shotgun blast while duck hunting; or Uncle Picheito's people fighting the Sioux who'd also fled there after the Minnesota wars. Here he'd met the only woman he'd ever loved. Lovely Catherine was the widow of Hudson Bay Company factor James Sinclair and daughter of Joseph Trottier of St. Mary's. In summer of 1869 they'd been married in the little Anglican church with Rev. Henry George officiating and Father and John Setter witnessing. Riel was urging his friends to join him but he himself wanted no further part of anything that might lead to bloodshed. Soon after the wedding Catherine and he'd headed West to make a new home.

* * * * * * * * * *

It's not certain whether Catherine and John Tanner took the overland route, famous Carlton Trail, to their new home, or travelled by canoe up the Assiniboine to Brandon House and then north up the Little Saskatchewan (now Minnedosa) River. An expert horseman, he probably took the former, rather than the river route his grandfather Falcon Tanner had frequently plied with fur-laden canoe and foster Saulteaux family. Nor is it absolutely clear exactly when he arrived at the Crossing which later bore his name. Years later, in a pension application, he gives the date as 1869; yet Portage la Prairie electoral lists carried his name as late as 1873.

John's arrival at Tanner's Crossing with bride wasn't the first time he'd been there. Long after he was to tell pioneer Norman Shuttleworth of Minnedosa "I was here at this Crossing 30 years ago, about 1848, and I saw the buffalo crossing over the Little Saskatchewan River at the ford just east of this Crossing. It took the main herd that year three days to go south in the spring and three days to go north up into the bush in the late fall when winter came on."

During the dozen years John and Catherine lived in what's now Minnedosa John made his living by helping settlers cross the river--in spring a cataract often hundreds of feet wide--in "sort of a coracle shaped, circular boat made of buffalo hide." From 1877-80 he served as first postmaster. Local historians indicate he was, despite loss of arm and small size, one of the town's star football players in 1879. A Dominion Land Grant document shows title to the homestead granted him March 29, 1881; where the heart of Minnedosa later grew.

About a year after the Tanners (likely) arrived at the Crossing John's father was killed. Manitoba's first Presbyterian minister John Black of Kildonan blames Wolseley's soldiers. A coroner's jury at an inquest conducted by Dr. Bird, where Dr. Lynch (later M.P. of Marquette) testified, listed the cause of death as skull fracture resulting from falling from a wagon drawn by a horse which "was caused to run away wilfully and maliciously by two persons unknown to this jury". "Alive, my brother preached your Gospel", Chief Picheito Tanner raged at Rev. Black who'd come to give his friend and co-worker a Christian burial. "You killed him. I take him to my people who do not kill their Medicine men."

Soon after Rev. Tanner's death Poopie came to live with John and Catherine. The chief and his band moved further west to Binscarth-Qu'Appelle Valley region, where Picheito is presumed by some historians to have died within a couple of years. His son John Tanner and family settled on Silver Creek Reserve, which later became reduced to Gambler Reserve when only Tanners remained on it.

In about 1881, because so many white settlers flocked to Minnedosa, Metis families like the Tanners, Peter and Maggie (Tanner) Sinclair, the George Sandersons and John Norquays (cousin to Manitoba's first premier) took to the Carlton and again migrated west. Several families settled 11 miles out of Prince Albert where John again operated a small country post office. The school district was called Ridge, post office Kirkpatrick.

During the quarter century the Tanners lived in Saskatchewan they somehow acquired an adopted son. On October 5, 1904, at 65 and in failing health, John applied for an American disability pension, made the error of stressing his amputated arm as major disability and it not being the result of his war service was rejected.

H.N. McNaughton, Ridge teacher in summer of 1906, paints a somewhat tragic picture of John at this point. "I do not know how long they had been living there but John told me he came from Minnedosa. I did have Granny (Poopie) Tanner's cane, given me by her before I left, I presume for man-handling John when I came upon him threshing her unmercifully. His ability was somewhat impaired as postmaster quite often on his return from Prince Albert with the mail." Soon thereafter, on January 17/07, Catherine died. John's mother left and headed back east along the Carlton, 1910 finding her living with nephew John Tanner's family near Binscarth. It was her photo, taken there that year when Poopie was 104, that was recently published in Manitoba Pageant causing somewhat of a stir among historians, not that of a Mrs. John Tanner as claimed.

After months of searching I located a descendant of John's adopted son. Mrs. Edna Struthers of Prince Albert (located with the help of John Diefenbaker's staff) wrote me recently, "My father was John William Tanner and I'm sure his Dad was the Tanner you referred to in your letter. I don't know much about him as I think my father was brought up by the Anderson family. My father passed away 20 years ago but I do remember old timers talking about my grandfather having one arm. My father had a step brother in Prince Albert by name of Norman Anderson."

Shortly after 1910 Mrs. James Tanner arrived in Kinosota district, accompanied by widowed daughter Maggie Sinclair. Poopie had briefly been married to a Baptiste Demerais, who apparently died. In about 1912 John joined them. Once again they lived together as family; until Poopie's death in 1914 at 108, Maggie's a year later. On May 11, 1912, John re-applied for an American service pension on basis of his rupture, was accepted. Three years later he applied again, indicating he now required personal care and the pension was increased. He hired sisters Lisa and Susan Moar to care for him. Susan died in 1929, Lisa recently. From 1929 until his death on Sept. 3, 1932, John's best friend was Gilbert Asham. After he'd bought the Tanner place, Asham built a new house, lives there still.

"He used to drive a sleigh pulled by a horse", old Gilbert Asham told me recently. "He'd built it himself; not a nail in it. John came here all the way with horses from Prince Albert. He used to talk about a stepson once in a while but had no children of his own. He was a very good worker, good repairman--fixed clocks, anything. He could really chop wood with that arm; built his log cabin all by himself. Liked to tell how he caught a pig running wild during the Civil War, butchered it and ate a hind quarter all himself."

Duncan Tanner of that district, son of a white man captured as youngster by Crees and later befriended by Rev. James Tanner after whom he named himself, told me that during the First World War John used to say, "Only if a man is brave enough to put his hand on a red hot stove is he brave enough to fight in battle." John Tanner himself was brave enough.

Today, a multi-million dollar new school at Minnedosa and that town's 1970 centennial park remind people John Tanner once passed that way. John's body rests in a quiet little cemetery on the west shore of his beloved Manitou-Waba Lake; his soul no doubt lives with The Great Spirit.

59. CAPTAIN JACK ALLAN   Free lance article, Minnedosa Tribune, Feb. 20 & 27/75

Of countless European immigrants who settled Canada's Prairies shortly before and after the turn of the century few possessed less aptitude for this formidable undertaking than did Captain John C. Allan of Fairmount district northwest of Minnedosa. Yet few brought to our Prairies a more fascinating heritage. Perhaps William Wood touched on the status of the Jack Allans of early settlement when in 1914 he wrote, "Canadian history is full of sea-power; but Canadian histories are not."

Red-headed Jack was born June 6, 1851 in Montrose, Scotland; son of Elizabeth Crabb and John Allan. His brother James was two years older, sister Elizabeth two years younger. Though his inept farming attempts during the last 15 years of life greatly amused neighbors, this well educated and highly articulate sailor - writer - amateur biologist enriched the lives of people he met in his own unique way. When he died November 22, 1915, and was buried in Fairmount cemetery near Minnedosa Valley, people whose lives he'd touched quickly realized one of our Prairie's most interesting pioneers had passed.

Virtually nothing is known about Jack's childhood. As his sister and brother never married and he himself had no children there are no descendants who might have such knowledge. Nor does he mention it in the 11 articles he wrote for British newspapers during his retirement from the sea. That he loved children Cam Ross, an eight-year-old son of pioneer Tom Ross and close neighbor when the old sea captain died, told me recently. Cam, who now lives in the 'Allan Place', in the same house and in whose yard Jack's wife lived out her widowed life until her death at 102 on her birthday, May 6, 1967, recalls, "He was a very friendly, pleasant man who used to tell me many sea stories."

In the only poem Jack Allan's known to have written (hitherto unpublished), he alludes to childhood, perhaps his own. He called it 'In The Dark' and it goes: "Who's afraid in the dark? Oh not I said the owl and he gave a great scowl and he wiped his eye and he fluffed his jowl--In whoo! Said the dog, I bark out loud in the dark-- Boo-oo. Said the cat Miew, I'll scratch anyone who Dares say I do Feel afraid Miew. Afraid, said the mouse of dark in the house Hear me scatter Whatever the matter -- Squeek. Then the toad in the hole And the bug in the ground They both shook their heads And passed the word 'round. And the bird in the tree The fish and the bee They declared all three That you never did see One of them afraid In the dark. But the little boy who had gone to bed Just raised the bedclothes and covered his head."

Undoubtedly there were many times since boyhood Jack Allan wished he could raise the bedclothes and cover his head. In his first newspaper article he tells of one such instance just after leaving "a comfortable home for that of one as an apprentice on board a sailing ship", waking terrified the first night with "my bed floating under me" buffeted by sailors' gear due to a lively squall. After realizing no one else was the least perturbed by such mundane happenings, Jack "thoroughly wet, cold and miserable and not at all in love with sea life" clambored onto an upper bunk to finish sleeping.

"I know of nothing so absolutely pitiless as weather", wrote author of In Flanders Fields, John McCrae, from the trenches January 25, 1917. The weather to sailors, as to Prairie farmers, has always been of vital importance. Jack quickly recognized its deep significance to his own personal well-being and recorded it dutifully on both sea and land the rest of his life, as diaries and ship logs reveal. Such a record for the S.S. Hispania of Glasgow he kept during a run from Liverpool to Calcutta and back in 1897 from September 22 to October 24 lists wind velocity and direction, cloud cover, ship's locations (with corrections), ocean surface condition; with additional comments "ship rolling heavily at times and shipping water fore and aft" frequently, "passed company's S.S. Britannica", "ship swinging to flood tide", mention of cargo like timbers unloaded and jute taken on during 20 days docking at

Calcutta. His log for the same ship on a Liverpool to Bombay via Suez Canal and return to Marseilles and Liverpool trip January 16 to February 10, 1898, recorded similar items and mentions passing the mail steamship S.S. Abram, a partial sun eclipse, taking a depth "rock hearing" reading, unloading timbers, a Bombay doctor coming aboard to inspect crew and passengers, "shipping water amidships".

Captain Allan's daily 'weather and remarks log' kept while farming later describes Prairie weather as only a seaman would. It seems Minnedosa district experienced frequent "fresh gales" which "take off towards evening" and "rain squalls", that the weather was occasionally "dull and gloomy overcast" with "light air from NE" and the "occasional glimpse of sun at intervals", the "sky misty".

He refers to episodes like: "Indians visiting us regarding exchange of horses", "started for town with steer but only got a half mile" because of weather, "today threshed 67 bags of wheat and 203 bags of oats", "carted hen manure away", "assisted to shift wood", "Indians called with fish", "fixed up sun dial", "assisted to put out fire at Ferguson", "put up fence rails on west side", "cut some trees at lake and some in alley", "laid up with sciatica", "put cow adrift on road allowance", "killed two cocks", "got three pigs heads and took feet", "killed a skunk and weasel", "a pedlar called", "Mother gradually sinking" and three days later "Mother died", "cut down some trees at N channel", "Indian called in search of horses", "had a visit from a wolf", "set a turkey with 15 hen eggs", "shifted plough share", "evening compared fence line with north star", "Lizzie and I struck by lightning rendering my right arm and hand useless for an hour", "saw Dr. Harrison about feet" and "went to Minnedosa to visit Dr. Andrew", "wee Cameron Ross called", "employed stacking all day, Anna assisting", "Nov. 27, 1912, no snow yet", "started cutting on brae".

In addition to such daily notations Captain Allan kept accurate records of mean, high and low temperatures for winter months, determined that Minnedosa was 3442 miles from his birthplace Montrose and 1690 feet above sea level, latitude 50+10 N and longitude 99-48 W, his own farm being 50-17 N, 99-56 W, the "difference of time slow of Greenwich" six hours and 40 minutes. Recipes for "condition powder" and for "home brewed ale" occupy prominence in his diary.

In articles to British newspapers Jack Allan expounded five intriguing adventures encountered as sailor. In 'A Dirty Night In Akyab' he described vividly living through a violent cyclone while aboard ship several miles off shore, all but colliding with another ship during that tempest. In another article he recounted the action, suspence, drama and tragedy of Spanish bullfights. 'An Adventure In Valparaiso Bay' depicted a vicious life-and-death struggle with three murderous thugs who try to rob and kill him while rowing alone to his ship. With intense clarity he portrayed his crew's dilemma when struck down with yellow fever in a South American port with several dying and he himself brought so low by this dreadful malady that shipmates "who had gathered round to see me die" believed him dead, Jack hearing the remark, "Poor fellow, he is gone". 'An Eventful Atlantic Voyage' deals with a voyage from Italy to New York in a badly rusted old ship under a vascillating captain, the ship springing a six feet by ten break in her starboard bow during a gale and starting to sink. Fortunately they were near Bermuda and managed to limp into port for repairs.

Undoubtedly a most memorable experience of Captain Allan's was being shipwrecked. In an unpublished report he relates the traumatic July 1, 1875, calamity and subsequent seven month ordeal, while a surviving passenger Spencer Joslen in the newspaper article 'The Wreck of the Strathmore' gives an equally stirring account.

Enroute to New Zealand with cargo and 88 passengers and crew the iron clippership crossed the equator without incident, crew and passengers enjoying the traditional ceremonies involved in entering Neptune's domain. "After getting clear of the trades we met with boistrous weather," Allan's report reads; which washed the sheep pen from off the main hatch "scattering the sheep all over the deck". The weather moderated slightly but the Strathmore had been driven off course and her officers no longer knew her position. Throughout this misadventure Jack, by now an experienced sailor, suffered an excruciating toothache. That night, during a second gale near the Crozet Islands about 700 miles southeast of Cape of Good Hope, the S.S. Strathmore struck hard a huge "rock shaped like a sugar loaf", capsized and slowly broke apart. Most lifeboats had been smashed on impact, 39 passengers and crew drowning soon after in the icy water. Allan was part of a boatload of 19 which eventually fought clear of the sinking ship and reached one of the Crozets, as did two other boats.

. Five of the survivors died during the long vigil on that bleak and barren rock but 44 eventually were rescued by the American whaling ship Young Phoenix, transferred to the Sierra Morena and conveyed to Ceylon. Inspired by descriptions and sketches by crew members and passengers a British artist of that era immortalized those months on Crozet in a painting. Almost within sight of Antarctic ice the island where Jack spent a winter, spring and early summer was about the same latitude in the Southern Hemisphere as his home in Minnedosa district later was in the Northern, his future neighbors then were simultaneously experiencing summer, fall and early winter.

On one of many sea voyages Jack met and married Anna. Born in Klagenfurt, Austria, her father a horse buyer for the Austrian cavalry and mother having died young, Anna was brought up by an aunt in Trieste. The Allans were perhaps the most mismatched couple in Fairmount district, neighbors recall. Anna was a highly practical, down-to-earth, 'no nonsense' woman; Jack, an intellectual dreamer. One neighbor remembers particularly the seaman's consternation upon entering the kitchen one morning where his wife was nonchalantly lighting the cookstove with his prized ship logs.

Besides Jack and Anna the Allan family at Fairmount included Jack's widowed mother, lay minister brother and his sister. One neighbor recalls the quarter section they were sold (under guidance of Canada's Dept. of Interior) was very poor and the house a mere shell.

Understandably, the Allan brothers knew nothing about farming. George Brown, 93-year-old pioneer who lived all his life in Fairmount district and whose family were good friends of the Allans, remembers Captain Allan as a "friendly, real nice, intelligent man." He recalls a neighbor watching the brothers struggle daily with a walking plow that just wasn't performing until one day he discovered the share had never yet been sharpened, a fact the two had not realized was necessary. Added to such everyday problems was Jack's uncertain physical condition, the long wet years having slowly taken their toll by crippling him with rheumatism forcing him finally to leave the sea (without pension those days) to seek a new livelihood.

That farmer Jack Allan failed to conquer physically his chosen portion of Canada's Prairies to the same degree as did many of his compatriots is readily admitted by those farmers who knew him best. That sea captain Jack Allan brought to Canada's Prairies a greater intangible legacy is even more readily conceded by those same peers.

60. CAPTAIN ALLAN'S JOURNAL Old Dartmouth Historical Society Whaling Museum,
Feb. 24/75

A century ago one of the more dramatic shipwrecks of Britain's far-flung sailing fleet occurred. A young Scottish sailor, who survived the terrible ordeal, eventually became a farmer near Minnedosa, Manitoba. Though he died 60 years ago his wife outlived him by 52, died in 1967 at 102. There were no children, nieces, nephews. For decades his journals, diaries and ship logs lay neglected, molding, chewed by mice in a little house in which his widow lived her final years.

Though Jack Allan learned to love the sea and remained with it a quarter century following that fateful shipwreck to eventually become captain, his wife Anna loathed the life of a sailor's wife—or later even her husband's sea mementos to remind her of those lonely years. On at least one occasion she lit the farm cookstove with her husband's prized logs. Based on pages of his recordings that did survive, the following is Jack's hitherto unpublished century-old story of 'The Wreck of the S.S. Strathmore'. Essential details of this shipwreck are well documented by British newspaper accounts of that era.

On April 19, 1875, the iron clipper S.S. Strathmore sailed for New Zealand. She encountered a strong gale southeast of Cape of Good Hope and was driven off course. That night, before the officers were able to determine her location, a second gale struck hard. On board were 88 passengers and crew members, many sheep and pigs.

"About 3:30 the mate told me to go forward and listen if I could hear or see anything, which I did. I had only got as far as the fore rigging when I observed something looming up in the darkness and the thought flashed through my mind that it was either breakers or an iceberg. I had not time to give vent to my thoughts in words when a shout came from a man on the forecastle head of 'Hard a starboard, breaker right ahead!'. I repeated his order to the watch and let go the starboard braces. Then the mate countermanded his order by shouting, 'Hard a starboard, shorten fore brace'; which I again repeated to the watch, at the same time running across and letting go the port braces. I now waited for the watch to fulfill the order but none ever came. The fore and main topsails halyards had been let go."

"While standing by the braces the ship apparently struck under where I was standing. I could now see all hands hurrying aft. Seeing that no one was going to attend at the braces I also made for the poop. I was met by the captain who told me to let go the mizzen topsail halyards, which I did but they got foul and I had to cut them. Just as I had finished the ship again struck very heavy, apparently right forward, causing her to tremble from stem to stern, and knocking me up against the mizzen mast. I took off my oilskin and coat in order to work more easily and in case I might have to swim. All the passengers were roused up by the sudden shock and before some of them got out of the salon the ports were smashed in, the water rushing into the cabins. The captain now gave orders to clear away the boats, also shouting to the cabin passengers to come up and save themselves as it was all up with us and shouting good bye to all."

The Strathmore had struck a huge rock, capsized and slowly began to break apart. Many lifeboats had smashed. Jack helps launch one boat. While so occupied he observes several incidents. An apprentice relinquishes his lifebuoy to a pleading passenger, who then jumps overboard and is never seen again. A brother and sister wait on the poop for a boat to be launched, the ship settles "down by the stern" and the "seas coming over the poop swept the sister off her feet and washed her along the poop past me down on the main deck and she drowned. The brother then made for the rigging. The next sea that came on board swept everybody off the poop. I had just time to catch hold of the davit guy."

Jack struggles to the mizzen rigging which is crowded with people. "I could hear some of those beside me saying good bye to each other. The mizzen mast was working a good deal and we were anxious to get off it as soon as possible in case it might give away. Several of us now made our way down, others not caring to venture remained in the top. When I got down I came across a GS who informed me the mate was drowned through the capsizing of one of the boats. It appears a lot of people had got into her thinking she would float off as did the other one but when the water reached her she capsized. He was in her but made his escape."

Jack fights his way to the main mast, meets shipmate Patsy Cogan who seconds later is "caught by a wave and swept away clear of the ship into the sea and was drowned." He starts climbing to the main top. "When half way I came across an AB who implored me to assist him into the top. Poor fellow, he was actually crying. I told him I was unable to assist him as I could just barely pull myself up. So I left him and had just strength enough left to get into the top. I ventured down the main stay, found several people which I had not seen before." Making his way to the top of the deck house Jack sees "several people in the fore crying, so I made for where they were. I think about 15 of us had got on the forecastle head."

The group clings to the weather rail waiting for daybreak, is appalled at "the terrible havoc the sea had made and was still going on" when dawn finally breaks. They now see they'd struck a huge rock shaped "like a sugar loaf", beyond it a 500 foot perpendicular cliff, watch helplessly an exhausted passenger on the mizzen rail lose his grip on the topsail sheets and drown.

"The poop was now little better than a collection of iron. The deck had been completely torn off and the beams were twisted in all directions. The booby hatch was away and the main hatch off. I observed a kitten in the carpenter's room near the roof trying to escape from the seas that were continually washing through it." The group locate two undamaged boats. Jack helps launch the second mate with one load. Some refuse to venture into the small remaining dinghy; which Jack's last to board.

The dinghy occupants struggle in the heaving seas, desperately bail water while trying to keep up with the larger boat, lose her in heavy fog. At long last the boat "hove in sight and told us where to go, also informing us they had picked up the life boat with 19 hands and had towed her to a landing. The gig was on her way to the wreck to receive those who had been left. On our way towards the landing we passed through a lot of wreckage. We picked up a tin of meat", observed a dead pig float by but couldn't retrieve it, manage to fight through the surf and land.

The lifeboat survivors tell of a mother refusing to climb aboard without her child. "She was told her child was safe in the mizzen top but notwithstanding she went back to find it but never returned. How strong must be a mother's love!"

Jack asks for volunteers to take the dinghy out past the surf where floated much wreckage "to try to pick up anything that would be useful. I got two volunteers but after we got a little distance off the rocks a light puff of wind came and so frightened one that he would go no farther so we had to return."

Of the 88 passengers and crew 49 reached the island; one of the bleak and barren French-owned uninhabited Crozets in the Indian Ocean some 700 miles southeast of Cape of Good Hope "almost within sight of Antarctic ice cap." Considering the fact July there corresponds with January here and latitude that of North Dakota, being 'saved' was for the survivors (one of them a woman---Mrs. Wordsworth---and another the baby of the mother who perished) really 'out of the frying pan, into the fire'.

Five of the 49 don't survive the long ordeal on Crozet. The trauma of shipwreck seems to have crushed the mind and soul of one passenger, who'd had to be pushed overboard to be rescued. Next morning "one of the men woke up with him (Mellor) lying across him---dead. I had never handled a dead person before. However I took off his watch and chain, which I afterwards returned to his parents." Following the burial at sea Jack and volunteers take out the lifeboat and collect useful wreckage, one item being a chest filled with blankets, two dozen forks and knives. The men in the gig salvage two large cases containing sheets, those in the dinghy a case of wine and one of rum plus a case of gunpowder.

For seven long months the Strathmore survivors lived on Crozet. At first, they killed birds like albatross with stones for food; then ate their eggs. On August 9, hundreds of mollyhawks landed, and being unafraid of humans were easy to kill. From that point on the food situation improved greatly. On September 20 the great penguins arrived and fear of starvation ended.

Several passengers had had their feet frozen. One (Stanbury) "suffered a good deal. Then he took lockjaw and was unable to take any food. Wine was tried to put into his mouth but without success. He lived for a day or two and died. We buried him (July 19) not far from the shanty, had severe difficulty getting sufficient depth for his body, the ground being only deep enough to hold the body so we had to heap soil on top of him."

On September 2 another passenger, Thomas Henderson, died. His sister had died during shipwreck. "Poor fellow, he mourned the loss of his sister very much. He never regained his former spirits as his idea was that people would say that he saved himself and neglected his sister."

Though outside the usual shipping lanes four ships did pass within sight of Crozet. If they saw the shipwrecked Strathmorites they took no notice. This despite a tall flagstaff and a constant lookout. Of one ship they learned later "those on board did see us. The passengers had seen the report of our rescue in the papers and they wrote to the effect that when in the vicinity of the Crozet Islands they had been running along with squally weather. The passengers said they had told the captain there were people on the island making signals but he heeded them not. The ship, I heard, was the White Eagle of London."

Every Saturday night the castaways had a concert. "In place of a newspaper each of us related our dreams." They named various parts of the island---Pleasant Valley, Near Flat, Far Flat, The Gully, The Spring. On October 23 an elderly passenger, William Husband, died. "He always said that he would never get off the island, but added that some of us young fellows would. We could not say what he died of. December 25, the child died and was buried beside Henderson. Poor little fellow! We mourned him much. His father did not attend him too well."

On January 22 the 44 survivors sight another ship. As usual excitement mounts. "As she drew near we could make out the Stars and Stripes. When getting sufficiently close she hove to and put out two boats." The long ordeal was over.

Despite countless hardships endured Jack Allan feels sorry to leave the island as he climbs into a boat. "In going off to the ship", the American whaler Young Phoenix of New Bedford commanded by D.L. Gifford on a three-year cruise, "several got sea sick and were forced to give up all they had to Father Neptune. The cooper made wooden crosses to place at the head of each grave and a bottle to be buried about how we had lived during our stay. These were taken on shore." With increasing nostalgia, Jack watches the island slip beneath the horizon.

"A strong smell of whale oil was our first greeting. The boiler lay on deck for breaking down the blubber which is afterwards put into casks; is again used as fuel to melt the next lot." The captain gives each a suit of clothes. "The crew were comprised of different nationalities—Scandinavians, Negroes, natives of St. Helena and Azores. The captain was very kind to all, serving out tobacco to those who used it. He had given orders to keep a look out for passing vessels in order to transfer us for he was now going away from his fishing grounds and would lose a great deal." Several days later they're transferred to two passing ships and taken home.

It was not to be Jack's only shipwreck. In a badly mouse-eaten journal of which only pages 58 to 67 are still reasonably intact, Captain Allan tells of a second one. The location's not given on those pages, but the survivors are on a tropical island with coconut trees, bananas and pineapples. His close friend Jim is with him. There they meet several other castaways. One is Peter Clark, a Scottish schoolmate of Jack's. There is a Willie and the mate, a Mrs. Gordon and her son, a Mrs. Paul. "Now eighteen months had passed since their first landing" he says of some of the castaways, indicates the trees are "identical with those of Brazil." However, to date I haven't been able to document this second shipwreck.

In 1887 a strange sequel occurred on the Crozets. Thirteen sailors from the French ship Tamaris of Bordeaux escaped the sinking vessel and in heavy fog reached one of the smaller islands. Here they lived nine months. A device to which they resorted to precipitate rescue was capturing an albatross, fastening a piece of metal to its neck with a message describing their plight. Finally, without food and despairing of rescue they left an account of their ordeal indicating they were embarking for one of the larger Crozets 80 miles away where they hoped life and chance of rescue would be better. Meanwhile, the albatross flew thousands of miles to Australia, was found dead on the beach at Freemantle just eight days before the group sailed for the larger island.

Both France and Britain conducted searches for the shipwrecked men, found the account written by them only. It was concluded they had perished on the 80-mile voyage. "Few stories of the animal kingdom," wrote a British journalist, "equal in pathetic interest that of this strong-winged bird, whose fulfillment of the mission entrusted to him set two nations at work to rescue men in sore distress." They were not as fortunate as Jack Allan and his peers—in whose destiny albatross too played a major role.

61. COWBOY CAMPBELL RIDES THE TRAIL OF '98   Free lance article, North magazine

Of many thousands who streamed into Yukon during the Klondike Gold Rush few were as colorful or made as lasting impression on Canadians as the man whom journalists would for the next two decades dub 'The Cowboy'. Lieutenant-Colonel Glenlyon Archibald Campbell, buried October, 1917 in a Canadian veterans cemetery in France, was that man.

"Tall, erect and swarthy, defiant of ordinary conventions" a Family Herald columnist described Glen—then federal inspector of Indian agencies—on Jan. 1, 1913 after falling heir to a fortune left by a New Zealand relative. "If early Manitoba had anything resembling a Tom Mix or Gene Autry, the distinction would go to one who ranched and farmed close to the Riding Mountains. Six feet four, built in similar proportion, soldierly in bearing, magnetic in personality and daredevil in nature" Grant MacEwan of Western Producer portrayed him. "On the surface Glen was a rip-roaring, wild-man-from-Borneo kind of man, but he had a heart in him as big as an ox, and would go the limit in a poker game or to oblige a friend" eulogized the Windsor Record upon learning of his death. "Straight as an arrow, lithe and athletic, much of his life was spent in performing physical skill and valor. His towering figure, bronzed swarthy face, large brown eyes, capped with a cowboy hat" a Winnipeg Tribune reporter depicted him. "The man known from one end of Canada to the other for his generous nature, the warmth of his friendship and his sombrero hat, died in France Monday" reported the Brandon Sun on October 13, 1917.

By the time of the Klondike Gold Rush Glen Campbell was already known to many Canadians. At 22 he'd fought with Boulton's Scouts, a cavalry unit, in the 1885 rebellion. Rendering such distinguished service The Cowboy had been promoted to captain—the only soldier so honored throughout the rebellion.

When man's mad rush to the Klondike gold fields commenced in 1897, the Campbell name was already a household word in Yukon homes. It had been Glen's father, Robert, who some 55 years prior had established HBC's first Yukon post—Frances Lake; followed quickly by Pelly Banks and Fort Selkirk. It was he who had discovered and named the Pelly River, exploring it up to Fort Yukon at the junction of the Porcupine and Yukon proving the Pelly was really the upper portion of the Yukon. Robert Campbell had also explored stretches of the Porcupine, Mackenzie, Liard. When he finally decided to marry he'd travelled back to Scotland--3000 of those miles on snowshoes--to seek out and eventually wed Glen's mother Eleanora Stirling in 1859.

Glenlyon was born Oct. 23, 1863 in Swan River district of Manitoba at Fort Pelly where his father was then chief HBC factor, was named after his father's birthplace in Perthshire, Scotland. In 1870, during the Red River Rebellion, Mrs. Campbell and three young children journied to Scotland to visit--via USA to avoid rebellious Red River. In Scotland she fell ill and died. Glen stayed on with relatives, attended Glasgow Academy and Edinburgh's Murchistone College.

At 19 Glen returned to Canada, drifting first to Montana where MacEwan says "he learned to ride and shoot and cowboy with the best of the range men. Briefly he lived on his father's Murchistone Ranch at Elphinstone, Manitoba, where Robert had moved following arbitrary dismissal in 1871 by HBC. "In 1883," a daughter of Glen's told Gilbert Plains Historical Society, "he rode his father's pony over the Riding Mountains, marking trees as he went along that he might be able to find his way back" to the Gilbert Plains area where he'd begun to ranch following discharge from Boulton's Scouts and become the first white settler there.

As rancher The Cowboy executed a feat that's still viewed with awe or scepticism by many--hiding in a tree to mount a full grown bull moose passing underneath and then riding the frantic, plunging, enraged beast for many miles until finally it fell exhausted. On his spread he raised Scotch Highland cattle, which after running with Manitoba elk became so wild many had to be shot to salvage their meat. Yet his stock, crossed with Shorthorns in the Rocky Mountain foothills, produced some of the hardiest and best steers to come out of Alberta in the 1890s. Glen's brother Jim became a prominent sportsman in Winnipeg, his sister married J.A. McDonald of Qu'Appelle, Sask. and later also lived in Winnipeg.

Just before the 1885 Rebellion the young rancher had married Harriet Burns. According to a fellow employee of Jim Campbell's the name was Bones, not Burns, Harriet being a full-blooded Indian. According to Campbell descendants she was the daughter of a French count and an Indian woman. According to John Martin, a cowboy who rode for Glen in 1912-13 becoming a close friend, in a letter to MacEwan (owned by Glenbow-Alberta Inst.) on Nov. 12, 1957 following that journalist's article on Campbell, "Glen's family were quite a hand full, his wife of Chippewas band from the Riding Mountain Reserve was dead" (deceased May 17, 1910). According to historian Roy Brown of Brandon she was a daughter of Chief Kesik-oo-wee-ne-en of Riding Mountain band. Whatever the precise genealogy, descendants today use the name Burns. A photo of Harriet I saw recently shows her behind two baby moose at a picnic at home about 1902--a small, fair, most attractive and pleasant looking lady.

Glen and Harriet Campbell had four children. Jack, who at 84 lives in Victoria, B.C., Eleanora Knott and Christina Waddy of Gilbert Plains, Mary Austin who died in 1920.

In a recent letter to me Mrs. Knott says, "Glen Campbell was my father but I was really young when he was away on the Klondike trip. I did have quite a few clippings but a preacher from Minnedosa wrote me for them, said for sure he would send them back but never did. Now he is dead."

It's inconceivable that a man of Glen Campbell's venturesome nature would remain quietly at home ranching while daring men and women everywhere streamed to the Klondike during the winter of 1897-98. Of thousands of single trails commonly called the Trail of Ninety-Eight, five major routes led to Dawson City: Pacific Ocean-Yukon River; Dyea-Lewes River; Skagway-White Pass; Edmonton-Mackenzie River; Peace River. The Cowboy decided on a variation of the last three.

Besides lust for adventure two factors motivated Glen to join the gold rush--neither being the urge to prospect personally for gold. Familiar with his father's Yukon explorations he was convinced that a shortcut existed for Prairie and eastern Canada gold-seekers. A knowledgeable horseman he knew a massive operation like this must initiate a strong need for pack horses.

MacEwan states Glen "bought ponies and bronchos of a type considered suitable for the miners and took them to Skagway and farther. Horses not sold at Skagway were taken over the Chilkoot Pass and on to Dawson City." "Campbell offered to lead a party over this route," reported the Brandon Sun. "Hundreds of those who started perished. Glen Campbell's party was said to have been the only one to successfully consumate the journey. The manner in which he faced and surmounted hardships and disappointments on that trip reads like wild fiction."

Of the dozen men in Campbell's party two were his brothers-in-law: David Burns, Harriet's brother, and Walter Scott who was married to Harriet and David's sister Victoria. A recent conversation with two of Scott's children—Walter A. Scott of Rapid City, Man. and his 86-year-old sister who was six at the time of the trek—proved not only fascinating but verified several seemingly exaggerated newspaper accounts. Historian James L. Parker and Eleanora Burns Knott also assisted greatly in separating fact from fancy.

David Burns quit the expedition in disgust at the end of a month, terming it "a lot of foolishness." Walter stuck it out for a full year, then turned back. Glen and several others, according to Walter A. Scott, remained on the Trail a full two years, until the horses were sold and those who wished to prospect could continue safely to Dawson City. Perhaps his indomitable father's 11 month 1833 expedition of 10 men on horses and carts riding almost 2000 miles from Red River (now Winnipeg) to Kentucky to buy 1370 sheep and drive them back the same distance, encountering unbelievable hardships arriving eventually with only 251 sheep spurred the son on during those terrible months.

Asked whether any members of the Campbell expedition had perished enroute both Scott descendants indicated definitely that none had—but almost starved, being reduced to eat soup made from items of clothing like mocassins and suffered considerably from blood poisoning. In succeeding years, prior to his death in 1935 in California where he'd worked on an Arabian horse ranch since the First World War, their father had frequently spoken of the Klondike ride.

Andy Baird, in his recent book SIXTY YEARS ON THE KLONDIKE, explains the real reason why some 3000 pack horses perished on the Trail; refuting the commonly held notion Gold Rush writers perpetuate that cold weather and impassable terrain mainly were responsible. Discussing Yukon pioneer A.H. 'Bert' Hartshorn he writes, "Instead of following the stampede to the Klondike Hartshorn mined his own kind of gold along the trail, which was literally lined with dead pack horses. He explains the packers wouldn't feed the unfortunate animals the expensive grain they needed to keep alive, so the horses died along the trail of undernourishment and overwork." Hartshorn removed the horseshoes, re-shaped them and re-sold them to others.

Although The Cowboy may have inherited riches later, the Klondike ride left him considerably poorer than when he started out. To finance the expedition, Walter A. Scott told me, his uncle had sold one of his two ranches—Riding Mountain—to a Lord Vivian of England. Scott too sold property to assist. Following the Klondike adventure Glen and his family continued to live on their Gilbert Plains ranch, which Duncan Cameron had managed during the interim, while Walter Scott now managed the other for Vivian. Glenlyon post office was named after the dynamic Cowboy, who served his constituency as MLA from 1902 to 1907 and MP from 1908 to 1911. Shortly after outbreak of the First World War, no longer young and suffering from a severe kidney ailment caused by stopping a terrified team of runaway horses charging down a street crowded with people at a fair in Dauphin many years before, Glen recruited the 78th Battalion and later the 107th. Walter Scott and Glen's son-in-law Jack Waddy too enlisted, serving in France where Glen died on active duty.

In his letter Martin describes two other equinal ventures The Cowboy conducted. "In 1912 I had the pleasure of meeting Glen at the Calgary Stampede where he had a lot to do to secure for Tom Three Persons, a Blood Indian, the first all-around bucking horse contest of America."

"Following the Stampede," Martin continues, "Glen bought three cars of wild unbroken horses at a sale near the Blackboot agency from Ryan Dafoe and Harry Scott. I was a range rider for the Blackfeet Indians and Glen borrowed me from the Indian agent J.H. Gooderham to go east with his horses to Gilbert Plains. I loaded the wild mustangs at Gleichen and took my saddle and cowboy outfit in the caboose, and after several days of being pushed around by cranky trainmen arrived at my destination."

"At Gilbert Plains Glen's son Jack rode in to town to meet me. I saddled a half broken pony and together we drove the horses, about 45 head to the farm. There were too many to break in to saddle so we tied sacks of tin cans on their backs; and did they buck! Glen came out of town with a major and veterinary sergeant. They were buying bronks for the army. All day I put horses through the squeeze for the vet to measure up. They had to be just the right size. The vet measured them around the girth, from withers to root of tail, across the forehead, hands high; each foot had to be lifted and examined. After an all day session, none of the horses would do."

Hubert Darrell, the legendary Arctic pioneer in letters to parents during the Gold Rush and decade following, frequently mentioned the important role horses played in the North in the lives of Mounties, HBC traders, prospectors. Cowboy Campbell, who undoubtedly rode the longest and hardest horseback ride in Canadian Arctic history, contributed to that role in his own unique way.

62. ROSE AND ALLAN, PIONEER LAY PREACHERS   Minnedosa Tribune, March 27/75

On June 10 half a century ago a Toronto sports arena jammed with Canadians representing 8,000 uniting Congregationalist, Methodist and Presbyterian congregations celebrated the creation of the United Church of Canada. This summer golden anniversary celebrations across the country will commemorate that historic event.

In Minnedosa district Methodism and Presbyterianism had already played major roles in the lives of many people a full half century before that historic union. In early years lay ministers played at least as significant a part in people's lives as did their more fully qualified superiors. Two interesting lay preachers who exemplified this in particular, I feel, were Methodist Henry Rose and Presbyerian James Allan. Neither men lived to see the union of their respective churches.

Henry Rose was born in 1852 near Smith Falls, Ontario, son of John and Harriet Coolidge Rose. John was a United Empire Loyalist whose father had been a lieutenant in the war of 1812. Both John and son Henry became local preachers in their district. Rose Bridge on Irish Creek and Rose S.D. there commemorate this pioneer family.

Henry's training as school teacher and his preaching experience caught the attention of Dr. John McLean, famous missionary of Western Canada and later superintendent of Indian Missions. McLean persuaded Rose to settle in Western Manitoba and help establish Methodism.

In April 1879 Henry and his school teacher brother Francis with their widowed uncle William Rose arrived at Tanner's Crossing, the brothers filing on adjacent homesteads east of here. "My first service as a local preacher in this country," Henry writes, "was held at Rapid City" on May 18, 1879 in the home of Mr. Gardiner. Methodism in this district was however not entirely new for by 1877 Sunday School classes were already being held in the home of John Norquay (cousin of Manitoba's first premier) where, in the words of one historian, "Mrs. Norquay gathered her own and other Metis children on Sunday and taught them to read English and the Bible."

While Francis began breaking the land Henry travelled to Portage la Prairie where for three months he replaced Rev. Wm. Halstead who'd gone East to a conference. His circuit, which included places like High Bluff, Dalzell and Burnside schools, Trimble and Gowler homes, Portage, was one of two circuits between Winnipeg and Gladstone. On his first preaching tour his horse Jessie got stuck in a mud puddle and Henry eventually reached his destination mud-plastered and unrecognizable. The $20 per month he earned there helped the brothers establish their homesteads.

That first fall, as soon as their few harvest chores were done, Henry Rose headed west on the Carlton for another stint as missionary. Enroute, wrote Dr. Robert Harvey in the Brandon Sun, his horse Doll got stuck in a deep mud hole and Henry almost didn't make it. He and C.M. Copeland, a Presbyterian who later became famous in the YMCA movement, arrived in Birtle almost simultaneously. Writes Marion Abra in her recent fascinating book A VIEW OF THE BIRDTAIL "Copeland and Rose arranged schedules so as not to clash. Each gave Birtle a service once in three weeks. ...He (Rose) travelled with a toboggan and a Mountie 77 miles to Winnipeg, preaching enroute, at various points. Through storms in March 1880, undeterred by snowblindness, he walked or rode over 300 miles to Shoal Lake, Birtle, Rossburn. ...came regularly to Solsgirth, walking from Birtle summer and winter, sometimes taking a route around Shoal Lake."

"On October 12, 1879", indicated Harvey, "he held the first service in Birtle at 11 in the morning in the home of a Captain Wood. In the afternoon he held a Bible class at the home of Alfred Norton. He was the first missionary of any church to hold service there." "He boarded with his cousin Richard Rose Brown at Rossburn," adds his daughter Florence Brown, retired teacher and well known local historian, "and taught the first school there in the Ross home during the week." Rossburn historian Reita Bambridge Sparling concurs.

In 1881 Henry Rose was elected recording secretary of Little Saskatchewan Methodist mission. The following year he returned to his homestead (the current Oliver and Jack Douglas farm) to work the land. That year he obtained his Manitoba license as local preacher. He often preached in Clanwilliam district, in early days in the homes of George McKay and at the Cudhies (current John Hutton home). When the church was built he became one of its trustees.

On October 2, 1884, Henry married dressmaker Prudence McKinney, daughter of Wm. and Mary Crawford McKinney of Campbell's Cross near Brampton, Ontario, who had come to Minnedosa the year before to keep house for Brother George. The first Methodist church here, Florence Rose Brown told me, was located where the creamery now stands, built largely by George McKinney.

Henry Rose was Odanah municipality's first secretary treasurer and a member of Hazelwood S.D.'s first school board and its second teacher, informs local historian George Harland. By 1898 he was not only local preacher at Minnedosa Methodist church but also recording secretary and trustee. "Through the years," wrote Harvey, "he was often in demand as supply preacher and made many trips to Neepawa, Rapid City, Clanwilliam and other communities as the need arose." When the mortgage for the new Methodist church (present Calvary building) was being burned in 1922 (a year before his death) Henry was one of the proud officials participating in the ceremony.

Two years ago when RCMP Cst. Peter Tremblay transferred here and moved into the Rose Apartments, he asked me who William J. Rose was. Despite the fact I considered myself somewhat of an authority on local history I couldn't tell him anything about one of Minnedosa's most famous native sons. A son of Henry Rose and graduate of Wesley College (later United College and now Winnipeg University), Oxford, Leipzig and Cracow universities, he was the second Manitoban to receive a Rhodes scholarship. A professor of Slavonic languages he taught in London, England many years; later during retirement briefly at United College. The plaster cast of Dr. Rose in the apartment block lobby is a replica of a bronze one created and displayed in London in 1950 by artist P. Vincze. It seems the architect who designed the building had attended United College when Dr. Rose lectured there, was so impressed he sought and obtained permission to name the building after his favorite professor.

Perhaps nowhere is Henry Rose's religious influence in his son's work more obvious than in Karpinski's beautiful Polish hymn which William translated for Methodist use in 1922. It begins "With the morn in radiance breaking Earth in all her glory waking, Sky and sea, Thine own creation, Hymn Thee, Lord, in adoration", and ends "Death hath many captives numbered, While in peace we calmly slumbered; Now the newborn day arriving Summons us to noble striving." Manitoba Historical Society's annual meeting in Winnipeg in May will feature Prof. Daniel Stone of Winnipeg University speaking on 'William Rose, A Manitoba Historian'.

Lay minister Jim Allan of Fairmount district was hardly the first Presbyterian preacher to come to Minnedosa district. In fact, he didn't arrive until 1900. This was 22 years after Rev. Alexander Smith, usually considered the first Presbyterian advocate in this area when he began preaching west of Tanner's Crossing and performing so many marriages that his Saulteaux friends called the church he built Cadurcis, "a place of marriages." Others like Wellwood, Todd, McKinley, Paradis and Sutherland had also come and gone. Actually, if the truth were known, even Rev. Smith had been preceded a decade by several devout Presbyterian Metis families like John, Catherine and Poopie (Mrs. James) Tanner, Peter and Maggie Tanner Sinclair, the George Sandersons (originally 'Sandson' but later anglicized). It is however not known whether any did actual ministerial or Sunday School work; though John, Maggie and Poopie certainly had the necessary background through long association with their missionary father and husband Rev. James Tanner.

It's rather interesting that unlike most Prairie settlements, in Minnedosa district the seeds of the theological teachings of John Wesley (Methodism) and of John Calvin (Presbyterianism) had already been firmly planted by Metis pioneers well before any white settlers arrived. Perhaps it's significant that as I write this the United

Church Sunday service bulletin this week features a Metis lay minister, Johnston Garrioch of Cross Lake "whose special ordination was approved by the 26th General Council."

James Allan was born June 3, 1849 in Montrose, Scotland, emigrating to Fairmount district with sea captain brother Jack and wife Anna, sister Elizabeth and mother. He himself never married. Like his brother he was unsuccessful at farming. And like his brother he too had something else going for him; in his case that 'something else' being lay preaching. Some old timers I've talked to who still vividly recall Jim Allan's inspirational preaching are Cam Ross, George Brown, Mrs. Arthur McNabb, Doug McNabb, Florence (Mrs. Ed) Brown. Of course, they were all youngsters then. But then, youngsters frequently are more critical of sermons than are their parents.

Captain Allan's diary contains numerous references to his older brother's ministerial duties. A few during the years 1904-05 include: "Tom Ross called and drove Jim to Cadurcis, Fairmount and Basswood to hold divine services." "Went to Rolling River with Jim who conducted divine services there. Got pitched out of jumper, no evil results." "Started for Cameron school house with Jim to hold divine services. Got half way but had to return on account of snow drifts." "Went to Cameron and Rolling River where Jim held divine services at both places." "Started for Rolling River, Mr. Clyde accompanying; stabled horses and went to Magnus' house where Jim held divine services." "Started to go to Cameron school house; got stuck on road through snow drift and returned." "Went with Jim to Cadurcis, Fairmount and Basswood where he held divine services. Had dinner with Mr. Feir." "Jim went to Rolling River, Clanwilliam and Murchison and stayed overnight." "Jim at Rolling River, Clanwilliam and Bethany conducting divine services." "Jim held divine services at Cameron and Rolling River, Bible class at Fairmount."

Captain Allan's effects also include the 1900-02 McBride Reading Union minutes book. The founding executive, March 19, 1900, were Rev. Kirkpatrick as president, M. Ferguson treasurer, Jim secretary. It had about 15 members, met bi-weekly, studied and discussed history and literature. A common format seems to have been "home study one week, dramatic reading the second." India was thoroughly studied; Macbeth, Twelfth Night read out loud. Occasionally Jim chaired the meetings.

To a relative 'outsider' like myself who grew up in a vastly different church setting and joined the United Church 15 short years ago, the Methodist, Presbyterian and 'other' influences in Minnedosa United church are still discernible—especially among older members. When Minnedosa and neighboring churches join their Union's golden anniversary celebrations this summer, may they pay sincere tribute to early Methodist and Presbyterian Metis families like Norquay and Tanner and white ones like Rose and Allan who tried to plant the seeds of Christianity and brotherhood as they knew it in the hearts of their friends and neighbors.

63. HUBERT DARRELL AND ARCTIC FURS   Birtle Eye-Witness, Feb. 19 & 26/75

Although the Klondike Gold Rush drew Hubert Darrell away from his brother Charlie's farm in Warleigh district southeast of Birtle, into the Arctic where he quickly earned the respect of northerners as explorer, mail carrier, RNWMP guide and prospector, it was really the trapping, hunting, trading of furs that usually sustained him through hard times and made his many remarkable exploits possible.

Darrell's copper and gold discoveries later made other men rich. His Arctic explorations rank with the best and famous explorers like David Hanbury, Vilhjalmur Stefansson, Roald Amundsen praise his accomplishments. Had he not mysteriously vanished in northern Yukon in late 1910, he would the following year have accompanied Amundsen to the South Pole. As mail carrier for HBC he carried word to a startled outside world of the plight of 500 starving American whalers whose ships were frozen in Arctic ice. His guiding of police patrols over vast areas of uncharted northern wilderness rivals those of the famed Jerry Potts in the southwest.

Writing his parents in England from a little shack on Great Slave Lake on January 20, 1900 (letters owned by Scott Polar Research Inst., microfilm by Glenbow - Alberta Inst.) Darrell indicates, "I sometimes knock over four ducks with one shot. We had ducks galore all fall. I once dropped three partridges with one shot and two with the other barrel without moving my posture. Prairie chicken and white ptarmigan abound in great quantities. Not many buffalo here. I have lines of traps in four directions of 2 miles; have caught fox, lynx, marten, mink, fisher. Have shot no moose since June." In July he writes his father that he's making excellent money in fur, that he was just offered a good job but feels he can do better trapping, buying and selling furs, that "Edmonton is the best fur market on the continent."

Darrell was the first white man to ignore water transportation and on foot in 1899 penetrate overland deep into the barrens northeast of Great Slave Lake when he accompanied some Yellowknife Indians (after whom Yellowknife is named) on their annual winter muskox hunt. Describing the hunt to his father, he writes, "I singled out a big bull and dropped him like a stone, then fired at anything. After about two minutes of firing, the animals broke away leaving five on the hill but I dropped one within 100 yards and two more fell within the same distance. Got another bull further on." One animal charged "close enough to grab him" but by then his fingers were too cold to shoot. However, he and an Indian killed him moments later. "We got 18 all told." They slaughtered the animals, "each skin weighing 40 to 75 pounds." The following winter he again "trapped in the woods for a while."

During most of 1901 and 1902 Darrell guided Hanbury's expedition through northern Mackenzie and Keewatin; hunting for food, hides and furs to sell, as well as specimens for scientific purposes. This included animals like white foxes, wolverines, caribou, muskoxen, polar bears, Arctic hares and wolves.

In Spring of 1903 Darrell worked on a fur boat—as he was to do frequently on others in subsequent years—between Athabasca Landing and Fort Resolution, belonging to Nagle and Hyslop. Writing his mother, he tells of one load of furs and hides consisting of 6200 marten, 1600 mink, 5000 muskrat, 210 muskox, 1500 beaver, 30 otter, 150 wolverine, 1500 lynx.

The winter of 1904-05 saw Darrell trading furs with the Eskimos along Mackenzie River Delta. The following year he bought furs in the Peel River district and "had to bring a dead trader in from Arctic Red River; the Roman Catholic looked after the soul while we looked after the body." The winter of 1906-07 saw him helping trader Dan Cadzow of Rampart House with furs. It was an exceptionally harsh year, "starvation prevails all over this and the Mackenzie district." Although they bought more furs than the Peel River post they managed to obtain "only 350 lynx, 250 marten, some red and cross foxes, four silver foxes, besides a few mink and beaver. There are no caribou in the country this year, no rabbits to speak of." Hunting with Cpl. Haylow of the RNWMP yielded "three bighorn sheep and a deer."

But the pendulum swung back quickly and prosperity returned to the Arctic fur trade. Next winter Darrell dined with one of Dawson's biggest business men, Scougale, who averaged an annual profit of £10,000 trading furs in the Peel River area.

In his last letter to his father, from La Pierre House, Bell River, Yukon on June 25, 1910, Darrell indicates, "I'm able to pick up a little fur now and again. I could, by little trouble, pick up thousands of dollars worth of fur, it is only a matter of having the goods. Money is of little account. Nagle traded here on arrival for over $3000 worth just in a few hours besides having a ton of fur which his nephew traded here during the winter. There is big competition; the Hudson Bay Co. and the traders are cutting one another's throats all the time."

Dr. Margaret Dudley of Winnipeg, younger sister of Hubert Darrell's fiancee, Agnes Dudley of Warleigh district, recently told me, "When Hubert disappeared he had some fine furs, destined for my sister, in the trunk—so she said. After he was given up for lost, the trunk was sent to his mother in England."

Darrell, who during the first decade of this century knew our Canadian Arctic better than any other human being (white or native), lived through an era of devastating effect on northern fur, game and native people by white men. Writing his mother from Fort Resolution in December 1902 during the early days of that turbulent era, he compares the killing power of white and native hunters. "I am armed with the latest improved rifle and ammunition and the poor Eskimo with a bow and arrow with which he cannot hit a deer over 10 paces." Of the deteriorating effect of trading posts on natives he writes his father from Rampart House in May of 1907 that Indians there come to the trader "and get something they don't require such as a string of bells or a watch or a fine silk handkerchief" with their hard acquired furs.

Though Darrell hired out as guide to hunters on occasion, he never hesitated to refuse a man whose motives he suspected. During much of 1909, for example, though quite broke, he repeatedly refused to guide a trophy hunter called Harry V. Radford despite strong insistance, a high salary offer and accompanied personal recommenda-

tion from a bishop. This American 'sportsman's' reputation in the north left much to be
desired and money had often bought him privileges not readily available to ordinary
white men like Darrell, or to his Indian or Eskimo friends. Writing his parents from
Dawson in the spring of 1910 he adds, "Radford is a bore, green, the people at McPherson have a low opinion of him. I heard a lot about him. I hear that he killed a very
large buffalo weighing 2400 pounds (the mounted head today displayed in Calgary Museum). Why he should be allowed to kill buffalo and no one else beats me." Radford, with
a hunting partner, eventually hire two Eskimo guides, are both killed by the guides
whose lives they'd threatened--resulting in one of Canada's most sensational manhunts
and murder trials.

For several years Darrell operated out of Dawson. This was during the time Canada's
popular poet Robert Service also lived there. The two quickly became acquainted. When
Service later penned lines like "I have flouted the Wild. I have followed its lure,
fearless, familiar, alone" and "I am one of you no longer, by the trails my feet have
broken" he may very well, I firmly believe, have been referring to Hubert Darrell specifically. However, this can't yet be verified. Recent correspondence I've had with
the poet's widow Germaine, living in Monte Carlo, reveals that "when my husband left
the Yukon and came to France he did not take with him a box full of papers, and he never found it again."

Since becoming interested in this remarkable Arctic pioneer from Birtle two years
ago, I've written articles about different aspects about Hubert Darrell's career for
various newspapers and magazines. The more I learned about him the more I wondered why
some Arctic geographical feature didn't commemorate his accomplishments. One island,
for example, once known as Darrell Island, was later called something else; a river
that should have been the Darrell River was named otherwise.

After much writing and complaining (to the wrong people) I learned shortly before
Christmas that on December 12, 1939, two features were eventually named after Darrell
and had appeared on northern maps since 1943. They are Darrell Lake at "63 degrees, 47
minutes to 105 degrees, 39 minutes", and Darrell River--a tributary of the Hanbury River which empties into the Thelon River which flows into Chesterfield Inlet of Hudson
Bay. The river is about 40 miles long, the lake about seven. Ironically, not far to
the south on the same map are Radford Lake and Radford River.

64. MANITOBA'S SANTEE SIOUX   Excerpts from a much longer article, 'American Sioux
                               in Canada', submitted to a US magazine and unable to
                               determine whether or not published.

Perhaps the most interesting American Sioux in Manitoba were a small band of Santee
(meaning 'Permanent Home') settling on Birdtail Creek reserve between Birtle and Miniota. And perhaps the most fascinating member of this little band is a most articulate
venerable lady steeped in Sioux lore and history languishing in a personal care home
I interviewed recently called Mrs. Naomi (nee Bunn) Kasto--a Sitting Bull grand niece.

One Santee Sioux chief who led his band to Western Manitoba after two years of
dodging US cavalry in the Dakotas and Minnesota was Red Cloud. Obviously not the same
chief who defeated Col. William Fetterman's force at Fort Phil Kearney in 1866 and died
as blind decrepid old man in the Black Hills at Pine Ridge, S.D. in 1909, he was nevertheless a cousin or brother. As Naomi explains it, until recently customs acknowledged identical status in a band to all siblings and cousins; in other words, one's
cousins were considered one's brothers and sisters, real uncles and aunts as one's parents, and so forth. To further complicate things, chiefs and important warriors frequently had more than one wife. "I had quite a few grandmothers as little girl", she
remarked with a chuckle.

Of similar age, both Red Clouds were born and raised in Nebraska. That they did
not have the same paternity is certain. Unlike the more famous Red Cloud who didn't
inherit chiefship and whose father died of alcoholism, his own father was a chief with
interpreted name of 'Sleepy Eye'. The Santee chief died two years before his namesake,
is buried in a cemetery at Birdtail. His wife outlived him by several years.

Perhaps because she became higher educated than other Birdtail youngsters of her
time (high school graduate when few peers completed elementary school) Naomi became
deeply interested in Sioux history and frequently questioned her elders about "the old
days". An excellent memory coupled with a keen mind helped preserve much of this history as seen through Sioux eyes.

The following is the story of how the Sioux-Caucasian war of 1860s and '70s in America began as told to her by her people:

"Some white settlers moved into Sioux territory, and my people let them stay. One day some Sioux men visited the farm of a white family; the man was away somewhere. So the men went into the house and stood around admiring all the homemade furniture, the like of which they'd never seen before. There were chicken eggs lying loose on a table near the door. One man leaned against the door, which bumped the table and some eggs rolled off and broke. The settler's wife became very mad, rushed at him and kicked and slapped him. The men went outside, laughing and making fun of their clumsy companion. 'How come you let a squaw beat and kick you?' they mocked him. Embarrassed and annoyed he marched right back into the cabin and shot the woman and both children. The men left quickly. The mother and one child were dead; the other--just wounded--mounted a horse and rode to a white neighbor for help. There was much anger among the whitemen when they heard of this."

"Shortly after, one Sioux band broke camp to move to new hunting grounds, stopped for lunch. A white settler in covered wagon came driving by, stopped, asked the Indians if they would like some food he had with him. They said they would, and he gave them a big pot of soup and drove off at a gallop. The men were suspicious because of the settler's strange behavior and because he wouldn't stay to eat with them after they had invited him. But most of the women and children did eat the soup anyways. Soon they became very sick, and many died in great pain for the soup had been poisoned. This made the Sioux very angry."

"One baby, who had been breast-feeding at the time eating no soup and didn't die, was Jessie Aakpi (River) who later as a man was constable on Pipestone reserve (Oak Lake) many years."

Naomi can't recall having heard an English translation of her grandmother's name, but roughly it means 'Beautiful Sky'. She was a sister of Birdtail's Chief Red Cloud and cousin of Sitting Bull. As young woman Beautiful Sky was traded by her father to an American soldier stationed nearby for a horse, rifle and blanket. Thus she became the wife of Irishman John Bunn and lived in army barracks until the 1860s uprising. The Bunns had three children--Moses (Naomi's father), Hagar and Gerrod. Naomi's eyes crinkle with laughter when she discusses her quarter Irish ancestry. Perhaps this Emerald Isle heritage adds to her remarkable sense of humor.

Beautiful Sky's mother persuaded her to flee with the Sioux for she was convinced her daughter's status as wife of a white soldier would not be enough to protect her from retaliation by angry whites. Young Moses was six when the tribe left Minnesota, eight by the time they finally reached Manitoba after running and hiding from pursuing cavalry. In a deadly hail of bullets the tribe crossed the wide and treacherous Missouri in the very spot the main highway bridge near Bismarck, N.D. today spans that river. Naomi is convinced that her grandfather John Bunn was one of Custer's soldiers later annihilated by her uncle Sitting Bull and his warriors.

For several years the American Sioux refugees wandered aimlessly about the south-central plains of Manitoba. The buffalo were rapidly vanishing and times for all hunting societies became extremely hard. The whites feared them. The Metis resented them. The native Canadian tribes, Cree and Saulteaux, had long hated them and fought bloody battles with them in former years. Remains of trenches utilized in at least one major battle between the refugee Sioux and the Saulteaux (led by Chief Picheito Tanner of Portage la Prairie area) can still be clearly seen near the southeast shore of Lake Manitoba.

Naomi was born on Birdtail reserve in 1898. Her father, Moses Bunn, farmed and she recalls especially following him around fields in furrows while he guided a horse-drawn handplow. Her mother trapped and hunted in spare time and frequently Naomi tagged along. She even learned to make bows and arrows for younger brothers in the traditional Sioux manner.

Mrs. Kasto remembers vividly her granduncle Red Cloud while as young girl she attended Birtle Indian Residential School. He was of medium height, slim; "no fat Indians those days for everyone walked a lot." She remembers the many mares and fine stallion he owned. However, students only returned to reserve life for July in those days and thus she saw considerably less of relatives during school years than did most white Canadians. Following his death in 1907 Red Cloud's beautiful horses were inherited by his sister, re-married to John Bopha.

Violet Keel recalled that pioneer Albert Bartley "made a treaty with Bopha that if the Indian horses got out on the plains he would drive them back; if the Bartley horses went to the reserve, Bopha would do the same. That treaty was kept through the years."

The death of Sitting Bull shortly after his return to America from Canada, Naomi's people told her, was hardly the accidental shooting some historians have depicted it. "The old chief was in his lodge," she informed me, "and refused to come out to be put on a reserve when authorities came to get him. 'Come out and tell us how you killed all those whitemen,' one reserve constable kept taunting him. Finally Sitting Bull no longer could stand this and came out. As he stepped through the door that constable shot him dead."

Moses Bunn married twice and had 25 children altogether; 12 by Naomi's mother and 13 by her stepmother. One full brother, Eli, still lives on Birdtail reserve; a half brother, Edward, does Presbyterian missionary work on that and two other reserves. The Presbyterian church there, of which Naomi's a member, was built the same year she was born.

In 1918, at 20, Naomi married William Kasto (who died seven years ago) in that same church. A brother-in-law, Private Thomas Kasto of the 27th Battalion, had been killed in action in Europe on August 21 the year before. A grandson, John Kasto, who raises fine horses descending from the Red Cloud band, was recently elected chief of Birdtail Sioux reserve--the destiny of which his great uncle Red Cloud helped shape the first three decades of its existence.

65. JOHN 'FALCON' TANNER'S DEATH   Manitoba Pageant, Spring, 1975

As columnist writing historical articles revolving around Minnedosa area I became deeply intrigued with ancestors of one-armed Metis American Civil War veteran John Tanner (1839-1932) who founded Tanner's Crossing (now Minnedosa) and serving as first postmaster, contributions recently commemorated by naming a multi-million dollar new school and beautiful centennial park after him. I've thoroughly researched the Tanners and written a series of articles about this remarkable family. That involved much correspondence with Tanner descendants and genealogists scattered across North America, searching documents, interviewing people.

Wilson F. Green's fascinating RED RIVER REVELATIONS deals with the famous grandfather of Minnedosa's founder. Several books and articles have been written about John 'Falcon' Tanner (1781-1846), son of Baptist Rev. John Tanner (1732-1812), who was kidnapped by Indians in Ohio in 1789 and lived as tribe memmber in various parts of Minnesota, North Dakota, Ontario, Saskatchewan and Manitoba 30 years. Green's description of events surrounding this 'white Indian's' tragic death, though historically accurate according to general consensus in 1846, is unfortunately incomplete. Nevertheless, he does recognize there's conflicting evidence concerning that event.

True, John Falcon Tanner was, as Green indicates, blamed for the July 6, 1846, murder of wild but influential James Schoolcraft, younger brother of John's employer --Indian agent/historian Henry Schoolcraft. The Tanner cabin on the outskirts of Sault Ste. Marie, several authorities concur, had burned down prior to the murder and John was seen heading into woods nearby with rifle at about that time, not the time of the murder. His youngest son John J., who built a new home on the same site, was living there with mother Theresa two years later.

Tanner's skeleton was discovered in adjacent woods one year later, not years later, and identified. How he died isn't known; though his Indian friends were convinced he was murdered and cabin razed by James Schoolcraft's murderer so he'd be suspected of this crime. The meeting near Rainy River of the (1823) United States' Long expedition with John in wounded condition occurred 23 years before the murder and was obviously not, as Green quoting Minnesota historian Neill suggests, connected with the homicide. Actually an Indian shot him that particular time. And he was trying to take two daughters to a private school--St. Vincent's Academy in Cape Girardeau, Missouri.

For many years after his own death John was blamed for the Schoolcraft murder. Fortunately he was eventually vindicated when an army Lieutenant Tilden, who had conducted a massive 'search' for John after the murder, confessed to having committed that crime because of jealousy over a girl.

John Tanner's return to white society brought much heartache. In 1810 his first

Indian wife Sky Dawn left him taking their two daughters and son. When he did finally with help of Lord Selkirk (whom he'd greatly assisted with negotiating Indian treaties permitting Selkirk Settlement to establish and with recapturing forts Daer and Douglas) locate his 16 white siblings he found that his father, who'd married thrice and become rich, had just died at Cape Girardeau disinheriting him believing him dead. Two children from his second Indian wife Theresa died in epidemics. The Sault Ste. Marie whites shunned him and took legal action in 1830 to remove a daughter to a private school because of his hot temper. Because the pension Selkirk awarded him for his services was too small to allow retirement he was forced to work to the end at various jobs like interpreting for Henry Schoolcraft. His assistance with translating the New Testament and hymns into Saulteaux brought some recognition but no remuneration. Theresa became Catholic and refused to live with him on strength of their Indian marriage and they quarreled bitterly over this.

John Tanner had nine children. Of these two died young and two presumably married Indian men and are probably lost to history. Several of the other five are better known.

His oldest son Picheito Tanner (called Little Pheasant when young) became a major chief of a large Saulteaux tribe in the Portage la Prairie-White Horse Plains region. He became wealthy in later years retiring to Portage, died in Qu'Appelle Valley in or after 1872. His log cabin was the first shingled house west of Winnipeg. A son John Tanner (1842-1936) was of Gambler Band living on Silver Creek Reserve No. 63 near Binscarth which entered Treaty 4 on Sept. 21, 1874 under Chief Way-wa-se-ca-pow. When most of this band moved to Valley River (Dauphin) and No. 63 was thrown open to homesteaders the Tanner family kept 860 acres (today Gambler Reserve) which descendants still farm.

Not much is known about John Falcon Tanner's youngest son John J. besides what is already mentioned, other than he was divorced and remarried in 1848 and was killed in action in the second battle of Manasses of the American Civil War.

Martha Ann Tanner studied teaching at Catholic St. Vincent's Academy and as a member of The Sisters of Loretto Order taught there many years herself and later in Mackinac, Mich. but never married. Highly popular, and deeply respected, she was buried on Mackinac Island where a tombstone commemorates her passing.

Mary Elizabeth married a LaVogue. Their sons Joe and George became prominent Duluth business men. Next she married Joseph Tall and had a son Joseph, late in life married a Hoffman. As the last living child of John's she developed cancer and died about 1883.

Best known of Falcon's children was Rev. James Tanner, father of the founder of Tanner's Crossing. During his last 20 years he was a deeply loved Presbyterian and Baptist missionary among his Saulteaux people in the Pembina, St. Joseph, Winnipeg and Portage la Prairie regions. Despite a lengthy inquest, his untimely death about mid-way between Portage and Winnipeg in late fall during the 1870 Red River Resistance aftermath is still shrouded in mystery. Kildonan's Rev. John Black, the first Presbyterian minister to Canada's Prairies and a close friend of Tanner's, in letters to family members attributes James' fatal fall from a lurching wagon drawn by a runaway horse to deliberate action of Wolseley's soldiers. The coroner's jury ruled that "the late James Tanner died from a fracture of the skull caused by his being thrown out of a wagon while the horse of said wagon was running away, and that said horse was caused to run away wilfully and maliciously by two persons unknown to this jury."

Rev. Tanner's wife (Saulteaux name 'Poopie') soon thereafter moved to Minnedosa, in about 1883 to the Prince Albert region, about 1906 to Binscarth, and several years prior to her death in 1914 at 108 to Kinosota on Lake Manitoba's west shore. I'm convinced that she was the 104-year-old Indian lady whose 1910 photo was featured in the Winter 1972 MANITOBA PAGEANT with caption "Mrs. John Tanner of Binscarth," a slight error having been made for Mrs. James Tanner was exactly that age in 1910 while at Binscarth. Rev. and Mrs. Tanner had two children, Mrs. Maggie Sinclair and John; the latter though married had no children except an adopted son. John Falcon Tanner's second wife Theresa was still alive in Sault Ste. Marie in 1860

This is my fifth article on Ara-Wel Ponies to this magazine, the last three involving mostly negotiations with our federal department of agriculture as regards Canadian registry.

Last year I mentioned a recent proposal by Hon. Eugene Whelan that Ara-Wels could be recorded in the General Stud and Herd Book until considered purebred; as are most exotic cattle breeds, for example. Though I had serious reservations about recordation as first step towards getting hitherto American-registered Ara-Wels accepted for registration in Canada as the case of exotic cattle being 'upgraded' by continual use of purebred sires didn't seem analogous to Ara-Wels, I felt the matter should nevertheless be checked out. I mailed the (American) registration certificates of our two full sisters, Glendosa Silver Blitz 159 and Glendosa Silver Comet 164, whose parents were registered Ara-Wels (Glendosa Silver Abi 142 and Glendosa Silver Beau 141) with covering letter to Canadian National Livestock Records for recordation.

As anticipated, the certificates were promptly returned (Sept. 26/74) with a letter from director F.G. Clark indicating in part, "this book provides for the registration of purebred animals and the grading up to purebred status by the use of purebred sires", this method not being applicable to Ara-Wels for "at the present time there are no provisions for this procedure in the General Stud and Herd Book." However, he agreed to take up the Ara-Wel matter with the Record Committee to meet in late October.

On Nov. 13/74 Mr. Clark wrote again, indicating "I wish to advise that until this species qualifies as a breed in accordance with the criteria established by the Canada Department of Agriculture, we cannot make provisions for registration of same in the General Stud and Herd Book."

Meanwhile, I had again contacted Mr. Whelan, explained what happened with the recordation idea. It seems Mr. Whelan had not simply ignored the Ara-Wel situation (as had his predecessors) since my previous communication with him but had subsequently created an Advisory Committee "to establish criteria for the eligibility of new breeds in Canada" like Ara-Wels and others that might be developed. In my opinion, this is a major step in the right direction as to date it has been virtually impossible for Canadian individuals and groups to develop new breeds of domestic animals; and I told him so.

Excerpts from Mr. Whelan's letter read: "After a number of meetings this Committee has recommended that the criteria for eligibility for registration of new breeds of livestock in Canada be--'animals of a newly developed breed from identified parents from a foundation population which has been recognized by the Minister as having resulted from a selective breeding program which was closed to outside breeding for at least three generations. The Minister may require that the individual animals making up this foundation be identified by an independent inspection body'."

"In order to include Ara-Wel ponies in the General Stud and Herd Book, and in order to be consistent with the newly established criteria for the recognition of new breeds, it is necessary to establish that the Ara-Wels you wish to register in the General Stud and Herd Book meet with these criteria, namely, that they are three generations removed from the originating cross, and consequently are a minimum of 87½% Ara-Wel blood. We are prepared to recognize Ara-Wel ponies on this basis, and Canadian National Live Stock Records will be governed accordingly." Though a far cry from what I'd hoped might occur regarding Ara-Wels, it's nonetheless a breakthrough for this movement and will undoubtedly encourage development of other new breeds in Canada.

Although this breakthrough will eventually help Canadian Ara-Wel breeders considerably, it won't be of great significance for a decade. It must be noted that what we normally call 'first generation' Ara-Wels on basis of US registration (ones with one Arab and one Welsh parent) are termed 'original cross' according to this regulation. What we call 'second generation' Ara-Wels (with two Ara-Wel parents), are 'first generation' Ara-Wels by Canadian standards. In other words, an American-registered Ara-Wel cannot become registered in Canadian National Livestock Records until its pedigree contains: 1. Two American-registered Ara-Wel parents 2. Four

American-registered Ara-Wel grandparents 3. Eight American-registered Ara-Wel great grandparents 4. Sixteen American and/or Canadian-registered Arabian and Welsh (most likely eight of each) great great grandparents.

At Glendosa, because of the small size of our Ara-Wel project, our chief problem has been getting the correct sex. When you get two stallions of a particular generation and only one mare or two mares of another and are waiting for a stallion, this slows things down somewhat. But we don't have pasture or facilities to operate a larger one—with 20 or more ponies as should be done. Though it is too early to say definitely, I forsee no problem whatsoever in standardizing Ara-Wels as to size and type. Our three youngest children (the two oldest have flown the coop), Kathy 14, Rod 11, Lisa 9 like them very much and break them to ride themselves with virtually no help from me.

We sold our second stallion, Glendosa Silver Arrow 129, last fall to Joe Wilson who raises horses near Whitewater Lake. Joe has grades, registered Welsh and Ara-Wels; is a good horseman.

I mentioned last year that we're toying with the idea of developing our own conception of 'ideal Canadian pony' breed by using Ara-Wel mares with a different stud. We're considering this more seriously than ever but are waiting to see whether an Ara-Wel mare that's bred to Arrow foals a filly or colt this summer.

Regardless what we ourselves decide to do about ponies at our little Centre, sincere best wishes to all Welsh, Arabian and Ara-Wel owners and breeders.

Note: Since this article was written we have purchased a three-year-old registered tarpan stallion, Thrallhalla's Leonardo, from Mrs. Ellen J. Thrall of Lilburn, Georgia for the above stated purpose.

67. KIDNAPPING AND TANNER'S CROSSING   Minnedosa Tribune, May 8, 1975

If there is one unique aspect of early Minnedosa district history that might intrigue people internationally, it probably would be the 'White Child Kidnapped by Hostile Indians' syndrome. Very few North American communities can point to a single such case. That three completely unrelated such kidnappings figure prominently in Minnedosa history is not only intriguing but highly unusual.

I doubt if there's a North American (or European for that matter) who hasn't heard of the 1789 Shawnee kidnapping of John 'Falcon' Tanner and his subsequent lifetime of living with the Ottawas and Saulteaux. I doubt if more books, short stories, articles have been written about a single kidnapping. I doubt if more detailed and accurate information about daily lIndian life in Manitoba, Ontario, Minnesota and North Dakota during the 1790-1840 half century has been recorded for posterity than by the grandfather of Minnedosa's founder. As historian Paul Radin indicated, "Of all the many narratives written by white people who have been captured by Indians, that of John Tanner easily takes first place."

Because so much has already been written about the indomitable Falcon by others and myself, I won't dwell on this fascinating saga again here. Suffice to say, the history of Tanner's Crossing would have been vastly different—perhaps much less interesting—had the Shawnees not kidnapped young John 186 years ago. I wonder how many Minnedosans realized that the recent tragic death of one of their fellow residents, that of Mrs. Louis (Julie Tanner) Ducharme, was that of a great great great granddaughter of the famous white Falcon and his beautiful Saulteaux wife 'Red Sky of Morning'.

Craig Stewart, who grew up in the district where our founder lived out his last two decades, mentioned to me a while back having heard of a second kidnapping years ago. Last summer when son Rod and I were camping in the Kinosota-Silver Ridge-Reedy Creek area, I ran the story down.

The founder of Tanner's Crossing had a white 'foster brother'; a boy kidnapped by Minnesota Cree whom John Jr.'s missionary father Rev. James Tanner befriended and who never did learn his true identity despite great effort. Even his descendants (and I talked with his son Duncan at length) still don't know it today. Because the boy was so impressed with Rev. Tanner he discarded his Cree name and named himself after his benefactor—James (Jimmy) Tanner. Later Jimmy married a prominent Minnedosa Metis girl, Elizabeth Sanderson (originally 'Sandson'). "She attended the little white Presbyterian church (now AA club house) in the eastern part of Town still there today," Duncan told me. Thus the remaining Manitoba Tanners are descendants of Jimmy and Elizabeth 'Tanner'.

Many Canadians and Americans eventually learned of Jimmy's kidnapping because of his deep conviction that he was Charlie Ross. Though you may never have heard of Charlie Ross, his name was a household word in your grandparents' day. Like that of Patti Hearst currently, or Charles Lindbergh Jr. in the '30s. His was North America's first 'kidnap-for-ransom' case. Countless articles and at least one book were written about it. In July of 1924 Ladies Home Journal ran a cover story on the tragedy's 50th anniversary. Upon Jimmy's death, Myrtle J. Broley in a July 7/34 Winnipeg Free Press article was still speculating on whether he was "the missing Charlie Ross." Both Philadelphia papers, Bulletin and Inquirer, still carry lengthy feature articles on the "first kidnapping case of modern times."

Four-year-old Charles Brewster Ross was abducted in the afternoon of July 1, 1874 from the front yard of his home on East Washington Lane, Germantown (now a suburb of Philadelphia). His father Christian Ross, who lived with wife Sarah and seven children in the large stone house, had kissed him goodbye that morning, promised to buy him fireworks for evening celebrations, and left for his store eight miles away. Mrs. Ross and eldest daughter were in Atlantic City on vacation, the two oldest boys in Middletown visiting a grandmother, the youngest four at home cared for by servants.

Two men in a buggy, who had stopped several days earlier to give the Ross children candy, pulled up at the curb and offered Charlie and older brother Walter a ride. The youngsters accepted eagerly, asked the men to stop at a store for fireworks. The men readily agreed, drove to a distant neighborhood, gave Walter a quarter to make the purchase and while he was inside disappeared with Charlie. A search and advertising campaign ensued. On July 4 a letter arrived warning not to contact police and await instructions. Two days later a second letter demanded $20,000 ransom.

Unknown to the kidnappers and Germantown residents Christian Ross had recently suffered severe financial reverses and was virtually bankrupt. Police and city officials decided to call the abductors' bluff and refuse payment. Although 21 more letters were received by the Rosses and more than enough financial assistance pledged by friends negotiations collapsed. The last letter came Nov. 7; $20,000 was promptly dispatched to a designated spot but no one came and no contact was ever again made.

"The greatest search ever undertaken by any city continued," wrote American journalist Jim Kelly. "Over 100,000 houses were entered. Graves were opened. Police from London to Berlin, and from Chicago to St. Augustine stopped anyone resembling Charles Brewster Ross." Meanwhile, police became convinced that one kidnapper was ex-Sing Sing convict Gil Mosher, then consorting with a Joseph Douglas.

At 2 a.m. Dec. 14 Mosher and Douglas were shot and killed in a furious gun battle with Bay Ridge, Long Island residents while burglarizing the vacant home of a New York supreme court judge. Mosher was killed instantly, but before Douglas died he confessed the two had engineered the kidnapping, Charlie was alive and well and would be returned soon, only Mosher knowing his whereabouts. But Charlie was never heard from again. Mosher's brother-in-law William Westervelt was later sentenced to seven years when evidence implicated him, served his time and emerged still maintaining innocence. The Rosses, what little money they had left having been spent searching, until Christian's death in 1897 and Sarah's in 1912 continued to hope, pray, search, interview boys and later young men believed to be Charlie to no avail.

According to Broley, Jimmy Tanner "claimed that he, the true Charlie Ross, was either put in care of Indians by the men who tried to get rid of him before they were caught or else that a band of Crees took him from the men—scalping them and leaving them to rot in some deep part of the forest. At any rate his very hazy memories of an earlier luxurious life, followed by a period when he seemed to be rushed from place to place, are swallowed up in recollections of the five years he spent with this tribe."

The tribe, wandering back and forth across Minnesota, were good to Jimmy, dyed his sandy hair and fair skin to make him appear one of them. Apparently his grey-blue eyes didn't worry them. But after a while the boy tired of this life and ran away, lived for a time with James Tanner "who made his living freighting goods from one part of the States to another." Eventually the tribe found him. The boy agreed to return, but rejected his former Cree name and refused to give up his new one.

A few years later Jimmy again escaped, met a freighter called Campbell and inquired about James Tanner. Campbell knew Rev. Tanner, who he said now lived "in the North-West Territories" (as the Canadian West was called). Campbell was travelling to Manitoba with a load of flour, hid Jimmy in a barrel and smuggled him across the border.

Though Jimmy couldn't find Tanner he decided to stay in Manitoba. Because of good knowledge of Cree he readily obtained work with HBC, for many years drove dog teams to outlying districts at Norway House. Later he moved back to southern Manitoba and worked for contractor George Greible.

During this time Jimmy heard men discuss the Charlie Ross afair, and the name was strongly familiar. One day he heard of the strange strawberry mark on the missing boy's arm, bared his own to reveal a similar one. He recalled dimly an old squaw saying to him, "Not Charlie--JAMES. Not Charlie--JAMES", as though teaching him a lesson and that when she lay dieing and asked to see him the chief prevented his going. He kept inquiring about James Tanner; some said he was dead, others that he'd gone to England. After years of searching he visited the Ross home in Philadelphia to try to prove his identity, but both Christian and Sarah were now dead and he got nowhere. He returned to Manitoba and worked on the CPR. Broley claims the Ross inheritance by then totalled millions of dollars (evidence refutes this), and that Jimmy made "two more trips to press claim to the money" without success.

According to Jimmy's son Duncan, in whose home I spent a most pleasant visit, his father fought in the Northwest Rebellion of 1885 "travelling from Winnipeg to Medicine Hat." In 1906 he was summoned to a police station in Winnipeg, his birthmark examined, although on correct arm was supposedly slightly higher than where it should have been according to experts. Mrs. Tanner showed me a large birthmark on her own arm, which she says was not only considerably lower when she was little but also a different shape. In February of 1916, says Duncan, his elderly father enlisted in the Canadian Army but though appearing much younger than his true age authorities eventually became suspicious and discharged him.

Both the Duncan Tanners, and other old timers there, remember well Rev. James Tanner's wife 'Poopie' living in that district with her son, Minnedosa founder John Tanner, and her daughter Mrs. Maggie Sinclair. Upon her deathbed Mrs. James Tanner asked for Jimmy, then living in Westbourne district, to come and see her for she had something important to tell him but by the time he got there she was too weak and died without uttering another word.

Despite strong evidence suggesting Jimmy Tanner was Charlie Ross, he could really not have been. First, Charlie Ross was kidnapped almost four years AFTER Rev. Tanner's murder (late fall of 1870). Second, Tanner's freighting days occurred prior to 1850, possibly again during the late 1850s and early 1860s when his missionary work was disrupted by Sioux hostilities. From about 1864 until his tragic death Rev. Tanner worked in the Portage la Prairie area as missionary, not freighter. Third, Jimmy was old enough to fight in the 1885 rebellion, Charlie Ross would have been barely 15. I personally believe that Jimmy Tanner was a boy called Charlie, one of many white Minnesota children whose parents were killed during the Indian-Caucasian hostilities and--similar to the father of the man he so admired after whom he named himself--was spared death and instead adopted into the tribe to replace a son who died.

Donald Murray of Neepawa-Minnedosa area mentioned the third kidnapping case to bookshop operator Mrs. Day who told me. A chat with Mr. Murray, who farms five miles south on 464 and one east where he operates a private museum, threw some light on the case. Much digging around has uncovered a bit. The case revolves around one of the earliest white settlers in this area, a young Anglican missionary called John B. Sargent (spelling of his surname varies in different reports).

MINNEDOSA MEMORIES indicates, "The first services of the Anglican church in Minnedosa were held by a young clergyman named Sergeant in 1881. He lived in Rapid City and only came here occasionally," was succeeded the following year by the first permanent rector Mark Jukes. These first services, say Anglican records, were held "in the old town hall."

A chat with Mrs. Robert (Ericka) Brandon of Clanwilliam produced evidence predating by one year services held here by Rev. Sargent. Her mother Ethel came to Tanner's Crossing as a five-year-old youngster June 10, 1880 with parents Octavius and

Emma Peacy Averill. Mrs. Brandon possesses Emma's hand-written journal which states, "There were only six houses in Minnedosa then, the rest were tents. The first Sunday morning the Church of England held their first service in Minnedosa, in the hotel, and the chaplain Mr. Sergeant preached the sermon." Octavius was a lay reader then. The Averills lived in a tent three months before building their home, which became the centre for Anglican services on numerous occasions. Emma Averill's journal, by the way, lays to rest a controversy that raged in a Brandon Sun column about five years ago involving the re-naming in 1928 of the Little Saskatchewan—the Cree word 'Saskatchewan' and Saulteaux 'Minnedosa' being synonymous.

Mrs. Bert (Adelle) Hulbert of Minnedosa was able to add information from her 1967 copy of ANGLICAN CHURCH BRANDON DIOCESAN WOMEN'S AUXILLIARY by archivist Miss Frances Lena Mary Code. Regarding Rapid City Code writes, "Records show Rev. J.B. Sargent was priest-in-charge in 1880 and Rev. Lorenzo Sheperd became resident priest 1883." For Rivers, "The first Anglican services in this district were held at Arva Farm, three miles east of Rivers, at the farmstead of Thomas Cousins in 1880. They were conducted by the Rev. John B. Sargent of Rapid City who walked 10 miles from there to the Cousins farm. These services were continued from the spring of 1880 until 1884 when the Rosevale Church was built." Referring to Souris she mentions that Rev. "Sergant of Minnedosa laid the cornerstone Aug. 13, 1883, and St. Luke's Church was dedicated October 13, 1884." Her book and A.F. McKenzie's NEEPAWA—LAND OF PLENTY indicate that Rev. Sergent conducted the first Anglican service in Neepawa district in 1879, six miles southwest of that town in the home of a Mr. Patterson, next in newly-constructed St. George's church (which was later moved to Bridge Creek and re-named St. Martin's).

Code, McKenzie, Neepawa Press, all refer to Rev. Sargent having "a 10-year-old daughter who was kidnapped by the Indians and was never returned." From that point on this case to date remains a total mystery. When and where did this kidnapping occur? What Indian tribe's alleged to be responsible? What kind of search was conducted? From where did the Sargents come and where did they go when they left this district? Generally speaking, when Indians captured white girls or women those days they did so simply to acquire white wives.

It's a most intriguing thought when one contemplates the many North American Metis descendants which undoubtedly resulted solely from the three kidnappings that figure prominently in Minnedosa district history.

And in the June 12 edition of the same newspaper:

"The Charlie Ross Story, in full detail, is now in my possession, thanks to you and the editor of the Tribune," E.S. Hopper of Powell River, B.C. wrote me recently. "As a child I can vaguely recall the name, Charlie Ross, spoken of by my parents in the early days at Rapid City. That was probably 80 years ago, and during the intervening years it had been my hope that the full details of what could be quite a fascinating story would be told."

Not everyone was as happy with the Jimmy Tanner-Charlie Ross story. A grandson of Jimmy's, who requested anonymity, phoned to inform that some of what's been written about his grandfather in years past was inaccurate. A cousin of his in the same district, Tribune, readers may remember as the lady who cut the ribbon to officially open Tanner's Crossing School. He referred me to his mother, a very nice elderly lady, who's a daughter of Jimmy Tanner.

A conversation with the lady elicited one surprising development—that her father had supposedly disliked and feared James Tanner when he lived with him and had avoided rather than searched for him after he came to Manitoba with Campbell. This lady, who grew up in Westbourne district, didn't know Minnedosa's founder and sister Maggie well but did meet them once. She reiterated her son's allegation that some of what's been written about her father in past years is incorrect, could not explain or understand why he would name himself after a man he feared and hated, who at one point allegedly threatened to kill him. "He believed until the end he was really Charlie Ross, and so did all his neighbors." She disagrees strongly with her brother Duncan Tanner that their father ever enlisted to fight in the 1885 Rebellion. "I think it's time people quit writing about my father."

My May article dealt with three kidnappings of white children by Indians that figure prominently in early Minnedosa history. It seems there were four. A recent letter from Pax Crawley of Clanwilliam, author of the booklet 'Lakelet School and its Pioneers', provides details.

"There was another one that you may not have heard of. My father told me of it many years ago."

"It was not strictly a kidnap, but an exchange and involved a man named George Campbell, who my father said, lived south and west of Clanwilliam. He homesteaded the SW ¼ of 2-16-18; west of Ed McFarlane's place. (A check with Arla Gowing showed that no one lives there today but that Ed farms it.) The exchange took place at a picnic in Ontario, which the Campbell family attended. A number of babies were left on a blanket in the afternoon and when the Campbells went to get theirs it was gone and an Indian baby left in its place. I don't know if they ever heard of their own baby, but they apparently raised the little Indian child and named him George Campbell. George (Sr.) probably took up the homestead in 1879 or early 1880 as all the land from there to the end of the survey, six miles north, was taken by the spring of 1880."

"My father told me a little story about George. It seems he bought a walking plow from an implement dealer, Arthur Shaw, but did not pay for it; as often happened in those days. So Arthur Shaw went to see George to try to get the money or reclaim the plow. Not having any success on the first count he asked, "Where is the plow, George?" to which George replied, "Arthur, I'll tell you what I'd tell nobody else--it's hid." And it was, in the cellar under the potatoes and Arthur was sitting right on top of it. History doesn't relate if he ever got the plow."

Pax referred me to Art Pollon of Minnedosa, who knew George Campbell Jr. (long his neighbor) very well. George, says Mr. Pollon, has been dead many years now; died in a 'home' somewhere. He never married. Wherever he went he took with him his dogs Scotty and Charlie. He had a (step) brother in Winnipeg. George was highly skilled at making fancy household articles like comb and soap holders. Somewhat paranoid, he was convinced that people "were after him" and strung wire throughout his farmyard to trip them in the dark. A tall man, thin of face, Art recalls he especially loved fiddling, that on one occasion his team of horses bolted because of a particularly loud musical rendition and that for a while all that could be heard were George's shouts of "Whoa! Whoa!" receding rapidly into the distance. In later years he built a cabin in Minnedosa; "a very sturdy one" which Art's father eventually bought and moved to his farm, where it still stands today.

68. WATER SPORTS AND SAFETY   :   Minnedosa Tribune, May 29, 1975

Back in '52 I completed Red Cross senior swimming in Sherbrooke pool, Winnipeg and instructor-life guarding at HMCS Chippewa under Bill LeBlanc and Bruce McIntosh. That summer I taught swimming and life guarded briefly at a leadership camp (under current United Church moderator Wilbur Howard) at Clear Lake. Thus began and ended my formal very short water safety career. Much had occurred in the program before I came along, lots more since.

Bill LeBlanc, just back from combat in Europe, became Manitoba's director and driving force in 1946; Bruce McIntosh, one of the first instructors to qualify, Manitoba's secretary-treasurer of Royal Life Saving Society the following year to quickly earn the title 'Mr. Life Saving'. Brandon YMCA helped LeBlanc establish the program in West-Man. "Minnedosa, Rapid City, Souris, Dauphin, Wawanesa and Ninette Red Cross branches," states one report, "adopted the program and graduated instructors." Later, Army cadets and many others became deeply involved in a program in which most Manitobans have had some involvement. In 1964 LeBlanc became assistant commissioner, the program having mushroomed from 300 to 25,931 participants during his directorship and programs from 8 to 105. Manitoba drowning deaths dropped from 10 per 100,000 in '46 to 7 per 100,000 last year.

Manitoba director James Fenske wrote me last fall that Bill LeBlanc recalls well that two pioneers "deeply associated early in the Minnedosa program" were Anglican Rev. Cecil Rothery and pharmacist Ross Cairns (now in Grandview). Today, he says, Manitoba has "some 900 water safety instructors and some 400 water safety leaders."

Mrs. Ivy Mummery, who co-ordinated Minnedosa Lake's program the past two decades and whom I've recently succeeded, told me that the Kinsmen, Elks, Town, Chamber were all much involved in launching our program. During her time quite a few instructors-life guards also became qualified, some early ones being Joan Erickson, Ray Orr, Faye and Bill Congdon, Linda (Delmage) Vint, Richard Clark, Devon Best. The number taking swimming instruction fluctuates from 160 to 260 per summer.

Last summer's life guard at Minnedosa Beach was Nancy Smith, daughter of local CPR operator Don and school teacher Bev Smith. She qualified in Brandon Y two winters ago, was employed by Minnedosa Parks Board, her boss being Jim Chipperfield who with Mrs. Mary Congdon did much to start the program. One highlight of Nancy's summer was the near drowning of a Brandon man with heart condition at the opposite end of the beach from her post. Bill LeBlanc Jr., son of the founder deeply involved in Water Safety also and former instructor of Nancy's and friend of the family, happened to be near and revived him.

Three instructors gave classes at the beach last summer. Lois Farley, daughter of farmers Ruth and Roy Farley of Minnedosa-Forrest area, taught four regular groups plus a bronze class. She qualified in Winnipeg, had taught at Carberry, Rossburn, Minnedosa and Brandon before, has been studying phys. ed. at University of Manitoba this year. Joyce Webb, daughter of mechanic-theatre operator Bill and Mary Webb and Peggy Mummery, daughter of Ivy and fire chief-ambulance driver-hospital custodian Mel Mummery, were the other two. Lois and Peggy will be back again this summer.

A highlight of last summer's water safety program here was the fact the examiner also was a 'local swimmer makes good', whom water ski fans will remember vividly, Ray Orr. Ray completed senior and bronze at Minnedosa Lake, qualified as instructor in Winnipeg in '62 and numerous bars since plus Award of Merit in '67. A director of the provincial water safety advisory committee, the popular six footer is married and had a son of four "learning to swim" last summer, is working towards a degree in personnel and industrial relations at U. of M., curls exceptionally well and takes karate lessons. Since '64 he's been examiner, has life guarded in both Minnedosa and Winnipeg. As one of the original Minnedosa Mallard Water Ski members he began skiing in '59, was near the top in provincial championships several years and took the jumping championship in '66.

Last fall daughter Kathy and I attended the day's ski lesson conducted by the Mallards. Most members are Minnedosa and Brandon area residents. I don't know the club that well but did get to know instructors Ray McPhail, Bud Wellman, Dan Mulligan, Terry Farley, Peggy Mummery and Betty Butler somewhat while swallowing more algae than absolutely necessary. Terry, the club's president, brother of Lois farming near Forrest, informed me then the Mallards would like to host the Canadian Water Ski championships at Minnedosa soon. As readers will recall, they've been held here once before, as have several provincial ones. A recent chat with Bud Wellman established that the club, who produced three of Manitoba's top seven skiers last year, feel they're not quite ready to host the Canadian open; perhaps next year. Besides their own tournament they plan to host Manitoba closed championships and possibly a Canadian regional.

Canoeing has become exceptionally popular and our district is typical. Minnedosa River upstream from the lake is one commonly used location. In early spring this stretch can be tricky; as a friend, son Rod and I learned the first Sunday in May when we went for a bad spill. You can get awfully cold when you're miles from home with your matches wet and your paddles preceding you downstream. Take the inside of curves as there are usually sweepers (trees fallen into the river) on the outside. If you hear or see fast water, beach your canoe for a look and PORTAGE if necessary. Wear your life jacket, instead of sitting on it.

One group that canoed the river from north of Basswood to the 'rock dam' in Minnedosa the second Sunday in May was the Manitoba Naturalist Club, led by Keith Vidal, a former Minnedosan. The 22 expert canoeists found the river a challenge, warned against country bridges when the river's high (they had to lie flat in their canoes for one), a few fast stretches of water and many sweepers, were especially upset over dead cattle carcasses floating about.

Since we moved here 14 years ago several drowning deaths or near deaths have occurred in Minnedosa Lake and River, the latest such tragedy on the recent long week end. If for any reason you find yourself in a river current don't fight the current but swim fast in the SAME DIRECTION while aiming for a point on the bank a fairly long distance ahead. Like all water, this lake and river must be treated with deep respect and common sense. Let's not have a second tragedy this summer.

69. GOLD IN THEM HILLS?   Minnedosa Tribune, July 24/75

Recent skyrocketing gold prices have rekindled interest in prospecting for that elusive legendary mineral. The 75th anniversary of the fabulous Klondike Gold Rush, a fascinating trek in which many Western Manitobans participated and at least four adventurers from this area (Hubert Darrell, Pat Burns, Glen Campbell, Henry Toke Munn) became famous for their Arctic exploits, has come and gone. It seems that particular scramble for this rare metallic element extended even to our own Minnedosa River and its tributaries.

About four miles downriver from Tanner's Crossing, the Jack Hare family operated a Crossing. Jack's ferry resembled John Tanner's, writes Rev. George Hambley, being "sort of a coracle made of green poplar and willow boughs ingeniously covered over with a large buffalo hide." His homestead later was purchased by Ed Taylor's parents. Jack, Ed told me recently, panned enough gold there to make a ring for Mrs. Hare. No fortune, of course, but it does establish the presence of gold fairly far south in Manitoba.

Ed, who's pushing 80 now, recalls vividly as six-year-old youngster watching in deep fascination a gold dredge operating slowly upstream on Minnedosa River in the vicinity of the 'swinging bridge'. Carl Erickson, who worked in a Northern Ontario gold mine as young man, remembers old timers telling of panning Minnedosa River, that none made fortunes but some were obtaining enough to pay expenses.

Unbelievable? Not so, feels Roco operator Warren Best who probably knows more about searching for gold than most of us having worked a number of years as diamond-driller in gold explorations in the Oxford Lake and Rice Lake (Bissett) areas. The Riding Mountains would logically possess the necessary geological attributes common to gold ore. He's convinced that mines like Bissett, which eventually closed when production dropped, will reopen soon because of current fantastic gold prices, believes that even countless tons of 'tailings' dumped in water bodies like Rice Lake by former mining operators could well contain sufficient gold to warrant further extraction today. Warren recalls reading an article a while back on gold panning in our district.

Mike and Paul Podruski recall that in about 1927-28 while clearing bush near the south boundary of Riding Mountain National Park just east of Sportsman's Park, they watched a gold dredge (or some such apparatus) working on what was known locally as Mud Creek. This machine, operated by two or three men, remained several months. The year previous, these fellows had been panning for gold on the very same creek. The brothers never could understand the significance of the name for that particular stream because it was exceptionally clear. In fact, early Indians of the district used to call it "clear as gold". Ethel Shuttleworth Leguee, who lived nearby briefly as a youngster, agrees; as does an elderly lady from Onanole with whom I chatted recently. One old timer believes the operators were connected with the same outfit that discovered gold at Bissett and Snow Lake.

On several occasions I've written about four kidnapping cases related to early Minnedosa history. A recent letter from provincial archivist John Bovey indicates "according to entries in the register of the Acts of the Lord Bishop of Rupert's Land, the Reverend J.P. (not J.B.) Sargent was collated to the Incumbency of Rapid City on 3rd May 1880. However the Parish of St. Thomas, Rapid City, was not officially recognized as an organized parish. The Rev. Lorenzo Shepherd received license as Missionary at Rapid City, Oct. 18, 1883."

Ed Taylor clearly remembers George Campbell, who had been 'exchanged' for a white child, and showed me a photo of him. To me he looks like a tall, slim and handsome Cree. In later years, recalls Ed, George became destitute and for a while lived in Minnedosa Jail because the Town had no other facilities for welfare cases. Seems that George couldn't resist poking fun publicly at the victuals served there; to the great embarrassment and annoyance of the Town fathers, one of them Ed's father.

As indicated in PRAIRIE VISTAS, of which this book is a sequel, the genealogy in question would be corrected and continued in the next book. Several genealogy books, history books and other sources of which I had not previously known have helped considerably, as also have a number of persons. Of the latter, I thank particularly the following: Dietrich & Helena Driediger of Clearbrook, B.C.; Kornelius Willms family of Hohenau, Fernheim, Chaco, Paraguay; my father and stepmother, mother-and father-in-law; Mrs. Adolf (Anna Epp) Ens of Winnipeg; John and Anna Willms of Lethbridge, Alberta; librarian Margaret Franz of Canadian Mennonite Bible College; Mrs. M. (Elizabeth) Schlichting of Springstein; Shirley Woodcock of Calgary; Mrs. Vera Fast of Sorrento, B.C.; Mrs. Alvin E. Wiens and Rev. Roland R. Goering of Hillsboro, Kansas; Roy E. Neufeldt of Tucson, Arizona.

Obviously this information is of value only to persons who own copies of PRAIRIE VISTAS. The following information relates to pages 73 to 85 of the first (1973) edition of that book, though no necessarily in sequence: PAGE 73: No changes. PAGE 74: First paragraph, 6. Jacob Klassen also had a son Peter, born 1901, who married a Klassen; 7. Johann Klassen's wife died and he remarried, had more children; 10. Jacob Neufeld (Sept. 27, 1865 to ?, 1944), correction, his second wife--whom he married in 1907 -- was a widow Mrs. Penner (nee Maria Plett of Hierschau) with seven children from her former marriage. Children of Jacob and Anna Willms Neufeld (who died in 1905) were: Peter, the oldest, deceased; Heinrich, next, deceased; Maria, died in 1972; Tina; Anna (Mrs. John Willms) of Lethbridge; Jacob, who remained in Russia, deceased. Heinrich married his stepsister Lena Penner and had children Jacob and Elsie living in Paraguay and Henry in Alberta. Lena and Henry later separated and Lena emigrated to Paraguay while Henry married a non-Mennonite and they had one child. The John Willms have four children: Verna, Anna, Henry, Johny Jacob and 15 grandchildren (8 girls, 7 boys). In January/75 John was 77, Anna 72, retired. Jacob and Maria Plett Neufeld had a son Bernhard who shot and killed himself in a hunting accident in Alberta in 1929. Third paragraph. There's a very good possibility that my great grandfather Peter Neufeld's sister, who married a Salesky of Prangenau, had four children: Johann, Peter, Heinrich, Katharina Salesky. Johann married Elizabeth Girsch, was a blacksmith and lived in Sowiefka (Tiegenhof) and later at Hochfeld. They had five children, Elizabeth the youngest being married to Martin Henry Schlichting (son of Martin and Katharina Marks Schlichting) who died Oct./74 in Springstein. The Johann Saleskys moved to Lockstaedterlager, Germany after WW I where they both died. Elizabeth and one brother were the only ones to emigrate to Canada, the brother being dead now but Elizabeth living in Springstein in Jan./75. Fourth paragraph. There's little doubt that the father of Dad's great grandfather Abram Enns was indeed Abraham Enns who came to Rueckenau from Pintzendorf, Prussia, as theorized. Abraham's wife Catarina had been a widow at the time of their marriage and Franz was her son from her first marriage. I feel there is a very good possibility that my great grandfather Peter Neufeld's parents were Jacob Neufeld and Anna Thun who in 1839 emigrated to Rudnerweide, Mol, to farm, where Jacob died in 1890. They were both born at Katznase, Prussia; Jacob on March 4, 1807 and being a cabinet maker there, Anna in 1806. Anna had an unmarried sister Maria who came then also. Ninth paragraph. This seems as good a possibility as ever. In 1811 Jacob Klassen was five, had siblings Abraham 21, who married Anna (daughter of Daerck) Wiebe of Lichtenau on May 8, 1813, Anganetha 19, Agatha 15, Elizabeth 12, Catarina 10, Margaretha 7. PAGE 75: First paragraph. I'm convinced more than ever that my great grandmother Margareta Buller Klassen was a granddaughter of Rev. Heinrich Buller, her father likely a Jacob. Third paragraph. Heinrich P. Lohrenz (born April 22, 1814) and brothers Peter and Johann were born at Muhle, G. Marienwerder and not as stated. This was an error on my part in translating from old German script in difficult-to-read handwriting. Fourth paragraph. It seems that great grandfather Peter Lohrenz was quite instrumental in paving the way for Mennonites to emigrate to Canada and the USA in the 1870s by persuading Russian officials through letters and petitions to permit such emigration. Fifth paragraph. Heinrich D. Penner served First Mennonite Church in Hillsboro, Kansas, as pastor 1897-1907, elder 1907-13, started the preparatory school in Hillsboro, taught at Bethel College 1893-97 and 1913-18; Anna Penner Bartel, upon her marriage became the stepmother of the 12 children of Leonard and Aganetha Funk Bartel. Gertruda Fast Penner's second husband, Cornelius Duerksen, whose first wife died in 1873 at almost

74, had been a village school teacher many years. Daniel Penner's father (Aug. 2, 1802) was likely Daniel Penner who emigrated to Blumstein, Mol. from Kalthof, Prussia with parents Johann and Anna Pankert (July 27, 1766, Danzig) Penner (born about 1759) and siblings Benjamin (Oct. 9, 1795), Catharina (May 30, 1798) and half sister Maria (Jan. 16, 1789), his father first having been married to Maria Epp who had died Feb. 27, 1794. Gertruda's father was likely Isaac Fast who came to the same village the same year at age 2 from Ellerwald, Prussia with parents Johann and Catarina Harms Fast and siblings Johann about 8 years older and Catarina born shortly after arrival. PAGE 76. Second paragraph. There's little doubt that my mother's great great grandmother Catarina Schmidt Penner's parents were Daniel and Barbara Schmidt as suggested there. Unless there's a typing error in Barbara's age it would seem that she is a second wife and could not be the mother of Daniel, Susanna, Peter and Heinrich. The Daniel Schmidt family came to Rueckenau in 1811, settling on a farm with 1 horse, 6 cattle, 5 sheep, 1 plow, 1 harrow, 1 wagon, 1 spinning wheel. On Feb. 25, 1813, Susanna Schmidt married Jakob Draksel (born about 1785) of Rueckenau who had a mother Magdalena (born about 1744) and sister Fronika (born about 1791). Fourth paragraph. I feel strongly that my great grandmother Eva Dick Neufeld's grandmother was widow Anna Born Dick who came to Gnadenheim, Mol. in 1819 from Koszelitzke (Warnau), Prussia. Her husband Jacob Dick had died in 1811. She had with her then children Jakob (born Jan. 20, 1790 and likely Eva's father), Isaac (Dec. 17, 1793), Anna (March 3, 1796, Sandhof), Abraham (April 26, 1798), Maria (June 18, 1804, Warnau) and stepsons Peter Reimer (Aug. 15, 1773, Sandhof) and Martin Dick (March 1, 1781, Sandhof). Grandmother's uncle Johann Balzer, who raised her, was likely a son or grandson of Rev. Heinrich Balzer who came to Grossweide, Mol. in the same migration from Schweingrube, having become a teacher-minister in Prussia in 1800. Seventh paragraph. I'm all but convinced that this is the right connection, with Heinrich Neufeld Jr. being my great grandfather Jacob Neufeld's father. Further, I believe that Heinrich Neufeld Sr. was a son of Jacob Neufeld of Tiegenhagen, Prussia, who was a son of Peter Neufeld of the same village. PAGE 77. Received a nice letter from cousin Katie Neufeld Froese' daughter Shirley in July/74. She is married to Roy, a son of Verna and John Woodcock, Wilfred's brother. At that time they had two sons, aged 3 and 5. This applies to the third paragraph. Fifth paragraph. Elizabeth (Betty) and Jessie (Jo) were also born on the first farm and not the second. Sixth paragraph. Uncle Jake Neufeld farmed at Purple Spring and at Grassy Lake, not Coaldale. On Dec. 15/74 Aunt Annie died of cancer, funeral service Dec. 18 with burial in Boissevain cemetery, not far from my mother's grave. PAGE 78. No changes. PAGE 79. Seventh paragraph. Jacob Neufeld's funeral and burial place likely was in Sofieoski and not Halbstadt. Eighth paragraph. It would certainly appear that the parents of Elsie's great great great grandfather Peter Epp were Peter and Helena Classen Epp of Pletzendorf, Prussia. Their one-year-old daughter referred to there was called Catarina. When they arrived in Ohrloff they had with them a wagon, half a plow, 1 harrow, 5 horses, 12 cattle, some corn and hay. Ninth paragraph I'm more convinced than ever that Elizabeth Epp Riediger's first husband was a grandson of Johann and Catarina Oehmsen Riediger, his father likely being Abraham Riediger, who arrived in Lichtenau with a wagon, half a plow, 3 horses, 11 cattle, some corn and hay. Tenth paragraph. I believe Jacob Neufeld's grandparents were Peter and Justina Neufelt as suggested here, his father being Abraham. They came to Ohrloff with 2 wagons, 1 plow, 2 harrows, 4 horses, 14 cattle, 6 sheep, hay and corn. PAGE 80. Fifth paragraph. Dr. Abram Gerhard Wiens, the retired language professor and author of the novel AND EVER THE SUN published in the Mennonite Weekly Review and of numerous Low German articles in magazines like Mennonite Life, Der Bote and Mennonite Quarterly, died July 25/74 of a heart attack in Norman, Oklahoma. A diabetic, he was married to Anna Loewen, had one surviving son, a nephew Gerhard Wiens in Vancouver. I'm convinced that a sister of Catharina Loewen Wiensz was Margareta 41 who with husband Cornelius Toews 42 and children Johann 17, Catharina 14, Margaretha 11, Jacob 9 and Elizabeth 4 settled on a neighboring farm in Lindenau in 1804. Possible other siblings who came to Mol. the same year were Dirk Loewen, and (sister-in-law) Anna Siemens Loewen who had an adult daughter Anna. My guess is that Catharina's mother was a Margaretha or an Elizabeth. There is a typing error in this paragraph. The comma following the words 'born 1762 W. Prussia' and the parenthesis mark following the words 'died 1885, Lindenau' should be transposed. Sixth paragraph. I believe Margaretha Riediger Baerg was a daughter of Johann and Catarina Oehmsen Riediger, already mentioned. PAGE 81. First paragraph. 7. Gerhard J. Fast, who gave me invaluable assistance with family tree data, died June 16/74 in Boissevain. He died of appendicitis and pneumonia, had been baptized May 24, 1908, by Bishop Jacob Toews of Lichtenau, Mol. Funeral services, in which my brother Rev. Jake Neufeld assisted, were conducted in Whitewater Mennonite church in Boissevain on June 21. Fourth paragraph. A typing error; the date '1878' should read '1778'. Fifth paragraph. Maria Neufeld Epp was born in 1882, not 1883. PAGE 82. First paragraph. Henry and Barbara Johnson Fast have a second daughter now, Alison. They've just left to teach in West Germany for two years. Second paragraph. Bishop Bernhard Peters' great grandfather was probably Hans Peters of Vierzehnhuben, Prussia. Third paragraph. Bernhard Peters also played a major role in producing legislation to govern the colony of Molotschna during the 1860-80 era, especially in connection with inheritance of property, welfare of orphans etc. PAGE 83. Fourth paragraph. Albrecht Fast had a daughter Kornelia, who became the second wife of Abraham Sawatzky who lived in Tiegerweide and later in Oklahoma. The death date of Johann A. Fast was Feb. 19/44, in Poland. Fifth paragraph. Justina Huebert Fast had three sisters: Aganetha (Mrs. G. Siemens); Helena (Mrs. H. Huebner), who was deaf-mute; Margaretha, who died single during the famine following the Russian Revolution. There's no doubt in my mind that the grandparents of Justina Dolesky Huebert were Jacob and Catharina Martens Dolesky as speculated. Though not positive as to which of the three sons was her father, it most likely was Jacob. Sixth paragraph. I no longer believe that Abraham Huebert could have been a son of Martin Huebert; more likely of Rev. David Huebert who was married to Agnetha Giesbrecht. This minister and his wife emigrated to Lindenau from Einlage, Prussia in 1803 at the age of 35 with children Catharina 4½ and Agatha 1½; David being ordained just after his arrival. Seventh paragraph. 1. Johann Fast born Sept. 20, 1880; died Oct. 6/33 in Alexanderwohl; born in Paulsheim or Tiegerweide, likely the latter. 3. Abraham Fast's wife was an Agata Haarms, born Feb. 28, 1894, of Friedensruh, Mol. 5. Mrs. Ben (Greta Fast) Sawatzky's full name is Margaretha. 6. Aganeta (Neta) Fast, born Sept. 18, 1884, died Feb. 14, 1916 in Peter Paul Mechailowka, Omsk, Siberia. Her husband was Wilhelm Heinrich Janzen, born Jan. 10, 1880, in Tiegerweide and died May 17, 1941, in Landskrone, Friesland Colony, Paraguay. Their children were: Wilhelm, born March 30/06, died Aug. 9/06, Mechailowka; Aganetha, born March 19/08 and in May/74 was living in Asuncion, Paraguay; Johann, born May 4/09, died Dec. 24/09 Mechailowka; Helena, born Jan. 12/11 Mechailowka and in May/74 was living in Chaco, Paraguay, and is married to Kornelius Willms, son of Heinrich Willms who was the oldest son in the family and who had a sister Justina married to a Janzen, son of Kornelius Willms of Fuerstenwerder in Mol.; Johann, born Dec. 21/11 Mechailowka, died Nov. 18/33 in Paraguay; Justina, born March 29/13 Mechailowka and in May/74 was living in Encarnacion, Paraguay; Peter, born Oct. 27/14 and in May/74 was living in Vancouver. 7. Lena (Mrs. Tiessen) has a daughter Lena (Mrs. Herman Froese) living in Russia. Eighth paragraph. 2. Lena Fast's husband John F. Martens of Rivers died suddenly on May 7/74. Born March 21, 1928 at Eyebrow, Sask., he moved to Rapid City district in 1944 with his parents Frank and Maria (Krahn) Martens. Married Jan. 30/52, the couple had three children: Richard, Gerald, Kathleen. John had a brother Frank and sister Mrs. Helen Isaak. A storekeeper in Rivers, John was a most popular and friendly person with a tremendous sense of humor, had with wife Lena (Elsie's cousin) and daughter Kathleen paid us a delightful visit about 10 days before his untimely death. Funeral service was held in Brandon, internment at Rivers. 3. Elsie's uncle Jacob Fast of Rivers, born March 2/13 at Tiegerweide, Mol., died of cancer Nov. 16/74 and was buried in Rivers Mennonite church cemetery on the day of his funeral there Nov. 20. Second last paragraph. Susanna Fast (Oct. 19, 1884, Tiegerweide - Feb. (20?), 1938, Rapid City). 3. Harry James Fast (April 1/27) on Sept. 14/54 married Vera May Moffat (March 5/30) and have children Steven James (Oct. 7/56), Jefferey Alan (Aug. 8/58) and live in Sorrento, B.C.

To bring our own family up to date. Elsie is studying part time towards a Bachelor of Teaching degree at Brandon University. Oldest son, Neiljonn Lory, was teaching at Duck Bay the past year and has transferred to Cormorant Lake this fall. On March 29/75 he married teaching colleague Audrey Mae Turton, born April 6/54, daughter of Wilfred J. Turton (son of Wm. John and Mathilda Kennedy Turton, originally from Cannington Manor, Sask. where they homesteaded and later of Rapid City where William died) and Janet Bakke (daughter of Melvin--stepfather an Everson--and Annie Whitelaw Bakke, the Bakkes originally from Minneapolis-St. Paul area and Annie from Scotland. Audrey has a younger brother Wally and younger sister Faye, the family living at Emerson where her father owns and operates a body shop. Oldest daughter, Verna Marie, has completed her second year of Fine Arts at University of Manitoba and plans to enter third year this fall. The youngest three are still at home; Kathryn Susanne entering grade 11, Roderick Peter grade 7, Lisa Ellen grade 5. All are doing very well and I'm sincerely proud of them.

Recent years have witnessed not only a sharp increase generally in interest in local histories and in genealogy by Canadians but also in heraldry. One of several companies that has researched family names and coat-of-arms is Sovereign Heraldry of Cornwall, Ontario. This particular company has researched Dutch, Prussian and German surnames common in Mennonite genealogies. Of the four which interest me particularly--Neufeld, Lohrenz, Fast, Epp--Shirley I. McDonald of Sovereign has located information on all except Lohrenz.

"Until about 1100 A.D.," indicates Shirley in a recent report, "most people in Europe had only one name. As the population increased it became awkward to live in a village wherein perhaps 1/3 of the males were named John". Thus developed a need for surnames.

The fighting man of the Middle Ages found it necessary to go a step further. He "wore a metal suit of armor for protection. Since this suit of armor included a helmet that completely covered the head, a knight in full battle dress was unrecognizable. To prevent friend from attacking friend during the heat of battle, it became necessary for each knight to somehow identify himself." Many accomplished this by painting colorful patterns on battle shields and weaving them into cloth surcoats worn over their armor.

As the practice mushroomed, "it became more and more likely that two knights unknown to each other might be using the same insignia. To prevent this, records were kept" granting the sole right to a certain pattern to a particular knight and to his family permission to display these arms.

According to data I purchased from Sovereign, the historiography of the Neufeld coat-of-arms can be documented in "SIEBMACHER'S WAPPENBUCH, Vol. 6F, p. 29, under the variant Neifeld. Heraldic artists of old developed their own unique language to describe an individual Coat of Arms. In their language, the ARMS (SHIELD) is as follows: 'Geviertet; 1 und 4: durchgehender Schragbalken; 2 und 3: Blumentopf mit gr. Baumchen.' When translated, the Arms description is: 'Quartered: 1 and 4, a left diagonal band; 2 and 3, a flower pot with a little green tree.' Above the shield and helmet is the Crest which is described as: 'Zum Flug geschickte Friedenstaube.' A translation of the Crest description is: 'The dove of peace, ready for flight'." Although my German is quite rusty and I took only a single university course in it, it seems to me the translation, though not incorrect, doesn't go far enough. The 'durchgehender Schragbalken' is more of a large beam used in construction, at an angle or slant as when used to help support a wall or dike. As regards the Crest symbol, the German words suggest the dove is being sent on a peace mission by its owner.

"The four primary sources for second names," says Sovereign, "were: occupation, location, father's name and personal characteristics. The surname Neufeld appears to be occupational in origin, and is believed to be associated with the Germans, meaning 'one who farmed newly cleared land'. Information available to us indicates there are approximately 2715 heads of households in Canada with the old and distinguished Neufeld name." Actually, the meaning of this surname is more specifically Dutch-Prussian in origin and refers to a very particular type of 'newly cleared land', that of land recently reclaimed from the sea--in this case, the lowlands in the Danzig (Gdansk) area on the Baltic Sea of Prussia, now Poland.

Personally, although I was quite prepared psychologically to learn of a little green tree and of the supporting beam on my family's coat-of-arms, the dove of peace came as a great surprise. The impression I had developed after some six years of digging around in closets of my particular branch of Neufelds had led me to expect a hawk but hardly a dove. Guess there must be more pacifistic Neufelds about than my own immediate ancestors. I'll require a bit of time to get used to this.

The following is the family tree, as I now believe it to be, of Peter K. Neufeld of Boissevain, Manitoba; the father of Anne Neufeld Unrau, Sarah Neufeld Shail, Dr. Peter L. Neufeld, Betty Neufeld Engbrecht, Jo Neufeld Nicol, Rev. Jake Neufeld, and husband of their mother Agatha Lohrenz:

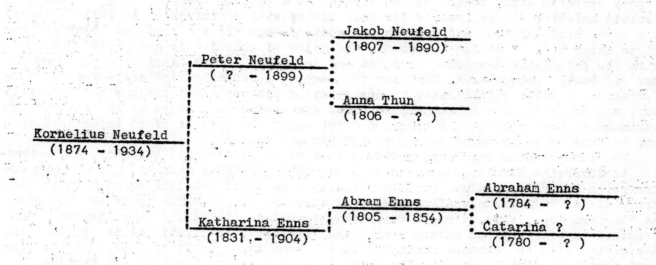

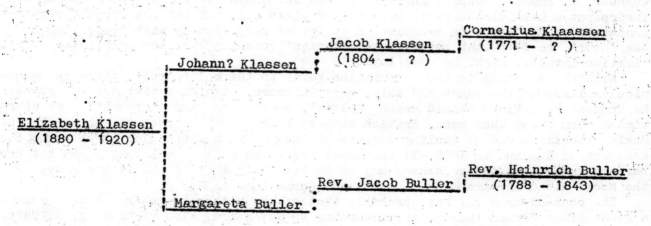

Note: A vertical dotted line signifies considerable circumstantial evidence to support the relationship, but not 100% direct proof.

NEUFELD COAT OF ARMS

Crest: dove of peace with olive branch
Shield: two seedling trees and two supporting beams or props.

William H. Whitmore, in THE ELEMENTS OF HERALDRY--a book dealing with coats-of
-arms related to Anglo Saxon families, warns "that there is no such thing as a coat-
of-arms belonging to the bearers of any particular surname". Strictly speaking, this
is of course the case; and no doubt especially holds true in the British situation.
Where persons of ethnic Mennonite origin are concerned, the era when surnames began
to come into popular use (1200s and 1300s) in west-central Europe coincides closely
with the time when coats-of-arms were also being registered there to particular families. To complicate matters somewhat, the early 1500s saw the creation of the Mennonites as a religious and ethnic entity. Thus it is not only conceivable but also
highly probable that, taking my own surname as a typical example, it was indeed my
Neufeld ancestor who registered (or made use of with registration to follow later)
the dove, seedling tree and beam as his coat-of-arms and yet that not many generations later all, or at least some of, the males of this family associated themselves
with the pacifistic Mennonite movement and denounced (or at least made no further
use of) their coat-of-arms. Whatever the case, I personally find coat-of-arms information of vital significance to any study of history and genealogy and sincerely
hope someone will soon thoroughly research coats-of-arms history as it relates to
surnames of Mennonite ethnic origin and not shrug them off as of no importance simply because of their relationship to knights and warfare.

The coat-of-arms for Fast, probably that of my wife's male ancestor, is, according to Sovereign Heraldry, documented in RIETSTAP ARMORIAL GENERAL. The shield's description is: "D'arg. a une echelle d'escalade de trois echelons de gu." which they
translate as "Silver: a scaling ladder of three red rungs." The crest is described
as "Un more iss., tort. d'arg." which they translate as "Half a moor issuing, and
wreathed in silver." The surname Fast, they indicate, is locational in origin being
associated with the Germans meaning "one who came from, or lived near, Fast"; the
most prominent variations being Fastert, Fastue, Fasting, Fastring and Fastida, and
that currently about 1125 Fast families live in the USA.

As my own knowledge of French is minimal, I checked with local collegiate French
teacher, G. Basset. Despite the fact he was not shown the coat-of-arms sketch, which
incorporates heraldic language of dots and lines etc. and was not given Sovereign's
translation, Mr. Basset's translation coincided very closely with theirs. Regarding
the 'Moor', he felt that perhaps a 'barbarian' emerging over the particular forti-
fication involved might be more logical.

Although no words in the description refer to the color 'red', there are perpendicular lines on the rungs and this, says Whitmore, signifies that color. Further,
he indicates, a blank shield means 'silver', as does the word 'argent'; the abbreviated form being used here. British history books show sketches of Norman knights
making excellent use of scaling ladders as they storm a particular tower during their
conquest of England in 1066. If the crest refers to Moors specifically and not bar-
barians generally, the reference may be to the 'Holy War' of the 11th century when
the Moors aided the Arabs in fighting the Christians in Spain.

The coat-of-arms for Epp, probably that of my mother-in-law's ancestor and of
a great great grandmother's, is, according to Sovereign, also recorded in RIETSTAP.
The shield's description is: "D'or a un singe assis de sa., tenant de sa patte dex-
tre une rose de gu., tigee et feuillee de sin", which they translate "Gold: a black
ape seated, holding in his right paw a red rose with stem and leaves of green". The
crest is described as "Le singe, entre un vol d'or", which they translate as " The
ape of the shield between two gold wings". The surname Epp, they indicate, appears
to be patronymical in origin and seems to be associated with Germans, meaning "descendant of Epp, a pet form of Eber (boar)", the most common variations being Epple,
Epplin, Eppelin and Eppo, and that about 500 Epp families currently live in America.

Mr. Basset's translation closely parallelled this one. The shield is engraved by
dots and, according to Whitmore, this (as well as the word 'or') signifies 'gold'.
The ape or monkey is criss-crossed with vertical and horizontal lines signifying
'black', the leaves have diagonal lines denoting 'green', the rose vertical lines
meaning 'red'.

As to why the Epp knights chose an ape for their crest and to decorate their
shields is open to conjecture until some future date when research may establish the
reason. Possibly because of similarity in both high and low German words of 'ape'
and 'Epp'. Perhaps the family had a pet monkey, or one as mascot in battle. Maybe Epp
was noted for hunting prowess; or as mimic, and crest plus surname refer to this.

The following is the family tree, as I now believe it to be, of Agatha Lohrenz Neufeld (1904 – 1963):

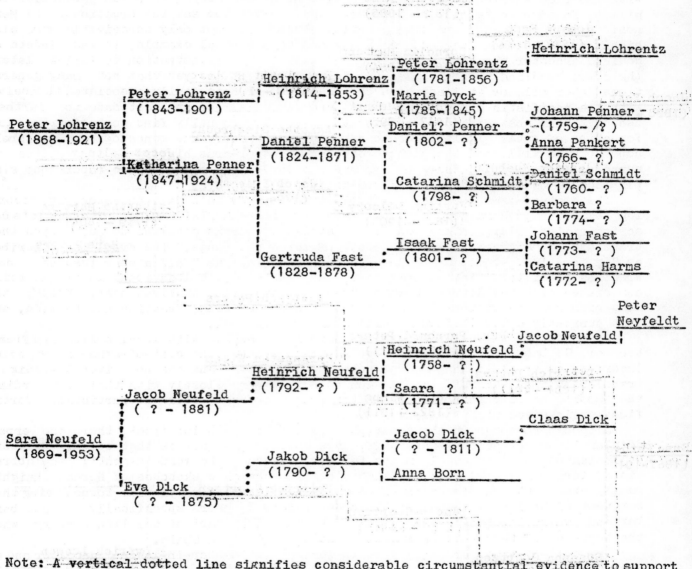

Note: A vertical dotted line signifies considerable circumstantial evidence to support the relationship, but not 100% direct proof.

NEUFELD COAT OF ARMS
Crest: dove of peace with olive branch
Shield: two seedling trees and two props

The following is the family tree, as I now believe it to be, of John J. Fast of Boissevain, Manitoba; the father of Elsie Fast Neufeld, Jack Fast, Vern Fast, Helen Fast Hildebrand, Henry Fast, and husband of their mother Maria Epp:

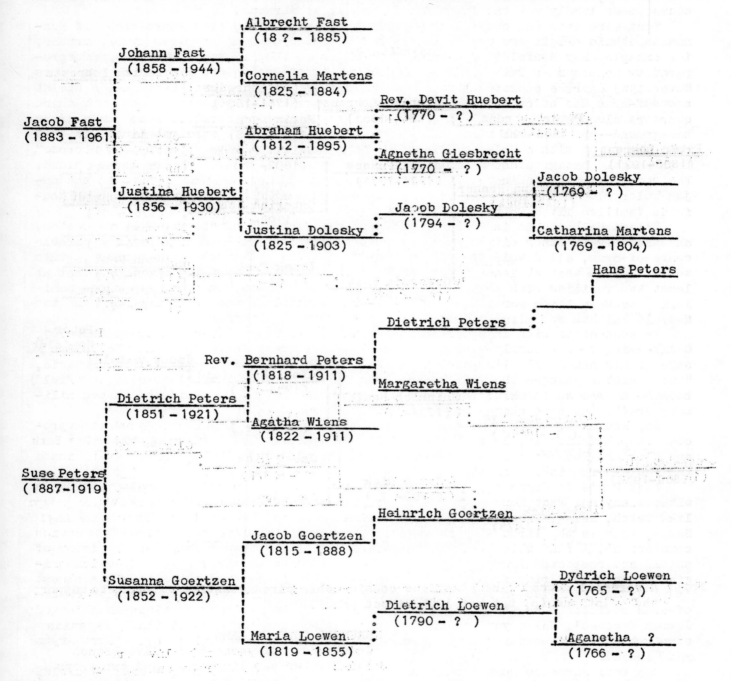

Note: A vertical dotted line signifies considerable circumstantial evidence to support the relationship, but not 100% direct proof.

FAST COAT OF ARMS

Crest: barbarian, wreathed in silver, emerging over parapet
Shield: of silver, portrays a scaling ladder with three red rungs

Personally, I don't agree with Sovereign Heraldry that the surname 'Epp' derives directly from 'Eber' (boar). Mennonite historians like Herman Epp of Hamburg, who have done exhaustive research on this surname, believe it derives from the Friesland Christian name 'Eppe', which in turn probably derives from the Christian name 'Eberhard'. Thus, the man first called 'Eberhard' undoubtedly was a swineherd; though of course most likely not the first Epp to use it as surname.

That more than one coat-of-arms per surname may exist, even where those of Mennonite ethnic origin are concerned, cannot be ruled out. As involves my own surname, for example, Roy Neufeldt of Tucson, Arizona had a (copyrighted) historiography prepared by Halberts of Bath, Ohio which (though it doesn't quote its source as does Sovereign) carries a sketch plus arms description. They indicate that the Neufeldt coat-of-arms has no crest; that the shield is quartered also, the second and third quarters also depict a plant--in this case "a red ancient heraldic rose" on a green background--and that the first and fourth quarters too have straight lines--in this case the first with a "black initial 'N'" and the fourth with "a narrow black cross", both on gold backgrounds. A small blue inner shield is centred on the large shield. The rose, Halberts indicate, represents "beauty, hope, grace and joy", that the major color blue being symbolic of "loyalty and/or splendor", that fewer than 300 Neufeldt families lived in the USA in 1972.

Unless Halberts is included in Whitmore's indictment of "in New York and Boston, and probably in other cities, seal-engravers and painters have produced innumerable coats-of-arms, all devoid of authority as far as the artists were concerned", this would suggest that at least two Neufeld(t) coats-of-arms WERE registered and that at least two families with that surname already existed then. In fact, the close similarity between these particular coats-of-arms would lead one to believe that the two Neufeld knights who first utilized them were probably brothers.

In connection with this particular surname, Dr. Duane D. Schroeder of Berkeley, California, in a recently-published genealogy involving Schroeders and Neufeldts, says of his ancestor's 1839 arrival in Molotschna, South Russia from West Prussia, "our ancestor changed the family name from Nifelt to Neufeldt, (literally, New Field) because he was so thankful for the freedom to worship and to avoid the hated military draft. The name change persisted...".

Roy Neufeldt, who's done much research involving his own genealogy and is in process of publishing it, learned that "a lot of Neufelds are Jewish, mostly in New York and Florida. They came from Rumania and Poland, all after 1900. I have even found two Neufeld rabbis". Fascinating.

That Roy's findings may prove of great interest to Mennonite genealogists goes without saying. That Mennonite ethnic origins trace to various European ethnic groups like Dutch, Swiss, Prussian, Polish, Italian, Belgian, even a little French and Anglo Saxon, this is the first time in years of research that I've come across 'the Jewish connection'. I find this highly intriguing. Especially when I consider the irony of an old and respected Prussian name like Neufeld quite possibly being of Jewish origin. Hitler would rise from his grave in horror if he learned that one of his oldest 'pure Aryan' families--a family that seems to have a minimum of two Prussian coats-of-arms registered to its members for past loyalty in military service--is of 'hated Jewish descent'. Makes you wonder how many Jewish families with similar Prussian ethnic ties Adolf murdered because of his misguided racist philosophy. 'Pure Aryan race' indeed!

The four surnames most prominent in the genealogy of my children are: Neufeld, Lohrenz, Fast, Epp. The origin of Lohrenz, as I showed in PRAIRIE VISTAS, is undoubtedly the Italian part of Switzerland. Probably because of this Sovereign Heraldry did not locate a coat-of-arms registered to a Lohrenz, as likely neither SIEBMACHER'S WAPPENBUCH nor RIETSTAP ARMORIAL GENERAL covered that particular area and the Mennonite Lohrenzes left that area for Holland and Prussia in the mid 1500s. To me it seems significant that the Fast and Epp coats-of-arms are found in the same registry, and in one different from that of Neufeld, as both those surnames almost certainly originated in the Netherlands-Belgium area rather than in Prussia. Blaupot ten Cate, for example, found the surname Epp (spelled Eppens then) occurring in early 'Mennonite' lists in Holland as early as 1569, while Juriaan Epes was a strong supporter of William of Orange (1533-84) in his fight to rid that country of Spanish anti-Protestant persecution. (About 75% of all martyrs in Holland during the Reformation were Mennonites.)

The following is the family tree, as I now believe it to be, of Maria Epp Fast:

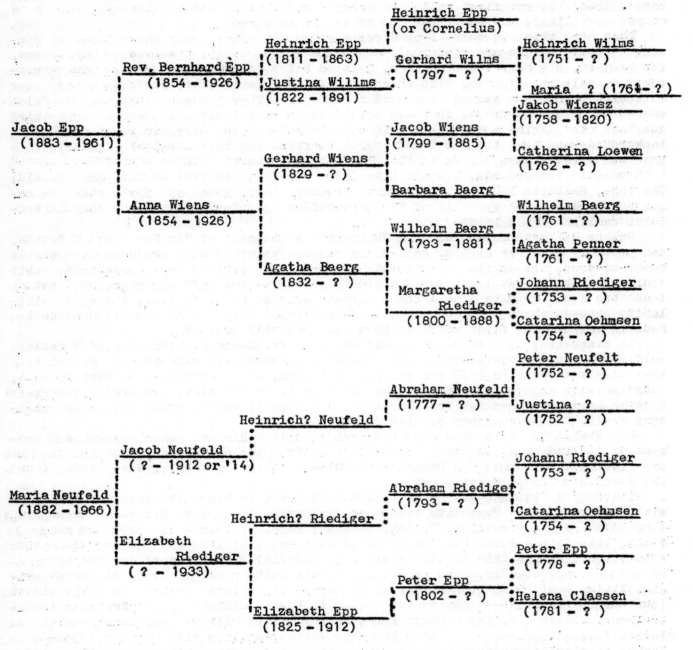

Jacob Epp
(1883 – 1961)

Rev. Bernhard Epp
(1854 – 1926)

Heinrich Epp
(1811 – 1863)

Heinrich Epp
(or Cornelius)

Gerhard Wilms
(1797 – ?)

Heinrich Wilms
(1751 – ?)

Justina Willms
(1822 – 1891)

Maria ? (1764 – ?)

Anna Wiens
(1854 – 1926)

Gerhard Wiens
(1829 – ?)

Jacob Wiens
(1799 – 1885)

Jakob Wiensz
(1758 – 1820)

Catherina Loewen
(1762 – ?)

Barbara Baerg

Agatha Baerg
(1832 – ?)

Wilhelm Baerg
(1793 – 1881)

Wilhelm Baerg
(1761 – ?)

Agatha Penner
(1761 – ?)

Margaretha
Riediger
(1800 – 1888)

Johann Riediger
(1753 – ?)

Catarina Oehmsen
(1754 – ?)

Maria Neufeld
(1882 – 1966)

Jacob Neufeld
(? – 1912 or '14)

Heinrich? Neufeld

Abraham Neufeld
(1777 – ?)

Peter Neufelt
(1752 – ?)

Justina ?
(1752 – ?)

Elizabeth
Riediger
(? – 1933)

Heinrich? Riediger

Abraham Riediger
(1793 – ?)

Johann Riediger
(1753 – ?)

Catarina Oehmsen
(1754 – ?)

Elizabeth Epp
(1825 – 1912)

Peter Epp
(1802 – ?)

Peter Epp
(1778 – ?)

Helena Classen
(1781 – ?)

Note: A vertical dotted line signifies considerable circumstantial evidence to support the relationship, but not 100% direct proof.

EPP COAT OF ARMS
Crest: two gold wings with black ape
     holding red rose between
Shield: gold with black ape holding
     red rose

NEUFELD COAT OF ARMS
Crest: dove of peace with olive
     branch
Shield: two seedling trees and
     two props

126

Thanks to considerable genealogical research by Anna Epp Enns of Winnipeg in connection with an Epp reunion in August/75, much new data has come to light involving Epp history. It's not my purpose to discuss in detail the various Epp branches but to simply sketch each briefly to show where they fit into the ancestral pattern of my children's grandmother, Maria Epp Fast.

Heinrich Epp was born March 3, 1811 in Rosenort, Mol., was a farmer, died Aug. 28, 1863. His first wife was Mary (Thiessen) Wiens, his second (my children's ancestor) Justina Willms, born March 17, 1822 and died 1891 in Rosenort. There is some uncertainty as to the identity of Heinrich's father. An article written by Heinrich's son Kornelius on which the Steinbach data card I consulted for PRAIRIE VISTAS was based and which I.G. Neufeld (a nephew of Rev. Bernhard Epp's daughter Anna) of Fresno, Calif. helped Anna and me locate recently, indicates his name is also Heinrich. According to another reliable source, three Epp brothers emigrated from Germany to the Old Colony, two stayed there while the third—Cornelius—moved to Lichtfelde, Mol. and was the father of Heinrich Epp (1811-63).

If this claim's accurate (and I see no reason why it might not be except that possibly the third brother was a Heinrich instead of Cornelius) there exists an excellent possibility the other two were Rev. David and Peter Epp. Not much is known of Peter except he was married there (by his brother), but David was born June 15, 1750 in Stadtgebiet (Danzig), Prussia, died in Rosenthal, O.C. Sept. 29, 1802. He was married twice, his second wife being Anna Barkmann (Bergmann) of Danzig (born Oct. 10, 1762). David had a daughter from his first marriage, Margareta, born March 13, 1777, and from his second marriage three children: David born Sept. 25, 1781, Anna born 1791, Catherina born 1793. David and Peter had come to Rosenthal in 1789. In 1791 David Epp Sr. became a teacher (minister) and the following year a bishop. Several teacher and minister descendants moved to Mol. later. I think David Jr. also became a minister. A photo of one early descendant of this family is almost an exact replica of Elsie's grandfather, Jacob Epp, and there's little doubt in my mind that David and Peter Epp were related to Heinrich Epp.

The following is based on the list of Heinrich Epp's 11 children and immediate descendants distributed at the recent reunion, the first two of his first marriage: 1. Heinrich, lived in Kleefeld, Mol., married Agatha Mathies (1833-1924) who later married a Klassen. These Epps had children: Heinrich, Jacob, Cornelius, Abram, Justina, Anna, (Mrs. Reimer), Aganeta, Katharina, Lisa (single). 2. Peter (Aug. 20, 1838 Rosenort - Nov. 11, 1914, USA; likely Mountain Lake, Minn.), farmer, married Anna Janzen (1833-63) and had children: Mary (1860-60), Henry (1860-61), Justina, Peter (1863 -63). After his first wife's death Peter married Elizabeth Enns (1844-1917) and had children: Elizabeth, Katharina, Peter who died in Russia, Jacob, Anna, Peter who died in Russia, John and Susie and Peter who all died in infancy in America, Susanna, Daniel, Marie, a boy who died at birth, Peter, Cornelius, Abram (3.6.1886-14.6.1906) Gerhardt. 3. Johann (31.10.1842, died Siberia), farmer and blacksmith, lived in Samara for a time, had a daughter Susanna who married a Kroeker and moved to Brazil, son Kornelius who died in Omsk, Siberia, son Johann born 15.3.1874. 4. Kornelius (4.8.1844-Rosenort-10.1.1916 Neuhof), farmer-minister-photographer who lived in Rosenhof for a time, married Anna (Harder) Schmidt Wiens who died in 1897 from whom he had children: Kornelius (3.8.1870- ? .8.1884), Nikolai (9.2.1872- ? .8.1873), Heinrich. After Anna's death he married Agathe Franz and they had children: Johannes, Kornelius, Petrus, Agathe, David, Anna, Abram, Gerhard (23.3.1896-31.10.1918), Helene. It is my belief that Agathe married Heinrich Tiessen on Aug. 26, 1910 and that by May 8, 1923 she was a widow. 5. Abraham (13.1.1846 Rosenort-28.7.1920), farmer-minister -carpenter-house parent (latter at Tiege Deaf and Dumb Inst.), married Katharina Fast (1850-1903) and had children: Justina, Katharina, Anna, Abraham, Helena. After Katharina's death he married Maria Friesen. 6. Gerhard (13.7. ? -1933), carpenter who lived in Kleefeld for a time, married twice with second wife being a Reimer, had children: Johann, Gerhard, Heinrich, Justina, who died February/52 in Winkler and was first married to a Toews and then to Abr. H. Funk who died July/65 in Winkler, childless, Elizabeth. 7. Jacob (17.4.1850-19.7.1919 Rosenort), farmer and houseparent in senior citizens home, married Katharina Boese (1853-1937 Manitou), had children : Heinrich (1875-76), Katharina (1876-81), Heinrich, Justina, Jacob, Katharina, Martin (1886-86), Cornelius (1888-1969 Chicago, Ill.), Johann, Abraham, Mariechen. 8. David (18.2.1854 Rosenort - before 1914), farmer-businessman who lived in Kuruschan, married

Maria Harder born 1856, had children: Heinrich, Justina, Baerbel, Mariechen, Katharina, Agatha who married Heinrich Woelk and had 8 children, David who married an Elizabeth but had no children. 9. Bernhard (18.2.1854 Rosenort - 26.8.1926 Lindenau) who was a farmer-elder-carpenter; no other new or revised information. 10. Katharina, married Daniel Boschmann (1851-1909) of Rosenort who later married a Peters. They had children: Jakob, Daniel, David, Johann, Tina, Justina. 11. Martin (6.4.1860-16. 7.1912), a merchant-farmer, married Katharina Penner (1863-95) having children: Justina, Kornelius (26.12.1887-6.3.1892), Martin (9.7.1889 and died), Mariechen (30.7. 1890-19.9.1899), Johannes. After Katharina's death Martin married Susanna Renpel (1873-1910) and had children: Susanna, Anna (3.2.1898-1944), Jakob, Tina, Heinrich, Bernhard, David, Gerhard. After Susanna's death Martin married Margareta Enns (1877 -1948) and had children: Greta, Martin (9.8.1912-22.11.1916). Anna Enns has great amount of data on Heinrich Epp's grandchildren and their descendants, which I assume she will have recorded in the genealogical centre at Steinbach. One interesting discovery was that these descendants today belong to at least 28 different church denominations in addition to that of Mennonite ones.

I have a strong hunch that Heinrich Epp, though he may have grown up and lived in Rosenort most of his life, was actually born in Altonau eight miles away. There were no Epps in Rosenort yet by 1805. The man I strongly feel was Heinrich Epp's dad came to Altonau in 1808 at age 25 from Danzig (probably having lived in the Old Colony the past 19 years with older brothers David or Peter), had a wife Anna 3 years younger and a year-old son Johann. On June 6, 1813 they had a daughter Anna in that village. Most of the 4th paragraph on page 81 of PRAIRIE VISTAS requires revision.

Further, I feel the first wife of Heinrich Epp (1811-63) was born in Laescky, Prussia in 1803 coming to Rosenort in 1805 with farming parents Frank and Catarina Tiessen and siblings Catarina 20, Abraham 19, Elizabeth 19, Margaretha 16, Jacob 15, Cornelius 10, Anna 8 and Franz 7. As regards his second wife Justina Willms, the information in the 3rd paragraph on page 81 of that book requires slight revision. I believe her father probably was Gerhard Wilms who came to Tiegenhagen (seven miles from Rosenort) in 1806 as youngster of 9 with farming parents Heinrich (55) and Maria (45) Wilms and siblings Heinrich 24, Adam 22, Maria 20, Peter 19, Simon 14, Agatha 13, Catarina 8 from Morefe near Marienwerder, Prussia.

To date I've been unable to determine the relationship between these various Epp families and that of my deceased step grandmother Justina Epp Neufeld to whom she was distantly related. She had a brother Heinrich born about 1903 who died (single) of typhus during the Russian Revolution. Mary Epp Friesen (deceased) of Lena, Man. was her oldest sister, Tina Epp Martens of Morden her youngest. It may well be the relationship traces through Heinrich Epp Sr. of Rosenort's brothers or cousins.

Going back to page 79 of PRAIRIE VISTAS for a moment, 4th paragraph, I believe that a daughter of Heinrich and Margareta Classen Neufeld of Sofiejewka was Margareta Neufeld who in October, 1906, became formally engaged to Eugen Wedell, whom she presumably married. In the 6th paragraph, I feel there's a good possibility Heinrich Neufeld's second wife was a Sara Bartel whom he married at Gnadenfeld in December of 1917.

Going back to page 78, last paragraph, the Jacob Epp killed in 1919 during the Revolution and buried in a mass grave in Blumenort, seems to have reported the murders of several of his co-villagers to the family of Jacob G. Dyck of Leamington, Ont. just prior to his own death. I.G. Neufeld of Fresno is currently researching that particular atrocity.

There is one other possibility regarding Epp relationships that can as yet not be ruled out. In fact, it's one I've often contemplated and would much like to prove or disprove. One ancestor of my mother-in-law was a Peter Epp. Was perhaps Peter Epp of Rosenthal, O.C., the elusive brother of Rev. David Epp of the same village, the father of this Peter Epp? Perhaps he even moved to Molotschna, as did (I think) his younger brother Heinrich (Cornelius?) and at least one nephew. Could it be too that my step grandmother's relationship with the Jacob Epps of Whitewater, which she mentioned several times during the years she lived with us, traced instead through Mrs. (Maria Neufeld) Epp's great grandfather Peter Epp rather than that of Mr. Epp's as I always assumed?

The study of genealogy fascinates me. God grant that it will fascinate others enough to dig deeper into the particular Fast, Epp, Neufeld and Lohrenz lines whose stories I've barely begun.

71. MINNEDOSA BEACH 1975 SWIMMING AWARDS   Minnedosa Tribune, Aug. 7/75

Of 156 persons who registered for Red Cross swimming lessons at Minnedosa Beach this summer the following 70 qualified for crests:

Pre-Beginner: Lori Birch, Barbara Habing, Michelle Kingdon, Paul Seel, Brenda Penner, Allan Robertson, Lisa Wade, Susan Penner, Mervyn Steen, Teresa Hampton, Alayna Bertram, Tammy Lee Johnson, Floyd Hampton, Suzanne Lillie, Scott Woodcock, Scott Burgess, Ricky Cameron, Audrey Gill, Allan Parenteau, Michael Bertram, Randy Penner, Ian St. John, Sharri Bertram, Jeff Bilcowski, Philip St. John.

Beginner: Karen Charles, Mike Konopski, Bradley Moad, Lisa Neufeld, Kevin Moad, Marcia Schatz, Sherry Seel, Leslie Stewart, Louise Sharpe, Kimberley Girling, Darcy Kowalick, Gwen Smith, Georgina Wade, Martin McNabb, Allison Bardsley.

Junior: Terry Burgess, Kevin Clark, Daryle Foster, Everett Wilkinson, Susan Tarlisky, Cheryl Cardy, Janice Girling, Craig McDonald, Kathy Neufeld, Ken Sharpe, Anna Wonsul, Valerie St. John, Paul Kruger.

Intermediate: Kelly Gray, Donna Hay, Heather King, Joan Hay, Barbara Kingdon, Rod Neufeld, David Brown.

Senior: Lois Briese, Shaun Clark, Terri Lynn Gray, Kathy Jardine, Marilyn Martin, Erliss McPhail, Arlene Ritchie, David Smith.

Bronze Medallion: Cathy Charette.

Bronze Bar: Ernie Cameron.

Instructors were Devon Best and Lois Farley, volunteer aids Rod Neufeld and Bruce Wishart. Main problems encountered this year were getting qualified instructors as one had an accident the week before lessons began and the one promised us by the Winnipeg office backed out at the same time. The accidental death of the father of two of the swimmers saddened everyone. The weather was somewhat better than most years.